Professionalism

for
Helen

Professionalism

THE THIRD LOGIC

Eliot Freidson

The University of Chicago Press

ELIOT FREIDSON, professor emeritus of sociology at New York University and now visiting professor at the University of California, San Francisco, is an international authority on professions. The University of Chicago Press has published the following books by him: *Profession of Medicine: A Study of the Sociology of Applied Knowledge* (1970, 1988); *Professional Powers: A Study of the Institutionalization of Formal Knowledge* (1986); and *Professionalism Reborn: Theory, Prophecy, and Policy* (1994).

The University of Chicago Press, Chicago 60637
Polity Press in association with Blackwell Publishers Ltd

10 09 08 07 06 05 04 03 02 01   1 2 3 4 5

ISBN 0-226-26202-2 (cloth)
ISBN 0-226-26203-0 (paperback)

Library of Congress Cataloging-in-Publication Data

Freidson, Eliot, 1923–
    Professionalism, the third logic : on the practice of knowledge / Eliot Freidson.
        p. cm.
    Includes bibliographical references and index.
    ISBN 0-226-26202-2 (cloth : alk. paper) — ISBN 0-226-26203-0 (pbk. : alk. paper)
    1. Professions—Social aspects. 2. Occupations—Social aspects. I. Title.

HD8038.A1 F74 2001
305.5'53—dc21

00-064877

This book is printed on acid-free paper.

Contents

Acknowledgments

The epigraph of this book expresses my sense of inadequacy in writing it, for now the doughy mass of print which frustrated Qfwfq is even larger, more doughy, and more indigestible than ever before. The logic of my enterprise required me to deal with a number of areas in which I am not a specialist, areas which I had to sample rather than command, and sampling, as we all know, is a risky business. I am burdened, as Max Weber (1946b: 134–5) put it, "with the resigned realization that at best one provides the specialist with useful questions upon which he would not so easily hit from his own specialized point of view. One's own work must inevitably remain highly imperfect." Furthermore, I am aware that much of what I write here is not really new, for I have used many of the insights of the admirable scholars of the past who have suffered the bittersweet success of having been so fully absorbed into the way we think today that we forget them as our sources. For all that, my hope is that I have presented the familiar from a different angle which can give a fresh perspective to the old, perhaps insoluble problem of the place of knowledge and skill in human life.

This book was part of a larger project on which I have worked sporadically over a fairly long period of time. It has certainly been influenced by the many informal verbal encounters that are the lifeblood of collegiality but which are unfortunately difficult to remember. Some of the content of those encounters has certainly found its way into this book, although I can only acknowledge the help of colleagues who must remain anonymous. On a more formal level, I had occasion to consult colleagues who read and commented on early drafts of one chapter or another. I acknowledge with gratitude the helpful comments and suggestions that I received from Robert Althauser, Thomas Bender, Michael Burrage, Burton Clark, Frederic Hafferty, Barbara Heyns, Burkhart Holzner, Caroline Persell, Seymour Spilerman, Anselm Strauss, and Dennis Wrong.

An even greater debt of gratitude is owed to those who read the penultimate draft of this book and made many useful critical comments and suggestions. They are Howard S. Becker, Steven Brint, Robert Dingwall, Magalí S. Larson, and Derek L. Phillips. Robert R. Alford went far beyond the call of duty in the detail of his comments and was especially helpful. None of those I consulted should be held responsible for any of the flaws in this book, if only because their recommendations led me more often to try to clarify my analysis than change it.

Some of this book was written while I was Scholar in Residence in the pleasant and stimulating surroundings of the Villa Serbelloni in Bellaggio, whose hospitality is gratefully acknowledged. I must also express gratitude to the European University Institute (Fiesole) for its subsequent hospitality, and for the more recent scholarly aid provided by the Department of Sociology, University of California, Berkeley, where I was Visiting Scholar, and the Department of Social and Behavioral Sciences, University of California, San Francisco, where I have been Visiting Professor.

Finally, I must say that whatever clarity this book possesses stems from the meticulous and expert editing of my wife, Helen Giambruni, to whom I dedicate this book with love and gratitude.

San Francisco

And I think how beautiful it was then, through that void, to draw lines and parabolas, pick out the precise point, the intersection between space and time where the event would spring forth, undeniable in the prominence of its glow; whereas now events come flowing down without interruption, like cement being poured, one column next to the other, one within the other, separated by black and incongruous headlines, legible in many ways but intrinsically illegible, a doughy mass of events without focus or direction, which surrounds, submerges, crushes all reasoning.

(from "How Much Shall We Bet?", in *Cosmicomics*, by Italo Calvino)

Introduction

Imagine a world in which we are all free to buy and sell anything we choose, individually competing with each other to buy at the lowest possible price and sell for the highest possible price. Nothing is regulated nor are there any large companies or unions to limit that competition. Such free and unregulated competition both encourages innovation, which increases the variety and quality of goods and services, and keeps prices down. Consumers are fully informed about the quality and cost of available goods and services and choose them rationally, to their own best interest. This world is organized around consumption, with consumer preference and choice determining whose services will succeed. Value is measured primarily by cost.

Now imagine a different world in which the production and distribution of goods and services are planned and controlled by the administration of large organizations. Each organization, whether a private firm or a public agency, is governed by an elaborate set of rules that establish the qualifications of those who can be employed to perform different jobs and that define their duties. The effective planning and supervision of a variety of specialized jobs standardizes production so as to assure consumers of reliable products at a reasonable cost. In this world, the executive officers or managers of organizations control those who produce goods and services, aiming primarily at predictability and efficiency.

Finally, imagine a world in which those workers who have the specialized knowledge that allows them to provide especially important services have the power to organize and control their own work. Legally, only they can offer their particular services to consumers or hold jobs performing them in organizations: neither consumers nor managers are free to employ anyone else. Furthermore, only members of the occupation have the right to supervise and correct the work of colleagues. They do not abuse those exclusive rights, however, because they are more dedicated to doing good work for their own satisfaction and for the benefit of others than to maximizing their income. Thus, consumers and managers can count on work of high quality at reasonable cost.

All three of these are pipe-dreams, of course. None of those worlds exists, and where some of their elements have existed, predicted virtues are always accompanied by unanticipated vices. In unregulated markets, consumers must contend with deception, fraud, and collusion to inflate prices. In organizations, there is inflexibility and perfunctory treatment of consumers. And when occupations are in charge, their members may put economic advantage ahead of the good of their clients. Nonetheless, faith in those imagined worlds, each operating from a different set of assumptions, lies behind policy choices. They represent three logics. But while two of them are quite familiar and well worked out in theory, the third, which I call professionalism, is not. In this book I will spell out that third logic, showing it to be a set of interconnected institutions providing the economic support and social organization that sustains the occupational control of work. I will do so by systematically contrasting it with the other two, more familiar logics, treating all three as pipe-dreams or, put more academically, as ideal types. The ideal type is a method of conceptualization that can both organize the abstract theoretical issues which concern scholars and highlight the practical issues confronting social policy.

A Question of Policy

The policy issue that concerns me in this book is the status of professions in advanced industrial society. For decades now, the popular watchwords driving policy formation have been "competition" and "efficiency," the first referring to competition in a free market, and the second to the benefits of the skilled management of firms. Those watchwords are being invoked in aggressive campaigns to change profoundly the governing and staffing of schools and universities, health, welfare, legal, and other institutions in which professionals perform key functions. Until recently those institutions and the professionals who work in them occupied a specially protected position. Now, especially in the United States but also elsewhere, their position is being seriously weakened in the name of competition and efficiency. It is charged that professions have monopolies which they use primarily to advance their selfish economic interests while failing to insure benefit to consumers, that they are inefficient, their work unreliable and unnecessarily costly. Strip away their protective licenses and credentials, urge some, and let there be truly free competition. Open the market to all who wish to offer their services. Consumers will separate the wheat from the chaff in such a market so that the best services and products will emerge at the lowest cost. Where services are complex, requiring the coordination of many specialists and expensive technology, as is the case for medicine, let them be organized by firms whose managers are devoted to efficiency. Then let the firms compete with each other for consumer choice.

In response, the professions have not defended themselves well. For one thing, as Brint (1994) has shown, they are divided. They are a varied collection of occupations working in different sectors of the economy and with different vested interests, more inclined to attack each other than to recognize that they all share the same basic institutional arrangements. Then when they do defend themselves they rely primarily on a rhetoric of good intentions which is belied by the patently self-interested character of many of their activities. What they almost never do is spell out the principles underlying the institutions that organize and support the way they do their work and take active responsibility for their realization.

These principles differ markedly from those of the market, which celebrates competition and cost, and from those of the firm, which invokes the virtue of efficiency through standardization. I will show in this book that monopoly is essential to professionalism, which directly opposes it to the logic of competition in a free market. Freedom of judgment or discretion in performing work is also intrinsic to professionalism, which directly contradicts the managerial notion that efficiency is gained by minimizing discretion. Those defending their professions have failed to defend those head-on contradictions as essential parts of a larger whole whose logic and outcome are distinctly different from those of the market and the management of firms and which cannot be eliminated without seriously damaging the whole. In this book I will show in some detail how the properties of professionalism fit together to form a whole that differs systematically from the free market on the one hand, and the firm, or bureaucracy,[1] on the other. Only when that difference is established will I finally evaluate the consequences of excessive emphasis on competition and efficiency in professional work.

My Analytic Strategy

In my last sustained work (Freidson 1986), I presented a detailed analytic description of the institutions supporting professions in the United States toward the end of the third quarter of the twentieth century. In this book, my central concern is quite different. It is not to describe what exists in a particular time and place but to present a model of the logic of professionalism that can enjoy the same privileged intellectual status as the logics of the market and the firm. I will first establish the basic institutional characteristics of ideal-typical professionalism and then analyze the circumstances which make those characteristics possible. In adopting this strategy, I have chosen not to follow the example of traditional scholarly discussions about professions, which are largely inductive, seeking to find a general pattern or "essence" of professionalism in the variety of occupations called professions in various times and places. The patterns found by this method are necessarily circumscribed by the concrete cases studied so that, for example, many students of Anglo-American professions have mistakenly emphasized formal codes of ethics and private associations as essential institutions for occupations to gain professional status. Furthermore, because scholars do not share the same analytic framework, the information that one collects and analyzes may be overlooked by another so that their analyses are incomparable. Thus, while the literature on professions has burgeoned over the past few decades, with studies being made of previously unexamined occupations, historic periods, and nations, conceptualization has been scattered and typologies have proliferated to the point of confusion. Instead of building a sturdy tower of knowledge, this activity has created a number of scattered huts, some very elegant

---

1   My usage oscillates between "firm" and "rational-legal bureaucracy" because the former term, whose virtue is that it is familiar to everyone and has no invidious connotations, generally refers solely to private corporations in capitalist societies. However, I mean to refer to *all* formal organizations which exemplify the managerial control of work, including the state civil service agencies that are often called bureaucracies, and I rely on Max Weber's ideal-type, rational-legal bureaucracy for my model of firms.

indeed, but huts nonetheless. It is the use of the inductive method that is responsible for this outcome.

I hold that a logical model based on a theoretically chosen foundation can provide focus and direction to empirical studies, at the very least by serving as a clear target for criticism and revision. Furthermore, if constructed systematically, a logical model can have the comprehensiveness that generalizations from limited empirical cases lack. The model I propose is general and grounded in the world of work, most particularly in the political and economic institutions by which workers gain their living. It assumes that the historic professions are occupations and that because, like all occupations, they cannot exist without some way of gaining an income, their position in the marketplace is the most appropriate foundation on which to erect a model. I further assume that the historic professions and crafts exemplify to a greater or lesser degree, though none completely, a circumstance in which occupations themselves rather than consumers or managers control work. It is this possibility that I will develop systematically as an ideal type, informed but not limited by what I have learned about some historic professions and crafts. In order to clarify and dramatize the characteristics of this third logic, I will compare them with those postulated for the ideal-typical free labor market and the ideal-typical rational-legal bureaucracy.[2] While the model I present is static, and cannot therefore reflect the real world of process and change, it has the considerable virtue of being able to provide a stable point against which empirical variation and process can be systematically compared and analyzed. Provided one never forgets that it is solely an intellectual tool, a heuristic device, and *not* an effort to portray the varied reality of professions and crafts in different times and places, it can be as useful as the more familiar theoretical constructs of the free market and rational-legal bureaucracy which are similarly abstracted from reality.

My theoretical approach is different from that of Larson (1977) and Abbott (1988), two of the most influential analysts of the professions over the past few decades on whose work I have drawn heavily. Larson constructs a historic narrative around the process by which a limited group of occupations in England and the United States undertook to raise their social status (collective mobility) and gain a monopoly in the marketplace (the market

---

2 Some of these comparisons are likely to seem elementary to the specialist, but they are essential for demonstrating to others the systematic differences between the three models.

project). She studies the historic process of professionalization, emphasizing how economic advantage for occupations is attained by restricting the supply of practitioners and striving for a special position of public respect and influence. In so far as her narrative is explicitly concerned with the historic development of the professions, and is linked to the broader literature of Marxist and Weberian theory, it has proven to be a very influential resource for historians as well as sociologists. However, it does not develop the *logic* of the concepts it suggests because they are developed within a limited historic framework. Unlike Larson, I shall not concentrate on analyzing the rise (or decline) of the historic professions. While I rely on many of her concepts and insights, I abstract them into a model of interconnected institutions whose realization depends upon the conjunction of a limited number of contingencies.

I also rely on much in Abbott's *tour de force* for my analysis, but I do not choose to employ his method. He does not postulate a specific process of professionalization as does Larson; rather, he expresses skepticism about the very possibility of discovering one. He analyzes instead the process by which occupations gain, maintain, adjust, and even lose their exclusive jurisdiction over particular tasks and the critical, largely functional factors involved in that process. His focus is primarily on the relation of occupations to each other in a division of labor, with the forces influencing their jurisdictional boundaries establishing their official and social identities as well as their economic fortunes. He does discuss the social, economic, and symbolic sources of challenge and support, as well as the significance of an occupation's particular body of knowledge, but his concentration on jurisdiction leads him well past the conventionally defined professions to include many specialists who have attained considerably less privilege, leaving the question of their status open. More importantly, although he offers a rich and imaginative analysis of the institutions connected with occupational jurisdictions, his method is idiosyncratic, embodying neither a clearly structured analytic procedure that others can emulate and refine, nor explicit connection to other bodies of data and theory that have been important for the analysis of work and employment.

By its very nature, my analysis cannot be as rich as Abbott's or Larson's. Its intent is to erect a systematic framework around the substantive processes that concern them both – the processes connected with establishing and maintaining jurisdiction as well as with establishing and maintaining a privileged position in the labor market. My intent is to create a *logic*, a systematic way of thinking that can embrace and order most of the issues with which they deal, and to demonstrate how that logic represents a third approach to understanding how work can be organized and controlled. These different approaches will be discussed in detail in the chapters that follow.

Structure and Process

Narrative history limns process, as does any other description which attempts to be faithful to human affairs. But the ideal type that I advance establishes structure, which is fixed and static. How can this be justified? It is its very fixity that allows an abstract model to serve as an unchanging point against which one can compare and sort out the constantly changing empirical world. This is comparable to the commonsense strategy of everyday life that allows us to understand and describe the variety of the creatures we call dogs by comparing all of them against an intuitive model of "dog;" Linnaeus and his taxonomist descendants use more refined criteria but employ essentially the same method.

Such a method allows us to point and classify. It does not, however, allow us to understand how deviations from the fixed model come to be, why some occupations in some times and places succeed or fail to resemble the model. That is why the second part of my analysis is essential. It describes and analyzes the institutions and circumstances which can advance or impede the development or maintenance of the political and economic status of occupations and their control over their work. They represent the contingencies of professionalization which vary with the concrete contexts of time, place, and industry or economic sector, and which interact with each other. While the model hangs together by virtue of its own consistency and logic, providing a stable point for imaginative comparison with the real world of time and place, the contingencies of professionalism provide the resources for analytic description of how particular occupations in particular times and places come to resemble the model and be called professions or, conversely, lose all resemblance to it and become on the one hand mere casual labor in a spot market controlled by consumers, or on the other, mere job-holders in firms controlled by managers.

Ideal Types and Reality

How helpful is it to postulate a fixed model by which to analyze the variety of occupations to be found in different times and places? Think of Adam Smith's conception of the free market. Certainly no one can question its enormous value to the discipline of economics even though it does not accurately portray the vast majority of markets anywhere in the real world and never did. It is enough for analysts that the elements of the model are present in one way or another, however grievously distorted by circumstance. If successful, the model's simplicity is strategic. It allows one to engage in systematic reasoning from its conditions to the varying circumstances of the real world and it can be grasped sufficiently well to be reasoned from.

The same is true of the ideal-typical model of rational-legal bureaucracy advanced by Max Weber. It is quite different from Smith's model, more structural and less abstract. It was initially formulated to make sense of a particular method of organizing and exercising authority over the conduct of state affairs, a method which displaces administrative structures organized around various forms of traditional authority or around charismatic authority. It was patently inspired by the state civil service of Imperial Germany. Weber did not make much use of his model to analyze the governance and administration of industrial or other economic firms, but the marks of his model are clear in the theories of management or administration by which scholars began to analyze business firms early in the twentieth century (see Massie 1965 and especially Perrow 1986) and always forms part of the background of present-day analyses of firms and "internal labor markets."

Nonetheless, virtually since its formulation many have demonstrated that the formal organizations of the empirical world often deviate markedly from Weber's model. Furthermore, during the course of this century but particularly over these last two decades, a number of scholars have asserted that changes in managerial practices, technology, and the environment of firms have been so profound that the fundamental bureaucratic principle of hierarchical control realized by formal supervisory and personnel policies has been displaced by new forms of organization and employment. For example, it has been claimed that open systems and even dynamic loose networks are displacing formal, hierarchical organizations.[3]

3 See, for example, Kalleberg 1996, and the papers in Littek and Charles 1995.

The degree to which fundamental changes have actually taken place and, if so, will be permanent rather than transitory, is of course open to question. Whatever the case, in the very expositions arguing such changes, the baseline, the foil, the organized point of comparison for delineating what is different about those new forms of organization remains Weber's ideal type or its reflection in traditional management conceptions of formal organization. Its coherence and intuitive sense are what give it value, not its faithfulness to transient events. It is no accident that it has survived so long while other, more processual and empirically accurate conceptions litter the dustbin of history. The ideal type provides a disciplined focus for the imagination when confronted by the variety of the world even after the world has changed so much that little of the model remains to be observed.

The same might be said about an ideal type portraying organization and control of work by occupation rather than by market or hierarchy. It can be intellectually useful even if present-day professions, crushed between private capital and the state, may be losing their special economic and social position as Krause (1996) claims, or if the "organizational [rather than occupational] dominance of expertise" will emerge, as Abbott (1991b: 39) believes. There are even more extreme predictions that occupations as such will disappear in a "postmodern" economy, and that jobs will be composed of "flexible skills" rather than clearly defined tasks. Casey (1995) goes so far as to project a "post-occupational" society. There are good grounds to question how both specialization and relatively stable occupational identities and careers can actually be eliminated,[4] but even if this is to be the case, the logical as well as

---

For a systematic review and appraisal of new forms of industrial organization and the claims made for them, see Smith 1997 and Tomaney 1994. For networks as neither hierarchy nor market, see Powell 1990.

4   The issue of flexible or multiple skills is put into perspective by noting that the phenomenon represents the reconfiguration of related skills into new jobs or occupational titles which can become stable either in a firm or across firms as an occupation. Outside of Marx's fantasy of a future communist society in which no one's potential is limited by specializing in one kind of work, a bundle of multiple skills cannot be composed of just *any* collection of tasks, from parking cars to programming a computer to lecturing on quantum theory and playing viola in a piano quintet. Those flexible skills must be related to each other. Furthermore, if firms no longer offer lifelong careers of internal promotion, salary increments, and pension plans, workers must participate in what Sabel (1995) calls an open labor market, where occupational rather than firm identity becomes essential for work careers. Casey's prediction is based on ignoring how those who left the firm she studied got another job elsewhere without using either their educational credentials or a transferable job description.

historic importance of such organized occupations as crafts and professions justifies our attention.

Audiences

In conclusion, I must note that I have more than one purpose in this book and that these purposes are likely to interest different audiences. This poses some difficulty for my exposition. First, as much of my discussion indicates, I address the scholarly audience of Anglo-American and European historians, sociologists, and political scientists who have studied and theorized about the professions over the past thirty or forty years. For them, my main concern is to present a framework that might clarify and organize their work. In addition, I hope to call their attention to the broader field of the sociology of work, where studies of the professions belong. With but few exceptions, the study of professions has been in an intellectual world of its own, completely separated from studies of more humble occupations, from long-standing and sophisticated studies of industrial organization, and from recent work on labor markets and status attainment. In the empirical study of some professions, engineering being the most obvious example because its work is often carried on in industrial plants, attention to such literature is essential. However, the study of all professions can benefit considerably from greater familiarity with the more catholic concepts and illuminating data to be found in the sociology of work. By referring to and sometimes discussing key studies in those fields, I hope to draw the attention of my colleagues who study the professions to the broader intellectual context that I believe our field needs.

Second, I hope that my effort to connect the study of professions to industrial, labor force, and labor market studies may stimulate specialists in those areas to pay closer attention to the systematic analysis of occupations, of which professions are the most well organized. It is common in a number of areas to distinguish three basic kinds of employment relations. In labor market studies, for example, three types of labor market are distinguished: secondary, or open labor market, which refers to the classic external free market; firm internal labor market, which refers to firms or bureaucracies; and occupational labor market, which refers to occupational control of employment relations. Occupation is almost always recognized as a distinct and separate basis for regulating employment and work. And in political analysis,

Streeck and Schmitter (1985) argue that "association" or "interest group," and most particularly occupational association, must be added to state, market, and community as the fourth basic source of social order.[5] But in spite of widespread recognition of occupation as a basic political, economic, and social category, it has not received the same amount of analytic attention as have market and firm, nor has it been elaborated systematically. It has largely been used as an indicator of something else – of class, education, status, or income. I hope that the ideal type I develop here may stimulate the development of systematic ways of analyzing jobs and occupations, not solely through occupational labor markets, but also through ways of organizing divisions of labor and educational systems.

Finally, I address those concerned with forging public policy dealing with the financing and governance of the legal, medical, educational, and other institutions in which professionals work. For that audience, my exposition is much different than most in that instead of discussing public policy issues directly, I present a systematic analysis of the rationale underlying policies upon which professionalism depends. I try to clarify and dramatize that rationale by comparing it to those which are quite different and intrinsically hostile to professionalism. Advocates of the market and of bureaucratic management treat professionalism as an aberration rather than something with a logic and an integrity of its own. I hope that my extended comparison of the institutions of professionalism with those represented by the attractive watchwords of competition and efficiency may help guide debate through the doughy mass of contemporary rhetoric that obscures the basic issues underlying policy. But since the early chapters must of necessity discuss fairly abstract, perhaps excessively academic matters in order to establish the basic differences of the three logics, readers more interested in policy may find it more interesting to begin with chapter 4.

For that audience I must also note that while I conclude this book with a discussion of professional ethics, my emphasis will

5   Indeed, it could be argued that in the present day occupation takes on the characteristics of community. This is of course the position of Durkheim's classic work (1964), revived in a much more sophisticated form in Grusky and Sørensen 1998. The latter note the present-day exhaustion of class theory and suggest that "disaggregating" class into component occupations might solve what have come to seem insoluble problems. They point to the fact that occupation, not class, provides social identity, and that especially in the case of professions and crafts it forms the basis for organized activities.

not be on the behavior of individual professionals. This is not because I do not consider individual ethics important for the performance of all kinds of work, but because I believe that the economic, political, and social institutions which permit, even actively encourage, ethical behavior are ultimately more important. Even when those called professionals are something more than average people, few can be immune to the constraints surrounding the work they do. It is the institutional ethics of professionalism that establishes the criteria by which to evaluate those constraints. If the institutions surrounding them fail in support, only the most heroic individuals can actively concern themselves with the ethical issues raised by their work. Professionalism requires attention to the ethical status of those institutions.

The Plan of this Book

A note about terminology before I outline the chapters to follow. I use the word "professionalism" to refer to the institutional circumstances in which the members of occupations rather than consumers or managers control work. "Market" refers to those circumstances in which consumers control the work people do, and "bureaucracy" to those in which managers are in control. Professionalism may be said to exist when an organized occupation gains the power to determine who is qualified to perform a defined set of tasks, to prevent all others from performing that work, and to control the criteria by which to evaluate performance. In the case of professionalism, neither individual buyers of labor in the market nor the managers of bureaucratic firms have the right to themselves choose workers to perform particular tasks or evaluate their work except within the limits specified by the occupation. The organized occupation creates the circumstances under which its members are free of control by those who employ them.

While few if any occupations can be said to *fully* control their own work, those that come close are called "professions" in English. A word for occupations meeting that criterion is not common in other languages, though "profession" has been adopted in some. To complicate matters further, even in English the word has other meanings as, for example, Bledstein (1985) and especially Kimball (1992) show. The most rational method of dealing with this problem might be to avoid using the word entirely, but because neologisms have rarely been successful, I feel

I have no choice but to use it. Still, wherever I can, I try to use "occupation" instead of "profession" in order to avoid the pretentious, sometimes sanctimonious overtones associated with the latter. As Everett Hughes (1971: 417) emphasized, "We need to rid ourselves of any concepts which keep us from seeing that the essential problems of men at work are the same whether they do their work in the laboratories of some famous institution or in the messiest vat room of a pickle factory." The concept of profession tends to keep us from seeing those with that label as workers. It does properly signal that they have a special position in the political economy which truly distinguishes them and the problems they have at work from those in other occupations. But it obscures with the fog of mystique much of what they have in common with more humble occupations, exaggerating their differences. It is primarily the logic I have chosen that leads me to put the economic and political foundation of work first, but doing so is also an effort to avoid that mystique by secularizing the issues.

In part I of this book I present the ideal type, professionalism. Chapter 1 provides a context for analyzing its mode of controlling work by portraying the broad range of knowledge and skill within which the special kind of knowledge ascribed to professionalism is to be found, knowledge believed to require the exercise of discretionary judgment and a grounding in abstract theory and concepts. Occupations believed to possess such knowledge are singled out for the public prestige and official privilege in the marketplace which are essential to what, in English-speaking nations, are called professions. Chapter 2 portrays three profoundly different ways by which the relations between specializations composing a division of labor can be organized. In the ideal-typical case of professionalism, occupations have the power to negotiate their jurisdictions with each other. This produces a markedly different outcome in the content and organization of their division of labor than would be the case in a free or a bureaucratically controlled division of labor – the degree of specialization, for example, and the hierarchical relations between occupations. My discussion of those systematic differences continues in chapter 3, where I address the ways entrance into labor markets and subsequent work careers vary as the source of control varies. I note that in each case there are characteristic differences in career-line and both vertical and horizontal mobility. And since it is characteristic of occupational control of the labor market that eligibility for work is determined by training credentials produced by the occupation itself, I am brought to examine more closely in chapter 4 the ideal-typical characteristics of the training institutions of professionalism and their implications for both the development and control of new knowledge and skill and for stratification within occupations. This leads to discussion in chapter 5 of the ideology of professionalism, comparing it with those which advance the logic of the market and of bureaucracy.

In part II I analyze the major institutional contingencies of professionalism – the circumstances that vary historically and nationally and that have critical bearing on the process by which occupations gain special status in the labor force, control the division of labor and the labor markets in which they work, and the way their members are trained. Chapter 6 discusses the consequences of variation in the organization and policy orientation (or political ideology) of the state, and in the organization of occupations themselves. Chapter 7 explores the way the substantive characteristics of different bodies of knowledge and skill pose requirements for successful practice that in turn influence the occupation's capacity to attain professional privilege.

Finally, in part III, I turn to evaluating professionalism empirically in light of the criticism and economic and political pressures to which it has been subjected in recent years. In chapter 8, I briefly summarize the ideal type and its contingencies, then give a practical demonstration of its use by analyzing the changing status of the profession of medicine in the United States. This is followed by a discussion of the direction that public policy toward professions has been taking in advanced industrial nations in Europe and the United States, influenced as much by ideology as by functional necessity. I conclude this book in chapter 9, where I show that the most conspicuous attacks on professionalism are largely empty rhetoric which fails to address the central question of how the development and practice of specialized knowledge and skill should be organized and controlled. After suggesting how professional work may be subordinated to the immediate needs of both capital and the state in the future, I note that this will not put at serious risk the economic and political institutions supporting the special status of professions. What *is* at risk today, and likely to be at greater risk tomorrow, is the independence of professions to choose the direction of the development of their knowledge and the uses to which it is put.

Part I

Professionalism: The Ideal Type

1

Professional Knowledge and Skill

In the most elementary sense, professionalism is a set of institutions which permit the members of an occupation to make a living while controlling their own work.[1] That is a position of considerable privilege. It cannot exist unless it is believed that the particular tasks they perform are so different from those of most workers that self-control is essential. There are other important ways of evaluating work which I shall discuss in later chapters, but here I want to establish the essential framework of distinctions that defines the type of knowledge and skill at the core of professionalism. The two most general ideas underlying professionalism are the belief that certain work is so specialized as to be inaccessible to those lacking the required training and experience, and the belief that it cannot be standardized, rationalized or, as Abbott (1991b: 22) puts it, "commodified." These distinctions are at the foundation of the social processes which establish the social and economic status of professional work, and while they are elementary, they are too important to take for granted. Here and in the next chapter I will analyze the technical and social assumptions employed in distinguishing different kinds of work with the aim of defining the particular kind of knowledge which is granted the

1 I deliberately avoid defining "work" here and elsewhere, though in this book I restrict myself primarily to activities of sufficient value to others that they provide the performer with economic resources in an exchange system. Professionalism is by definition the creature of an official economy which defines work as a legal gainful activity. I have discussed some of the problems of defining work elsewhere as, for example, Freidson 1990.

social and economic privileges required for the institutions of professionalism.[2]

The Growth of Specializations

Specialization – the use of a circumscribed body of knowledge and skills thought to gain particular productive ends – is inherent in work, for it is rare that individuals are either able or willing to perform all of the tasks required for producing the food, shelter, and clothing they need for survival, let alone the amenities of life. After all, even Robinson Crusoe finally had his Friday. And since people do different kinds of work, it follows that they will be evaluated in some way or another. The degree and kind of specialization required by particular jobs, quite apart from their function, is widely used to establish their social, symbolic, and economic value and justify the degree of privilege and trust to which they are entitled.

Some degree of specialization in the work that people do is probably generic to social life. Most writers today believe that gender has been a universal basis for organizing specialization in human societies, even the most ancient, and that there has always been some specialization based on age as well, with children performing some kinds of tasks, adults others, and the aged still others. These rudimentary (but fluid) axes of age and gender upon which specialization has probably always and everywhere been based, order the various work roles that individuals adopt during the course of their daily lives in households and communities. But in daily life people perform a *number* of different tasks, each having different productive aims and requiring different skills. That is very different from my concern here, which is occupational specialization: people performing only the bundle of tasks connected with a defined productive end in an occupation.

When this narrower range of specialization becomes the source of a living, its practitioners are dependent on more than family or immediate community to provide them with the resources by which they can live. Should they specialize only in producing food, they need to enter into exchange relations with people who can provide them with everything else they need. They may specialize more narrowly – producing only one kind of food, for

2   For a much broader analysis of the establishment and use of "expertise," see Trépos 1996.

example, or, like the miller of grains, only processing food, or even, like the shaman, witch doctor, or priest, performing activities having no direct connection with material subsistence. Each additional degree of specialization increases the complexity of the exchange relationships needed to gain the resources for a living.

Full-time specialized work is generally thought to have become common first in the large, dense settlements of the early high civilizations of the Middle East, the Indus Valley, the Far East, and Central and South America (Childe 1965). There, those who performed particular tasks developed distinct and stable social identities as "trades," many of which are still familiar to us today. In general, the convention is to characterize such trades as being specialized in producing a single product or service as a whole, from the beginning to the point where it is ready to be consumed. So one can speak of shoemakers, potters, bakers, and the like. But by the end of the eighteenth century in England, most particularly during the nineteenth century in England, western Europe, and North America, and elsewhere not until the twentieth century, the Industrial Revolution created a new kind of specialization. Adam Smith was its best-known early celebrant.

Manual Specializations

In *The Wealth of Nations*, published in 1776, Smith's very first chapter began with praise for the way specialization increased productivity. He was not referring to the traditional trades, though they are certainly specialized. He wrote about a much less traditional form with which his vocabulary could not deal adequately. As the nouns "specialist" and "specialization" were not available in English before the middle of the nineteenth century nor in French before 1830 (*OED* 1971: 2948; Robert 1978: 1851) Smith used the phrase "division of labor" instead, and characterized the specialized enterprises of the workers he discussed as "trades," even though they were not defined as occupations. This new kind of specialization was exemplified by Smith's discussion of pinmaking, where the conventional, recognizable trade of pinmaker was replaced by a number of smaller and narrower, highly repetitive jobs created by assembling a number of workers under one roof and having each specialize in one of the separate tasks that together are employed to make a pin. Some workers devoted themselves to drawing out the wire, others to straightening it, still others to cutting it, or pointing it, or grinding it at the top for receiving the head. Some made the heads, others fastened the heads to the pins, others whitened the pins, and still others put the completed pins into a paper.

By means of this kind of specialization, the occupation of pin-maker is broken down into separate, limited tasks, each part of a coordinated plan designed to result in the production of pins. Thus, the pinmaker is no longer an individual practicing a trade; the organization and its production plan become the pinmaker, and each of the tasks created by the plan becomes so narrow in scope and simple and repetitive in execution that outside the organization it is unrecognized as a trade or an occupation. It is seen only as a job or as work within the pinmaking establishment. Neither in general official statistics nor in everyday life do those jobs gain social identities based on the particular specializations of wire-straightening, pin-head making, pin whitening, and the like, though in detailed labor statistics they might be so distinguished. Outside the firm, both officially and in everyday life, the primary social identity of those who perform such jobs lies in being an unskilled or semi-skilled industrial worker, or in being an employee of a particular firm, identified by working at the firm rather than by the specific job in that firm. The work is not defined or organized as an occupation.

This form of specialization was not entirely new for the Industrial Revolution. In the fourth century BC, Xenophon described a range of specializations at the end of which there was something "less than a whole trade" that resembled what Smith described:

> In small towns the same workman makes chairs and doors and prows and tables, and often the same artisan builds houses ... In large cities, on the other hand, inasmuch as many people have demands to make upon each branch of industry, one trade alone, and often even less than a whole trade, is enough to support a man: one man, for instance, makes shoes for men, and another for women; and *there are places even where one man earns a living only by stitching shoes, another by cutting them out, another by sewing the uppers together, while there is another who performs none of these operations but only assembles the parts.* (Kranzberg and Gies 1975: 40, italics added)

If the fragmentation of pinmaking into something less than a "whole trade" during the nineteenth and especially the twentieth centuries was not absolutely new to history, it was certainly new for it to be the form of work common to a large proportion of the labor force. It became so common that it was used to characterize an entire class of workers – the industrial proletariat.

Intellectual Specializations

But it would be a great mistake to use either pinmaking or Charlie Chaplin in *Modern Times*, for that matter, to typify all of the specialization that developed during the Industrial Revolution, for at the same time that manual specialization developed in factories, another very different kind grew up in other institutions. From the second half of the nineteenth century to the present day there has been a continuous increase of specialization in the pursuit and application of complex, formal knowledge and technique. Scholarship and scientific research, once the pastimes of such serious amateurs[3] as Charles Darwin, developed into full-time, paid occupations during the nineteenth and especially the twentieth centuries. The few intellectual occupations trained in the medieval universities, the original "status professions" (Elliott 1972) of law, medicine, the ministry, and university teaching, expanded in size and were either transformed or split up into separate disciplines, many of which developed subdisciplines that split off again to become established as distinct, organized disciplines in their own right.

The practice of most was sustained by the host occupation of university teaching, but those who could practice in the marketplace became self-supporting occupations, whether self-employed, like some physicians and lawyers in some times and places, employed by the state, like jurists and some engineers, or by industrial enterprises, as was early the case for chemists and most engineers. The development of that form of specialization, which involved the middle rather than the working class, led to the coming of the "expert" and the "technician," along with the

3   Any number of great scientists and scholars of the first half of the nineteenth century could not, by present-day official standards, be considered active members of the labor force. Indeed, most had no occupation at all, though some who lacked a private income were successful in obtaining sinecures in a government agency or clerical benefice. I call such sinecures "host occupations," which provide a living for "parasitic" occupations like scholarship or art which cannot gain their own living. University teaching is a modern host occupation for most scholars in the humanities and many in the social sciences who cannot gain a living practicing outside them. Waiting tables is often the host occupation for American actors today.

English words (which did not exist earlier) to designate them conveniently (Freidson 1986: 12–13; Barley and Orr (1997b: 12–14). The new "occupational professions" emerged, some evolving from the old "status professions," some from the informal economy, as uroscopers evolved into urologists, bone-setters into orthopedists, and domestic workers into trained nurses (see Dingwall 1983). Some, closer to the present day, grew up with new technology to serve the needs of established professions (see Elliott 1972; Reader 1966; Larson 1977; and, for technicians, Barley and Orr 1997b).

Types of Specialization

Mention of pinmakers and scientists as new specializations makes it clear that there is a whole range of specializations and that the differences among them are too important to ignore. Here, I shall present them as simple polar opposites although, as Littler's analysis makes clear (Littler 1982: 6–11), to do the issue justice we must ultimately include additional criteria.[4] Those who *celebrate* the virtues of a work-life of specialization (as did, for example, Durkheim) do not celebrate the work of the pinmakers. As we shall see in chapter 6, their kind of specialization might have been praised for its productivity, but was deplored for its effect on those who perform it. It is specialists and specializations of a different order that are lauded – the crafts practiced by skilled workers (sometimes tellingly described as the aristocracy of labor),[5] on the one hand, and on the other, in Smith's words, "the employments ... [of] people of some rank or fortune [which] ... are not ... simple and uniform ... [but rather] extremely complicated and as such exercise the head more than the hands" (1976b: 305).

Two major types of specialization seem evident, representing quite different *qualities* of work, with quite different consequences for those who perform them and those who consume their products. On the one hand there is the type of specialization represented by those who perform different parts of the process of Smith's pinmaking – the type of specialization that Marx and

4 Littler restricts his analysis to industrial work, which limits its range considerably, and he does not seem to recognize how problematic it is to determine the boundaries of tasks – that is, whether there is one or many in any particular instance. I will discuss in chapter 2 the troubling issue of relativism in delineating specializations.
5 See the discussion of what is in fact a very complex notion in Hobsbawm 1984: 252–72.

subsequent Marxist writers called the "detailed division of labor." This unwieldy and literally uninformative phrase is employed largely to characterize the work performed by semi-skilled workers in factories organized under the historic circumstances of capitalist production (though state socialist nations also organized factory production in the same way). The phrase is intended to convey the idea of the exclusive performance of tasks that are so simple and repetitive that they can be performed by virtually any normal adult – indeed, as was the case in the nineteenth century, even by children. In this form of specialization, usually called "semi-skilled labor" in English, there is said to be little or no opportunity to vary the tasks to be performed or the way they can be performed. Because the conventional Marxist adjectives "minute" and "detailed" do not capture the essential character of this form of specialization, I propose to employ the term "mechanical" instead, and speak of *mechanical specialization*. In Fox's analysis (1974: 16), whether or not these are tasks with a narrow, minute, or detailed range, their performance is specifically organized to minimize individual discretion.

In contrast to this mechanical specialization is what might be called *discretionary specialization* (see Friedmann 1964: 85–8). What distinguishes it from the other lies in the fact that the tasks it involves, however narrow, minute, detailed, or "specialized" the range, are tasks in which discretion or fresh judgment must often be exercised if they are to be performed successfully. Whatever the case may be in reality (and that may be a matter of opinion), the tasks and their outcome are believed to be so indeterminate (see Jamous and Peloille 1970; Boreham 1983) as to require attention to the variation to be found in individual cases. And while those whose occupation it is to perform such tasks will almost certainly engage in some routines that can be quite mechanical,[6] it is believed that they must be prepared to be sensitive to the necessity of altering routine for individual circumstances that require discretionary judgment and action. Such work has the potential for

---

6 Obviously, I am using logical rather than empirical distinctions. Just as no human work is ever likely to be completely mechanical, so is no human work ever likely to be completely discretionary. In the latter case, perhaps the work of the *bricoleur*, which I will discuss shortly, comes closest. (For industrial jobs, see Fox 1974: 19–21.) As to terminology, those writing about skill in industrial work link "autonomy" with high skill (for example, Spenner 1990), referring to the amount of discretion exercised at work. Fox develops this elaborately in his comparison of high-discretion and low-discretion jobs in industry.

innovation and creativity, thus distinguishing it from that of Adam Smith's pinmakers.

It may appear that I am merely echoing the conventional distinction between mental and manual labor which has a long history in Western philosophy (see, for example, Applebaum 1992; Tilgher 1958) and which was implied in Adam Smith's mention of the specialized "employments" of the higher classes cited earlier. Moreover, it is one still used by Marxists today. But used uncritically it conflates important symbolic, class, cognitive, and analytic distinctions. Certainly the implication that manual or physical labor does not involve the use of the mind is false, for little if any human work can be separated from symbolization and thought. What underlies it is not the use of the mind instead of the body but rather the *kind* of knowledge and thought that is believed to be used in different kinds of work. Mechanical specialization by definition requires primarily the knowledge and concepts that normal adults learn during the course of their everyday lives. Discretionary specialization, on the other hand, is thought to require the employment of a body of knowledge that is gained by special training – which is why its practitioners are called experts or specialists and pinmakers are not. What is needed to clarify the mental/manual distinction and refine our conception of work and specialization is an adequate conception of the different kinds of knowledge and skill that are used to guide the performance of work.

Skill and the Tacit

I have deliberately used the word "skill" in the same breath as "knowledge" because while I believe it necessary to distinguish the two, they are both essential to work and complement each other in its performance. Like all keywords, however, the word "skill" is ambiguous (see the discussion in Becker 1998: 112–16). In official statistics it is used to represent the amount and kind of specialized training that distinguishes members of the labor force. In the Marxist debate on proletarianization, where the "de-skilling" of labor[7] is a central issue, it is used in a quite different fashion.

---

7   In the context of the "de-skilling" debate initiated by Harry Braverman, a brief but intelligent review and discussion of conceptions of skill in industry is provided by Littler 1982: 7–11. He concludes that the development of "specialization [in industry] is not so much a de-skilling process as one which concentrates skill into

However, in his review of the various ways the term has been used, Attewell (1990: 423) concludes that "at the core of all definitions is the idea of competence or proficiency – the ability to do something well. The word encompasses both mental and physical proficiency (i.e., skill implies understanding or knowledge), but it also connotes physical dexterity." Similarly, the *Oxford English Dictionary* defines it as the "capability of accomplishing something with precision and certainty" (*OED* 1971: 2847). Skill may thus be taken to refer to the capacity to *accomplish* a task, which may be kept analytically separate from the substantive knowledge connected with the task itself. While skill is itself a kind of knowledge, namely, of the techniques for using or applying substantive knowledge, it is *facilitative* in character. Thus, to solve an abstract problem, one must not only have command over the body of knowledge connected with the problem, but also the rules of discourse (that is, logic, mathematics, rules of evidence), and the capacity or skill to employ them so as to arrive at an acceptable solution.[8] In the case of work involving physical activity, one must not only know, for example, that operating a machine produces a particular result, but also how to operate the machine. People with the same substantive knowledge can differ in their skill at solving abstract problems and using tools or operating machines.

Some of the skills required for applying knowledge to the performance of a task are formal in character, codified in texts, or otherwise described clearly and systematically in the course of training for work. Other skills, however, are *tacit* – unverbalized, perhaps even unverbalizable, but in any case not part of a formal corpus of codified technique. This is certainly, as we shall see, the case for work that has little connection with theoretical thought, but according to Polanyi (1964), it is also the case for such exalted enterprises as scientific research. He argues that skills are an essential component of scientific discovery and knowledge, and that they are exercised according to a *tacit* art that is based on experience rather than formal theory. Such skills are learned not in classrooms, but rather during the course of working in the labora-

---

a smaller task range" (1982: 186). See also Lee 1981, Darrah 1994, and the essays in Penn et al. 1994 for other discussions in an industrial context, and see Block 1990: 85–118. There seems to be little validity in notions that a unidirectional de-skilling of work is occurring in industrial nations today, for in a significant number of cases there is a complementary "re-skilling."

8   Much of Schön's (1982) discussion of "reflection in action" in professional work can be seen as the skill of application.

tory.[9] They are what he calls the "tacit dimension" of scientific knowledge, neither formal in character nor systematically articulated (Polanyi 1967). He regards knowing as

> an active contemplation of the things known, an action that requires skill. Skillful knowing and doing is performed by subordinating a set of particulars, as clues or tools, to the shaping of a skillful achievement, whether practical or theoretical. . . . Clues and tools are things used as such and not observed in themselves. (Polanyi 1964: p. iii)

Tacit skills are also to be found in the performance of physical tasks, of course. Harper's study of the mechanic and craftsman Willie, characterized as a *bricoleur* because his work consists of using and adapting whatever odds and ends are at hand to create or repair things, is particularly instructive (Harper 1987: 74). Trying to understand how Willie can do what he does successfully, Harper must invoke a "kinesthetic sense [that] infuses all of the work" (p. 131), "knowledge in the body" about "how hard to hit or twist a tool, or how to interpret the sounds of a running machine," "how much pressure may be applied to steel rather than ceramics and the like" (pp. 117–18). Those skills cannot be codified or described systematically; they must be learned by practice, become part of the eye, ear, and hand. Ryan (1984: 192) discusses a "manual dexterity that can be developed fully only with extended practice and experience. It is this manual knack, *common to all uses of the skill*, that endows it with a high degree of transferability."[10] There are other elements of skill which have probably not yet been analyzed, to take but one example of recent papers, fresh substance is added by the analysis provided by Pinch et al. (1997) of what is entailed in learning how to spay a ferret and remove the testicles of a horse.

The same tacit intellectual skills are involved in writing a research grant, an essay, a scholarly or scientific paper, a poem, or a novel. Formal rules of grammar, spelling, and discourse can be specified and learned (some reduced to a computer program), but no set of rules can specify, for example, how much to emphasize or repeat a point, what points need examples or supporting citation, when ordinary rules and conventional forms can be

9   See the interesting paper by MacKenzie and Spinardi 1995, that discusses the role of tacit knowledge in nuclear weapons design.
10   Transferability of knowledge and skill is an additional distinction of some importance that will be discussed in chapter 3.

fruitfully violated, how much (if any) dialogue is appropriate and how much narrative, and what words or phrases, should be used to characterize a point. Such issues of skillful intellectual technique are matters of style which are analytically separate from but not independent of substance. Intertwined as skill and substantive knowledge may be, therefore, their different roles in work dictate that they are best kept analytically separate.[11] And as we shall see in a later chapter, the distinction between codified and tacit skill and knowledge plays an important ideological role in the arguments of workers defending their discretionary freedom.

Everyday and Formal Knowledge in Work

The productive human activities we call work are sharply distinguished from the activities of other living creatures by the fact that they are directed by knowledge. An adequate sociology of work, therefore, must also be a sociology of knowledge.[12] Unfortunately, scholars in the latter field have largely restricted their study to the cognitive work of philosophers, scientists, and scholars. An adequate sociology of knowledge must range far more broadly than that.[13] Above all, it must recognize that all work presupposes knowledge, that it is the practice of knowledge, and that the social and economic organization of practice plays a critical role in determining both what knowledge can be employed in work and how that knowledge can be exercised. Here I will make a tentative effort to portray the full range of knowledge that is used in work, distinguishing different types by their origins and their relation to social institutions. Then I will be able to clarify the distinction between mental and manual labor, elaborate my distinction between mechanical and discretionary specialization, and delineate

---

11 My guess is that the best known and most admired practitioners of a craft or discipline are those with superior skill, or facilitative knowledge (style of discourse) rather than necessarily those with superior substantive knowledge (or erudition).

12 I do not discuss a third dimension of undoubted importance in many kinds of work, manual as well as intellectual – the "gift," whose source is probably genetic. See Lioger 1993, 1996 for an interesting case study of French dowsers and their gift. My only justification for omitting it is that while it can be very important for success in doing some kinds of work, it is an individual attribute not learned in a classroom or routinely acquired by experience.

13 Swidler and Arditi 1994 report on recent efforts to extend the reach of the field.

the kind of knowledge that establishes the foundation for the institutions of professionalism.

Of the varieties of knowledge and skill connected with work we can first and most fundamentally distinguish that knowledge and skill which all normal adults must possess in order to perform the everyday tasks of daily life from the knowledge and skill needed only by those who work at particular jobs and occupations. This of course varies in time and place. Virtually everyone in our present-day society learns, for example, how to sweep a floor, use a shovel, and drive an automobile – all are part of what we may call *everyday knowledge and skill.* Some of that everyday knowledge and skill is shared by all normal adults, but the ubiquitous division of labor between the sexes results in some being gender-specific. In our society, for example, women are more likely than men to know how to cook, iron, sew, and care for infants, while men are more likely than women to know how to care for and use tools and machinery. In addition, I would guess that some kinds of everyday knowledge and skill are differentially distributed by social class, with working-class men, for example, more likely than middle-class men to know how to maintain and repair engines.

This corpus of everyday knowledge and skill, somewhat segmented by age, race, gender, and class, is used unselfconsciously: people do not reflect on it and may not even be able to verbalize it. Some is certainly tacit. It includes what Schutz (1970) and Garfinkel (1967) would call taken-for-granted activity, and what Geertz (1983a: 73–93) discusses as common sense. It is an essential prerequisite for the performance of virtually any kind of work in a society. In not yet industrialized societies, everyday knowledge is taught informally to children during the course of their lives in the household and community. In advanced industrial nations, children have been required to attend formal schools where teachers are responsible for teaching much more – such skills as reading, writing, and arithmetic, and a considerable stock of information.

It is important to note that some of what is taught in the primary and secondary schools that all children must attend is formal in character, based on abstract theories and concepts created by the intellectual classes.[14] While that formal knowledge (see Freidson 1986: 2–16) becomes part of everyday knowledge, it is only a part, and a small part at that, of a much larger corpus. Some of it – what Machlup (1962: 21–2) calls "intellectual knowledge" – is taught to

---

14 One must not overlook the important role of the mass media, television in particular, for their contribution to everyday knowledge, if not skill.

children who obtain a higher education, and becomes incorporated into the everyday knowledge of the educated middle class. The largest part of it, however, is taught only to those seeking specialized vocations.

Unlike everyday knowledge, formal knowledge is institutionalized into what Foucault (1979) called "disciplines" and Holzner (1968: 68–70) "epistemic communities." These are of course inevitably rooted in everyday knowledge but are organized in institutions set apart from everyday life. Special groups of intellectual workers embody the authority of those disciplines, their work being to create, preserve, transmit, debate and revise disciplinary content. The formal knowledge of particular disciplines is taught to those aspiring to enter specialized occupations with professional standing. Much of it is abstract and general in character, however, and cannot be applied directly to the problems of work. For actually performing work, formal knowledge may be needed in some cases, but so also are specialized knowledge and skill of a more concrete nature and, of course, everyday knowledge.

Working Knowledge

Borrowing from Kusterer (1978), we might call all the knowledge and skill used in work, whatever the source and the content, whether everyday or formal, *working knowledge*. His conception of it is drawn from his study of industrial and clerical workers:

> All working knowledge appears to fit into one basic subject area, knowledge of routine processing procedures, and four supplementary subject areas: knowledge of the variable properties of the materials ... processed; knowledge of variable and potentially manipulable aspects of the equipment or machinery; knowledge of patterns of client or customer behavior and knowledge of patterns of work behavior of others in the work organization, especially including managers ... The workers' knowledge about each of these subject areas invariably contains two elements, the diagnostic and the prescriptive. The diagnostic is made up of all the background information about that aspect of the situation that is necessary for workers to ask and answer the question, "What is the source of this problem?" The prescriptive element consists of a repertoire of previously tried and tested procedures or coping techniques that will (at least partially) solve this problem. After the problem has been diagnosed

prescriptive knowledge enables workers to answer the question, "How can this problem be handled?" (Kusterer 1978: 138)[15]

If we take "working knowledge" to be a general category for the knowledge employed in *all* kinds of work, however, we can only conclude that Kusterer's conception is too narrow. For one thing, it only implicitly includes the taken-for-granted everyday knowledge that supplies the background skills and understandings necessary to perform "routine processing procedures." Kusterer himself notes that "although, conceptually, knowledge acquired outside the work place and put to work on the job is just as worthy to be considered working knowledge as knowledge learned on the job itself, nobody in fact concedes this. Workers themselves . . . invariably neglected to include those procedures, such as sweeping, driving, reading, and writing, that are a normal part of their life off the job as well as on it" (1978: 138). Part of this neglect by the workers may be due to the fact that "it is the knowledge required to perform particular tasks that is more conspicuous and given more respect than commonly-held, everyday knowledge" (p. 137).

In addition to the necessity of including everyday knowledge as a component of working knowledge (and remembering that concepts and theories are not absent from everyday knowledge), there is also the necessity of including formal knowledge for at least some kinds of work. This becomes immediately apparent when we compare Kusterer's reference to the diagnostic and prescriptive elements of working knowledge with Abbott's analysis of diagnosis, inference, and treatment as "the three acts of professional practice" (Abbott 1988: 40–52). Woven through Kusterer's analysis is reference to the importance of specialized formal knowledge in conducting those activities, but it is by no means the only kind of knowledge that is employed. One component of the knowledge and skill that he examines in the work of industrial and clerical

---

15   Burchell et al. (1994: 159), who studied British industrial workers, put it this way: "The undertaking of different types of tasks requires of job holders varying combinations of a wide range of attributes, exercised at varying degrees of intensity. These include the ability to manipulate tools, machines, and materials; knowledge of products, processes, machines, organizations, and procedures; the capabilities of cultivating and maintaining social relationships; the acceptance of responsibility for property, output, standards, and people; physical strength; mental ability; tolerance of working conditions; the ability to organize, coordinate and exercise discretion in undertaking task requirements; and the exercising and acceptance of authority."

workers is neither everyday nor formal but somewhere in between. I suggest that most of what he discusses may be called *practical knowledge* – knowledge largely free of formal concepts and theories, learned by experience, and instrumental for performing concrete tasks in concrete settings.

In many kinds of work, what Scribner (1986) calls practical thinking involving little formal knowledge is dominant in the constitution of working knowledge. She characterizes it as "thinking that is embedded in the larger purposive activities of daily life and that functions to achieve the goals of those activities. . . . So conceived – embedded and instrumental – practical thinking stands in contrast to the type of thinking involved in the performance of isolated mental tasks undertaken as ends in themselves" (Scribner 1986: 15). Much of the knowledge and skill it employs is developed and learned situationally, on the job, as information about the tasks to be performed and as skills to be employed in performing them, and consciously used in work.

We may assume that some of that practical knowledge and skill is tacit, and therefore neither verbalized nor codified. Tacit knowledge of the concrete circumstances in which virtually any kind of work must be performed is as essential to performance as the tacit skills employed to use it. What is tacitly known and used of course depends on the particular work: it is one thing for business executives and college professors (Wagner and Sternberg 1986), quite another for tellers in a bank and machine operators in a paper products factory (Kusterer 1978), and still another for the *bricoleur* (Lévi-Strauss 1966: 21; Berry and Irvine 1986: 271–4). Scribner emphasizes the discretionary character of the practical thinking which is involved in the use of working knowledge: "one artful aspect of practical thinking is to construct or redefine a problem that experience or hunch suggests will facilitate a solution or enable the application of a preferred mode of problem-solving . . . *Skilled* practical thinking is marked by flexibility – solving the same problem now one way, now another, each way finely fitted to the occasion. . . . Only novices use algorithmic [that is, mechanical, formatted] procedures to solve problems" (1986: 21–2, italics added). Patently, by definition, those performing mechanical specializations do not indulge in Scribner's "skilled practical thinking."

All forms of work thus require both everyday and practical knowledge and skill in varying degrees, but only some require the specialized formal knowledge that has not been incorporated into everyday knowledge. This assumption allows us to distinguish on analytical grounds the most important element of the mental/

manual contrast – namely, that specialized formal knowledge which is not part of everyday knowledge, but rather gained through special vocational schooling, and which is a prerequisite for some kinds of work but not others. Even when the actual tasks required by a specialization such as surgery are predominantly manual, they are defined as mental because of their grounding in abstract concepts and theories. Furthermore, in recognition of the widespread and largely arbitrary distinction between skilled and unskilled or semi-skilled manual work, it is possible to delineate skilled work as a discretionary specialization based upon everyday and practical, but not necessarily formal knowledge. Manual skilled work, of course, is identified with the historic crafts,[16] and is based largely on training in practical knowledge and skill. Historically, the work of the technician belongs somewhere between the crafts and professions, relying extensively on practical knowledge but also employing a significant amount of formal knowledge.[17] On the other hand, discretionary specializations which do include a large component of formal knowledge in their training are identified with the historic professions. Those special-izations which embody values held by the public at large, the state, or some powerful elite are given the privileged status of monopoly, or control over their own work. *This monopolistic control is the essential characteristic of ideal-typical professionalism from which all else flows.*

---

16   The mental/manual distinction is especially interesting in the cases of the painter and the sculptor, for not until the Renaissance did they rise above the undignified status of manual worker, or artisan, and to this day the line between art and craft has been unclear (see Becker 1982). As late as the 1970s the French census classified painters and sculptors as "artisans," while writers were classified with the intellectual professions. See Moulin (1992: 249–74) for a brief history of the status of artists from the Middle Ages to this day, including comments on changes in their official classification in the French census and social welfare system. I might add that not until comparatively recently was surgery given more than craft status.

17   Perhaps one can conceive of an ideal-typical technician, "between craft and science," as Whalley and Barley (1997) put it, neither profession nor craft, but something distinctly different. However, those with the job title of technician are much more heterogeneous than those called professions and crafts. Many are so newly created as to be still unformed, and as Whalley and Barley themselves recognize, are created in many different ways and for different purposes. Tech-nicians are much too important to ignore, both because of their rapidly increasing number and their critical position in many productive institutions, but I believe it is premature to declare them a generically new form of occupation. All that is certain is that they are a relatively new bureaucratically defined job or personnel category.

Specializations

In this chapter I have located in a broader context the knowledge attributed to those workers who are given the privilege of controlling their own work and have distinguished it from other kinds of knowledge and skill. *Skill* is the capacity to use knowledge in accomplishing a task. Like substantive knowledge, it can be tacit, embedded in experience without being verbalized, codified, or systematically taught. Substantive knowledge connected with work takes different forms and is distributed among different populations. Some is consciously articulated informally and concretely during the course of everyday life, but some is so taken for granted as to be virtually tacit and not self-consciously taught. Such *everyday knowledge* is shared by all adult members of a community and, in advanced industrial societies, is composed of both the informal knowledge of everyday life and the knowledge that is taught in schools and by the media, some of which involves abstract theories and concepts. It provides the foundation for all other kinds of knowledge and skill.

Working knowledge on the other hand, has narrower scope than everyday knowledge because it is addressed solely to accomplishing work and, apart from that portion addressed to the performance of everyday tasks in the household and community, is not shared by the general population. Rather, it is segmented into bodies of *practical* knowledge and skill, both conscious and tacit, shared only by those who do the same work, sometimes in but one work-setting. Finally, there is *formal* knowledge, which is composed of bodies of information and ideas organized by theories and abstract concepts. Some of it inevitably rests on the taken-for-granted (which is to say, tacit) assumptions stemming from both everyday and working knowledge, and some of it becomes part of everyday knowledge in advanced industrial societies, but most of it is divided among specialized disciplines practiced by different groups of specialized workers.

This analysis allows distinguishing specializations by the degree to which they are thought to employ these various types of knowledge.[18] A mechanical specialization is thought to employ

18   These distinctions should not lead us to forget that formal knowledge is less protected from diffusion today than it was yesterday. Knowledge and skill are not permanently imprisoned within different specializations. The schools, the internet, the media, occupations, firms, and segments of the public all interact to distribute once esoteric knowledge to lay persons, though never completely.

largely everyday knowledge and skill, some of which is of course tacit, and a fairly small proportion of practical knowledge connected with work in particular settings. A discretionary manual specialization employs a large proportion of practical knowledge, and moderate proportions of everyday, formal, and tacit knowledge. A mental discretionary specialization, on the other hand, is distinguished by its reliance on a relatively small proportion of everyday and tacit knowledge, a moderate amount of practical knowledge, and a high proportion of formal knowledge. Table 1.1 presents these distinctions in skeletal form.

These are not the only distinctions one must make in thinking about work in general and the kind of work connected with professionalism. I shall make more distinctions in the chapters that follow, including the important characteristic of *transferability*, which frees specialists from being dependent on work that can be performed in only one place and for only one employer or client. But those established here allow one to specify the ideal-typical character of the knowledge and skill imputed to practitioners who receive official sanction to control their own work. The concept of discretion is central to it and deserving of special status. As Fox (1974: 26–35) has shown at some length in analyzing industrial work, the right of discretion implies being trusted, being committed, even being morally involved in one's work. As the assumption is made that failure in work is not due to willful neglect, externally imposed rules governing work are minimized. Thus, when the practice of an occupation is believed to require the use of discretion, this ramifies into a number of critical areas having to do with the organization of work and the way the participants in that organization regard both each other and the work they do. The ideal-typical position of professionalism is founded on the official

Table 1.1   Relative proportion of each type of knowledge and skill in each type of specialization

Type of specialization	Everyday knowledge	Practical knowledge	Formal knowledge	Tacit knowledge
Mechanical	High	Low	Low	Moderate
Manual discretionary	Moderate	High	Moderate	High
Mental discretionary	Low	Moderate	High	Low

belief that the knowledge and skill of a particular specialization requires a foundation in abstract concepts and formal learning and necessitates the exercise of discretion. When so recognized, a number of distinctive institutional consequences follow, the first of which has to do with the organization of the division of labor.

2

Divisions of Labor

In the last chapter I wrote of specialization in the abstract, as representing different types of knowledge and skill involved in a task or set of tasks. Furthermore, I discussed specialization as a property of individual workers rather than as a social phenomenon. However, I am not concerned with tasks alone – which machines can perform, after all. I am concerned with work and occupations, which are social enterprises. Therefore I need to make sense of the ways in which they are organized, most particularly the way work is coordinated and controlled when individuals are performing different but related tasks. Here, therefore, I will extend the idea of work as specialized knowledge and skill into an explicitly social context, using the concept of the division of labor to represent the organization and coordination of the relations between workers performing different but interconnected specializations. I will show how the division of labor of ideal-typical professionalism is constituted and organized, comparing it with the distinctly different ways to be found in a free market and in a bureaucracy.[1]

The Intrinsic Relational Properties of Specialization

Part of the fluidity and complexity of the concept of specialization lies in its intrinsic relativity. This is to say that an activity can be

---

1 This chapter is an extensive revision and updating of a paper originally published in 1976 and reprinted in Freidson 1994b: 49–60.

defined as specialized only in relation to something else. Bücher, for example, asserts that specialization involves the transfer of "an economic task . . . from one person hitherto performing it to several persons . . . so that each of these performs but a separate part of the *previous* total labour" (Bücher 1907: 289, italics added). Thus, he identifies specialization by its relationship to a *historically prior* task rather than to some intrinsically whole or complete task.

Specializations can also be defined by comparison. Take Laski's (1931) denigration of the role of "specialists" in politics; yet the statesmen he lauds are no more generalists than are corporate executives, for they specialize in statecraft and management, performing those tasks full-time and for their living. They cannot be considered generalists in the absolute sense that Robinson Crusoe was. They are generalists only relatively, in comparison to others doing different kinds of work. A physician who is head of a department of health is also a generalist in comparison to, let us say, one who practices pediatrics, but is a specialist in comparison to a minister of health, or a prime minister. And so it is with the examples provided by Xenophon: the shoemaker who makes shoes for both men and women is a generalist compared to the one who makes shoes for men or women alone, but is a specialist in comparison to a leatherworker who makes belts, saddles, and bridles as well as shoes for men and women.

Thus, while it is indeed possible to define "generalist" and "specialist" abstractly in absolute terms, neither can be identified empirically in any other than relative terms. The same may be said of the idea of a "whole task." One person's "whole task" is another person's "specialty." Specialization can be delineated only by reference to some imagined or historically real *other* task that is considered to be the whole from which it came. It is not in practice a stable or an absolute concept. And since it is intrinsically relative, its invocation is likely to be subject to strong ideological winds.

It follows from the relativity of the idea of specialization that it must represent a *relationship* rather than a free-standing position. One cannot talk of a single specialization: for one specialization to exist there must also be another. There must be at least two specializations and they must have some sort of relationship to each other in order to be considered specializations that together are able to create the product or service that was once produced by only one set of activities. A specialization thus presupposes both a more general set of activities from which it is thought to derive or which it is designed to replace, and at least one other specialized activity that arises with it in the course of the division or differentiation of the more general set. Perhaps this is why in some discussions "specialization" and "division of labor" are used interchangeably. The question is how particular specializations are constituted and most particularly how the relationships among a number of them are organized into a division of labor.

The Concept of the Division of Labor

Both Adam Smith and Karl Marx made heavy use of the phrase "division of labor" to refer, at least in part, to specialization. So far, I have tried to restrict my usage to mean only "specialization." Its importance was established by the work of Smith who did not, in his day, have the term "specialization" available to him. Thus, through no fault of his own, he established a tradition of usage that is confusing, and that has unfortunately been carried down to our own time through the work of Karl Marx and Émile Durkheim.

The division of labor is a poorly developed concept, shot through with ambiguity (see Salz 1933: 279). For all its patent importance and for all the extensive use of it by a host of writers, 117 years after the publication of *The Wealth of Nations* Durkheim could write that "the theory of the division of labor has made . . . little progress since Adam Smith" (1964: 46). And more than a half-century after Durkheim, Clemente (1972: 31) could still claim that the concept is "one of the most neglected," that "it has received far less attention than it merits." Some two decades after that it could be said accurately that "surprisingly little research takes the division of labor as problematic and examines its social and political determinants as well as administrative and technical factors" (Strang and Baron 1990: 480). This may be because the classic writers – Smith, Marx, and Durkheim – had a larger, more central purpose and gave it little direct attention. They used the phrase to represent two quite different things – a synonym for specialization in the abstract, on the one hand, and on the other hand the manner in which specializations are constituted into occupations or jobs and their interrelationships organized.

As to Adam Smith, most of the time he clearly meant merely specialization, and as we saw in the last chapter, while he recognized the existence of more than one kind of specialization, he did not attempt to analyze them all. Had some other writer than Smith been responsible for popularizing the concept and with some other purpose than his, the received notion would no doubt have been different. But he was not really interested in the division of labor in and of itself. Like the other classical writers, Smith was concerned with understanding and conceptualizing the deep changes going on in European political economies, the movement from feudal, pre-industrial society to what we call modern, industrial society. He was concerned with explaining the sources of productivity and capital accumulation. Unlike many other classical writers, however, he advocated a particular national economic policy that he believed would lead to "universal opulence." Given his purpose, the concept of the division of labor warranted little extended analysis (see Meek and Skinner 1973). As Bücher (1907: 284) complained, "What division of labor is we can nowhere learn from Adam Smith," for it figured as a source of productivity and little more.

Smith saw the division of labor through the lens of his prescriptive conception of the free market, a state of perfect economic freedom. The market was seen as a fluid process composed of shifting demands by consumers of labor and its products and competition among workers to satisfy those demands, with tasks arrayed in a dynamic, functionally interdependent and efficient productive system through free and unfettered individual competition. His conceptual scheme could not tolerate any purposeful social organization that interfered with the operation of a free market. Indeed, the system was seen as automatic, self-adjusting, and efficient only when unobstructed by organizations. For Smith, if tasks were stabilized and organized by feudal corporations or worker or employer "combinations" (which is to say unions, trade associations, and other collective arrangements), a comparatively unproductive division of labor would result. A productive division of labor, by contrast, would result from keeping tasks responsive to demand alone, performed by workers who compete for work solely as individuals.

Like Smith, Marx sometimes used the idea of the division of labor to represent specialization in the abstract, sometimes to represent something quite different. In his earlier writings (Rattansi 1982: 59–85), when he deplored the division of labor and wished to abolish it entirely as a barrier to the development of the full potential of human beings, he clearly meant to refer to specialization. While he did make some distinction between the mechanical specialization to be found in factories and those to be found in the crafts, he did not dwell on them or address them analytically, and he rejected them both. For Marx, specialization was by its very nature undesirable, a position about which I shall have more to say later in this book.

His usage in other contexts was quite different, however. His concept of the detailed division of labor of the factory included within it not only what I call mechanical specialization, but also the formally structured social organization of the capitalist-owned factory in which mechanical specialization is instituted and sustained by "officers" and "sergeants" in managerial and supervisory roles. He saw both the mechanical specializations and the organization of supervision as stemming from the specific historical circumstance of capitalism (Marx 1967: chs 13–14). For him, the "detailed division of labor" contains within it both a variety of tasks which are all mechanical in character and a formal social organization that is employed to constitute, direct, and coordinate them. In contrast, the "social division of labor" is composed of all the different occupations or tasks that exist in a society as a whole, regardless of the type of specialization or the social method of organizing it. Marx portrayed the social division of labor as being composed of "independent commodity-producers" (Marx 1967: 350–5). His analysis is richer than Smith's or Durkheim's, including other distinctions not mentioned here but discussed in Rattansi (1982: 129–35), yet, as an abstract concept the division of labor still remains untidy and ambiguous.

Like Smith, Durkheim was concerned with the division of labor less for itself than for another purpose. As Kemper (1972) correctly noted, in *The Division of Labor in Society* (1964), Durkheim was preoccupied with refuting the Utilitarians, and especially Herbert Spencer.[2] He claimed that Spencer saw the division of labor as a precondition for the possibility of exchange and contractual relations and thus in some sense prior to and independent of established, organized societal arrangements. Durkheim argued precisely the reverse, and was not so much concerned with a close examination and articulation of the concept of the division of labor as with considering the kinds of social regulation and cohesion it presupposed. He used the phrase to represent "the apportionment of functions" (1964: 56).

While Adam Smith did his best to establish the artificiality of a socially regulated division of labor, Durkheim argued precisely the opposite. "The division of labor can be effectuated only among members of an already constituted [and organized] society," he

---

2 It has been argued that Durkheim misrepresented Spencer's theories "in an effort to hide his borrowing of Spencer's ideas" (Turner 1985: 64).

wrote (1964: 275). Worker and employer organizations, as well as what Durkheim called "restitutive law" – that is, the civil and administrative law governing the property, job, and contractual rights and obligations of participants in the economy – composed a part of that "already constituted society" without which agreements in the marketplace could not hold. Durkheim insisted that the division of labor was socially regulated, not a mere aggregate of individually contracted exchanges. Although that proposition obviously implies some kind of social organization or structure rather than free competition, he did not discuss such organization in any but the most general terms.

In so far as the concept of specialization is itself relative, any single instance presupposes another against which it is contrasted and by which its position is established. And in so far as any single specialty presupposes a relationship to at least one other that derives from the division of a more general task, then a structure or organization of relationships must be assumed. With this in mind, I will use the term "division of labor" to represent the structure of social relationships that organizes and coordinates the work of related specializations or occupations. One can conceive of a division of labor on a number of levels – in society as a whole (as in Marx's idea of the social division of labor), in a given economic sector or industry (such as health care, construction, manufacturing, agriculture), and in a given firm, work organization, or work-setting (where Marx located the detailed division of labor, and Smith his pinmakers). On each level the relevant productive tasks would vary in both content and number. On a society-wide level of analysis one would have to account for the entire range of tasks upon which the economy rests; on an industrial or sectoral level of analysis one would have to account only for the tasks performed within that industry or sector; on the level of the bureaucracy or firm, one need explain only the tasks performed within it.

Following Durkheim,[3] I assume that the relationships among specializations in a division of labor are socially regulated rather than the result of either spontaneous individual exchanges or the constraints of technical necessity. To make sense of such a socially regulated division of labor one must specify the source of the exercise of power that shapes it. But this argument depends upon

3 I deliberately omit Max Weber's discussion of the technical, social, and economic aspects of the division of labor here because of its cryptic, almost purely taxonomic thrust. See Weber 1978: 114–50.

first showing that the division of labor cannot be effectively conceptualized as a purely functional adaptation to ecological or economic necessity.

The Ecological Approach to the Division of Labor

It is a truism that specialization grew rapidly when the early high civilizations found the means to support large concentrations of population – a connection observed by early Western thinkers like Xenophon and Plato and many others in later times. Adam Smith connected specialization with "the extent of the market," which can of course be increased both by population density and by improved transportation. And Durkheim asserted social or moral density and "social volume," or population, as a cause of increased specialization (Durkheim 1964: 262; and see Schnore 1958.) This idea, perhaps borrowed from Spencer by Durkheim but in any case fairly common in nineteenth-century writing, has been used by human ecologists to postulate a direct relationship between the size of a population and its degree of specialization, a relationship in which they claim that culture or social norms (or in Durkheim's terms, social regulation) play no part (see Gibbs and Martin 1962: 677).

Gibbs and Martin made an essential distinction between two general ideas associated with the concept – first, differentiation of the workforce into different occupational specialties, which is designated as the *degree* of the division of labor, and, second, the *basis* on which occupational position in the division of labor is established (Gibbs and Martin 1962: 669). The basis of the division of labor represents the source and the nature of the criteria by which specializations are established. In a subsequent paper, Labovitz and Gibbs defined the degree of the division of labor as the *number* of different occupations in a population and the evenness of the distribution of the population into those occupations. "The maximum degree of division of labor occurs when no two people have a common occupation" (Labovitz and Gibbs 1964: 5). Rushing, using those distinctions in a study of formal organizations, called them "structural differentiation and structurally determined *individual differentiation* (or extent of dispersion)" (Rushing 1968: 235). The *basis* for determining whether or not a particular specialization should exist and what kind of people will be allowed to perform it was ignored, though it represents a critical factor.

Ten years after the publication of the Gibbs and Martin paper attention to the distinction between the degree and the basis of specialization had disappeared. The number of occupations and the distribution of the workforce among them became the accepted best representation of the division of labor as such (see Clemente 1972; Smith and Snow 1976). The division of labor was assumed to be simply an aggregate of individuals performing different tasks. No attention was paid to the social forces that organize tasks into roles, jobs, and occupations, breaking down tasks into more particular specializations, and organizing the relationships among those tasks.

Yet this mode of analysis relies on empirical data created by those very forces. How can one get information about the division of labor? The existence of the variety of specializations is determined by examining official labor force statistics, the number of specializations being the number of separate occupational titles to be found in such statistics.[4] However, those titles are created and defined by the functionaries of both firms and the state, and as Form (1968: 24) observed, "occupational classifications are made to fit administrative needs." Their very existence as occupational titles presupposes social organization in which culture and social norms, not to speak of power, play a major part. Stark notes that in large firms

> the regulatory bureaucratization that has rationalized the employ-
> ment relation operates through a set of codes – systems of classifica-
> tion that delineate various categories of persons and practices, and
> demarcate boundaries of eligibility and liability. . . . Unlike the codes
> of everyday life (without which bureaucracies themselves would
> cease to function), bureaucratized conventions are rationalized in a
> dual sense of the word. Their codification is standardized and their
> rationale . . . is made explicit. These explicit rationalizations are both
> a resource and an object of struggle among contending groups and
> classes. (Stark 1989: 643–4)

Strang and Baron's study of job titles in the California civil service (1990) clearly demonstrates a variability in the number of job titles (that is, specializations) or degree of the division of labor that can only be explained as "an object of struggle among contending groups and classes." What we know of the division of

---

4 For a number of excellent studies of how official statistics are created, see Anderson 1988, Conk 1980, Desrosières and Thévenot 1988, Irvine et al. 1975, and Starr 1987. And for insight into the various ways in which the job title "technician" is created, see Whalley and Barley 1997: 36–9.

labor from official statistics, therefore, cannot fail to be at least a partial function of arbitrary decisions on the part of those who create the classification system and those who influence them. Quite clearly, the conventional data by which the degree of the division of labor is determined are sufficiently arbitrary and artificial to cast considerable doubt on their validity. They reflect the basis, that is, forces or powers which create a particular division of labor rather than some functional necessity.

Apart from the methodological difficulties connected with the source and nature of the data used to test the predictions of a narrowly ecological approach, there are theoretical reasons for arguing that social forces play a major role in shaping both the degree of specialization and relationships among specializations. The aggregate of specializations representing the degree of the division of labor is merely that, an aggregate. But since no single specialization can exist without having a functioning relationship with at least one other, one cannot portray, let alone understand, a division of labor by simply adding up specializations to get a total. They must be treated as part of an organized set of relationships.

Furthermore, since there is more than one way to make a pin or skin a cat or produce a steel beam, the number of specializations needed to reach some production goal is indeterminate, not automatically given by the functional needs of that goal. This is not to say that a productive end and the technical means of gaining it pose no *limits* to the range of methods and tasks that can be used. But within those broad limits there is room for considerable variation in the number, type, organization, and content of specializations which can fulfill different functions. That variation can best be explained by the use of economic or political power to choose and enforce alternatives.

Finally, an issue that has not received as much theoretical attention as it deserves is the life-span of specializations – their persistence over time, the speed at which they are replaced by or broken up into other specializations (see Dingwall 1983). That issue cannot be addressed by the ecological approach because it is concerned only with number, not content. It cannot show whether, over time, a constant *number* of specializations represents the persistence of a particular set of specializations or the replacement of one set by another of the same number. But surely the relative permanence or transience of specializations is a matter worthy of attention, bearing heavily as it does on the work life of those in the labor force. If specializations are unstable and transient, the career-lines[5] of the labor force involve constant movement from one specialization to another. If they are stable and long-lasting, career-lines will be more orderly and predictable. The differing consequences of each alternative are much too important to ignore.

In sum, an adequate conception of the division of labor must be able to deal systematically with a number of different issues. Certainly the number of specializations in a division of labor is important, but so is the organization of the relationships among them – that is, whether they work alongside each other as equals or whether some are subordinate to others – and their relative permanence or transience. These are not determined mechanically, for the same productive end may be reached by different methods of constituting and organizing a division of labor. A critical task is thus to delineate the different criteria used for establishing a division of labor and drawing out the consequences of each. Professionalism represents one of three logically different bases, each of the three leading to quite different consequences.

Smith and Marx on the Division of Labor

Economists deal with society-wide, even global economies, but are concerned less with social organization than with their fiscal policies and productivity. Those who deal with the social organization of relationships among specializations, on the other hand, tend to focus on smaller units. The greatest attention is paid to the organization of the firms that employ a large proportion, even if not a majority, of the working population of industrial nations. Some writers have argued, like the ecologists, that the demands of efficiency require one form of organization rather than another for the accomplishment of specific tasks, but recent work has cast serious doubt on the existence of some "one best way."[6] Indeed, the issue of efficiency itself is problematic. Rueschemeyer (1986) correctly argues that the determination of what is efficient and what is not is arbitrary, that there are no objective and fixed criteria for efficiency, and in his sensitive and sophisticated discussion Reinhardt (1992) argues that the concept of efficiency always contains ideological elements. In fact, no inevitable functional

---

5 I shall deal with career-lines more systematically in chapter 3.
6 For a classic review of organizational theory, including an analysis of efforts to explain modes of organization by reference to technical imperatives, see Perrow 1986.

necessity determines efficiency. Rather, those with the power to do so select the criteria and on that basis encourage or create a division of labor that establishes a variety of jobs and organizes the relationships among them. That is, the organization of work is *chosen*. Which kind of organization is chosen for any particular time, place, and division of labor depends in part on the technical limits imposed by the productive goal itself and the resources available for reaching it and in part on who holds the power to choose among alternatives and establish particular criteria of efficiency.

That there is choice among ways of organizing the division of labor was certainly recognized by Adam Smith in his discussion of how the "policies of Europe," guided by mercantilist theory and, one might guess, political expediency, interfered with the free operation of the market. It was not that Europe could not survive under those policies, but rather, Smith believed, that its economy would grow more strongly under the conditions of a free market supported by laissez-faire policies on the part of the state. And Marx, as is well known, asserted over and over again that capitalists determined the concrete historical form of the division of labor in the factory, not technological necessity or nature as such (see, for example, Marx 1963: 127–44). Of course, Marx's view of an ideal society differed from Smith's. His was a society in which the working class supplants the capitalist and in which the division of labor is organized by collective choice and control (see Ollman 1976–7; Weiss 1976; Rattansi 1982: 163–79). In one way or another, however, both Smith and Marx were preoccupied with delineating how specialized tasks should be organized. The same may sometimes be said of Max Weber. Taking them together with Weber, two logically different models or ideal types to guide the organization of the division of labor can be seen. These are purely logical constructs, in part abstracted from and in part imposed upon the forms of the division of labor to be found in history.

Division of Labor Based on Free Competition

Adam Smith clearly suggests one way of organizing the division of labor in society. Within his state of perfect liberty labor can be organized solely by exchange relations in which all workers are free to compete with each other as individuals to perform any kind of work they choose without constraint. He presents what a critic has called "Crusoe economics" (Lavoie 1991). A particular way of creating a division of labor flows from those conditions of perfect freedom. "Combinations" by which workers or employers conspire collectively to gain an advantage in the marketplace must not exist. Without combinations, the division of labor can be very fluid, with occupational specializations and productive enterprises freely emerging and disappearing as market demand and competition by others change. Those manufacturers and tradespeople who survive must not only produce goods and services at the lowest possible cost (which is interpreted as efficiency) but must also be capable of shifting from one product or service to another when market demand shifts or when competition reduces the possibility of profit, or else they will disappear and be supplanted by competitors.

Similarly, in that situation of perfectly free competition within markets, workers are both geographically and occupationally mobile so as to be able to perform whatever task gains them the largest income wherever that may be. Without any restriction on movement from one locality to another in search of work and without reluctance to move or any protective laws or customs to prevent workers from offering to do any kind of work, work-roles, jobs, or occupations cannot have clear boundaries or jurisdictions. Much work is likely to be performed in jobs whose very existence may be fleeting, and whose tasks may change. Such jobs can develop no coherent identity, and those performing them are unlikely to be inclined or able to develop common occupational identity and consciousness. Indeed, a great deal of work is likely to involve everyday specializations that can be performed in a wide variety of circumstances. The content of work involving mechanical and discretionary specializations is likely to be unstable, varying even if in only minor ways to satisfy the different demands of each employer or customer.[7] Thus, the relative *number* of different specializations will be extremely high, though the substantive differences among them will probably be minor. Because many if not most jobs are likely to be short-lived, few if any will be based on extensive experience or training. Work careers, or career-lines, which I will discuss more systematically in chapter 3, will become a succession of diverse, temporary market positions which by their nature cannot require the application of complex skills for which a long period of training or experience is required – "disorderly careers" (Wilensky 1961, and see Spilerman

---

7   It is characteristic of both classical and neoclassical economists to maximize the capacity of consumers to make well-informed, rationally calculating decisions.

1977), with the work classified as unskilled or semi-skilled. Without jurisdictional protection or other sources of stability and definiteness, the content of jobs will vary to satisfy the differing demands of each employer or customer. Standardization is discouraged.

As I have already noted, a reasonably comprehensive picture of the divisions of labor in a society must be able to portray them on three different levels of analysis – first, in society as a whole, what Marx called the social division of labor, second, in particular industrial or economic sectors of that society, and third, in the productive organizations or firms and labor markets within those sectors. But given truly free individual competition and the fluidity it presupposes due to the absence of organized social constraints on workers and consumers, it is difficult to imagine how such a division of labor could exist in anything but a small and simple society where there are relatively few consumers and sophisticated demands. It is even difficult to imagine how the modestly organized pin manufactory described by Smith could exist, let alone the larger, more elaborately differentiated organizations analyzed later by Marx. Furthermore, such an arrangement would have to contend with the process that Smith (1976a, 74–5) deplored, when "masters" collude with each other against labor and exploit the intrinsic advantage of their possession of capital and capital equipment over workers who possess merely labor power. Such collusion contradicts the terms of the free-market model, of course, as does collusion among workers.

Seeking to show why the pin factory's organization into a hierarchy of masters and workers is efficient even though it violates Smith's simple model, Williamson (1975: 50) explains that it is a means by which to economize on "buffer inventories and mitigate costly haggling." That "simple hierarchy" he introduces is a crude version of a second, quite different method of organizing a division of labor. It was elaborated by Max Weber as the rationalization of administration or management by monocratic or centralized authority.

The Bureaucratic Division of Labor

In a political economy as a whole, in its differentiated industrial or economic sectors, and in particular work-settings, it is possible to conceive of a hierarchically controlled plan that specifies in detail what each task of a division of labor shall be, who shall perform it, what the relations shall be between tasks, and who shall be empowered to exercise direction over them. Marx (1963: 135) imagined how the division of labor of an entire society could be organized hierarchically:

> Society as a whole has this in common with the interior of a workshop, that it too has its division of labour. If one took as a model the division of labour in a modern workshop, in order to apply it to a whole society, the society best organized for the production of wealth would undoubtedly be that which had a single chief employer, distributing tasks to the different members of the community according to a previously fixed rule.

In this prophecy Marx sketched what we call a command economy, but he denied that in his time the social division of labor (which is to say, the division of labour in the entire economy) was organized in that manner, concluding that "while inside the modern workshop the division of labour is meticulously regulated by the authority of the employer, modern society [as a whole] has no other rule, no other authority for the distribution of labour than free competition" (1963: 135). In short, he inaccurately characterized the social division of labor of his time as what Adam Smith hoped it could be and conceived of an efficient method of organizing an entire political economy in direct contradiction of Smith's hopes. It was Weber who formalized the principles of that hierarchical or bureaucratic division of labor.

In Weber's analysis, authority could be exercised in a number of ways, including by the collegiality characteristic of professionalism (Waters 1989), but he gave the greatest historical importance to the monocratic, rational-legal mode. When rational-legal authority organizes work, formal, written rules establish the duties of each position, occupation, or job as well as their relationships. The organization of positions is pyramidal, establishing clear lines of authority leading up to the ultimate executive officer. Furthermore, while that organized division of labor is rationalized, it is not fixed. It can be altered, but neither consumers nor workers control such change. Should the occasion demand or a new conception of efficiency arise, administrative authority is empowered within the limits and by the means specified by the formal rules to reconstitute the tasks composing jobs and the titles attached to them, to eliminate or revise them, and create new ones. We would therefore expect some instability in the particular specializations or jobs in the bureaucratic division of labor, but since bureaucratic rules protect personnel, they are more likely to be assigned different jobs during the course of reorganization than lose their jobs entirely. Thus, individuals may not always perform any one specialization or set of tasks but may nonetheless continue to have secure places in the bureaucratic division of labor.[8]

Still, movement of workers from one specialized position to another within the firm is likely to be less frequent than would be the case when changing jobs in a free market. This is because the number of possible jobs is likely to be lower and their boundaries less permeable because they are established and maintained by a deliberate plan. Jurisdictional boundaries between tasks in a bureaucratically organized division of labor are likely to be specified in formal detail as job descriptions in a table of organization, and not subject to change without the use of formal administrative procedures. The rationalized division of labor is thus likely to be considerably more definite and stable than when there is competition among individual workers in a free labor market.

As writers like Edwards (1979) have recognized, there is some affinity between Weber's model of rational-legal bureaucracy and the organization of the factory that Marx attacked in his discussion of the detailed division of labor. In Marx's day, however, the authority of owner-capitalists was personal and arbitrary, based on what Weber called "patrimonial authority" and unhampered by formal rules. In Williamson's terms, it was a "simple hierarchy." Edwards argues that, more recently, strictly bureaucratic authority has become the major force in determining the substance as well as the organization of the division of labor in the large firm and, through planning, in industries. And of course conspicuous empirical examples of the bureaucratization of the division of labor of an entire society were to be found in the command economies of the former Soviet Union and similarly organized nations.

Bureaucracy and the "New Division of Labor"

Hierarchical authority to formulate, distribute, and supervise specialized tasks is the essence of the bureaucratic model, but there is

8 Miner found that in the university she studied a significant number of staff jobs disappeared over a period of time, and concluded that "we cannot automatically equate job formalization with job stability. It may be more appropriate to conceptualize formal organizations as skeletons of some stable, impersonal jobs – such as Controller, Director of Finance, and President – surrounded by other jobs of varying stability that are routinely contested and replaced" (1991: 782).

within it considerable room for variation. The historic forms of state civil service organizations and particularly of the large industrial firms of the twentieth century have rationalized work into detailed, minute, or mechanical specializations that deeply influenced the way analysts have thought about the model. Recent changes in the way a few firms have reorganized their division of labor have been described as new forms which replace the bureaucratic hierarchy and the detailed division of labor by "flexible specialization," "multi-skilled tasks," and flatter hierarchies (see, for example, many of the essays in Littek and Charles 1995).

It seems appropriate to comment here that in such circumstances the basic bureaucratic method of constituting a division of labor persists: only the concrete form has changed. Hierarchy remains, but is flattened to reduce the number of levels of authority. Specializations remain but are reconstituted to merge what were previously separate but functionally related specializations. Close reading of this literature shows that executive authority is still exercised to reorganize the division of labor and that both executive authority and subordinate managerial specialists evaluate its efficiency. Such reorganization does not eliminate specialization but reconstitutes it. When a number of related mechanical specializations are brought together into a "flexible specialization" so that workers no longer perform what were previously considered single, detailed, repetitive tasks, but instead exercise "flexible skills," it is in fact new specializations that have been created, not the dissolution of specialization as claimed. Furthermore, by their nature the substance of those previously separate specializations performed by individual workers that are now brought together into a flexible specialization must be functionally related: it is not as if everyone is able to perform everyone else's tasks. Thus, the essential principles of managerial control and the deliberate creation and supervision of a division of labor to pursue administratively established productive goals remain, though they may be manifested today in a different form than yesterday.[9]

9 For a very useful historical perspective on recent claims of deep changes in the industrial division of labor, see Bögenhold 1995.

Marx, Durkheim, and the Occupational
Division of Labor

In marked contrast to these two modes of organizing divisions of labor is the third, the *occupational division of labor* of professionalism, in which workers themselves rather than consumers or managers determine what tasks they will perform and the relationship of the specialization of each to the other. This third form is not a merely logical or wishful construct, for it has conspicuous historic precedent in the guilds, and exists today in the crafts and professions, though never in ideal-typical form. The work of both Karl Marx and Émile Durkheim has some bearing on it.

In his early work, Marx was hostile to the idea that people would devote a lifetime to practicing a single specialty, however complex and discretionary it might be. A stable division of labor among workers was anathema to him even if organized and administered by the workers themselves. In his later work, though he seems to have accepted occupational specialization of some sort as an imperative of the technical needs of production, he provided no hint of the way the division of labor in productive enterprises should be organized when it was created by workers rather than capitalists (Rattansi 1982: 163–79). He envisioned ownership by the working class, and collective decision-making to guide production as well as day-to-day management of firms, but as Rapaport (1976: 33) noted, he did not deal with "authority relations in the sphere of social production, social authority in planning and directing production, and the social division of labor among planners, managers and producers." This prejudice against specialization and the division of labor on the part of analysts influenced by Marx continues to this day, a fact which Sayer and Walker (1992) properly deplore.

In contrast to Marx, Émile Durkheim was a virtual apostle of specialization. He argued that specialization is not merely a functional necessity, but something positive in human life, something that stimulates the development of freedom and individuality. His *The Division of Labor in Society* (1964) argued that specialization has so seriously undermined the old "mechanical solidarity" of clan, kinship, and nationality which once bound people together that a new foundation for social cohesion was needed. That foundation, he believed, lies in the functional interdependence, or "organic solidarity," of the varied specialized occupations constituting the division of labor itself.

As he wrote in *Professional Ethics and Civic Morals* (1957), Durkheim believed that the resources for morality and ethics lie within occupations and are not available in other modern groupings. They have not been used in a positive fashion, however, because the division of labor has been organized in ways that breed exploitation, class conflict, and anomie. Durkheim proposed a corporatist solution to the problem, one based on occupation and industry. He argued that the various productive spheres of modern society should be organized into industrial associations composed of *both* the workers in particular occupations within an industry and their employers. These corporations would create and presumably enforce the rules governing conduct at work. And within their occupational groups workers would find the source of ethics and rule-making that would give meaning and direction to their lives and establish organic bonds with others. (For a discussion in the context of political theory, see Black 1984: 220–36; see also Lukes 1977: 536–41.)

There has been much misunderstanding of Durkheim's position, some stemming from confusing one particular usage of the word "profession" that is shared by both French and English – the general sense referring to *any* sort of occupation – with another that is more limited to English usage – the specific sense that refers solely to *particular* prestigious occupations distinguished by the intellectual or artistic character of what is done, or by their social standing.[10] Durkheim clearly had only occupation in general in mind and not solely what, in French, are sometimes called *professions libérales*. Another source of misunderstanding appears to lie in conceiving of Durkheim's recommendations for reorganizing the division of labor as reliance on strictly *occupational* associations like the old guilds or present-day professional associations such as the British Medical Association and the medical syndicates of France. But, on the contrary, he opposed programs of "administrative syndicalism" which relied solely on worker organizations, and explicitly included both workers and employers in the same "self-governing" unit. He did not support the organization of the division of labor by exclusive occupational groupings like guilds, unions, and associations of the crafts and professions.

---

10 For traditional French usage, see Robert 1978: 1538. As I have noted elsewhere (Freidson 1994b: 5), European sociologists and historians have recently become interested in those special occupations and have adopted the English usage. "Profession" was temporarily expunged from the official German vocabulary by the Nazis, but has re-emerged as a term of convenience.

In fact, Durkheim had a singularly vague conception of occupation itself. For all his rhetoric about occupations as groups with the potential to develop a common body of ethics, one cannot find the resources in his work which permit conceiving of them as viable, organized collectivities. He included semi-skilled workers performing quite limited, mechanical specializations in his discussion and, as Friedmann (1964: 68–81) noted, made some exceedingly dubious recommendations for creating meaning in their work. In all, he provides a viable foundation neither for his own vision, which is to join management to labor in industries, nor for the capacity to think of a truly occupationally controlled division of labor. Yet he does, like Marx, provide precedent for interest in the idea.[11]

We can visualize an occupationally controlled division of labor in two quite different ways. On the one hand, we can think of it as controlled *collectively* by all those working in it – that is, as worker-controlled, or controlled by the working class. This is at least the implicit image in Marxist thought and ideology. Should such a method of organizing work seem possible, it would surely have to be counted as a fourth logic, for the third does not involve control by a class but rather control by identifiable occupations interacting with each other. But while it is not difficult to visualize how collective control could establish general policies governing the organization and evaluation of work in a society, an industry, or a workplace, it is extremely difficult to visualize how it could control a division of labor. How can a body of workers who do different kinds of work so that their working, practical, and formal knowledge and skill vary markedly formulate *collectively* what the various specialized tasks or jobs in a division of labor shall be, their number, their stability or permanence, and how and by whom they will be coordinated? That question is even more difficult to answer if all the workers have been performing semi-skilled, mechanical specializatnder conditions of automation, which Weiss (1976) argues is Marx's view of work in communist society. While we can imagine workers exercising collective control over an established production process, it is difficult to imagine them changing that production process collectively, redesigning and

---

11 Weber (1978: 271–82) devoted a few concentrated pages to collegiality as a guiding principle for exercising power, and a few other pages here and there, but was concerned more with appraising its stability and efficiency than with its implications for constituting a division of labor. See, however, Waters 1989 and Sciulli 1990.

reallocating the tasks of a complex division of labor. (See the review of recent forms of work organization by Smith 1997.)

The most plausible method of control by an entire working class involves delegation of authority to managerial and technical specialists who then constitute and direct the concrete forms of the division of labor. Workers might collectively review the performance of those specialists, and vote to replace them with others, but they would not themselves create and control the production process. This is in fact what has happened when workers have gained collective control of a workplace, as Form (1981) notes and as Green (1983) seems to concede reluctantly.

True worker control must involve direct determination and control of the work by those who perform it, a possibility that presupposes a division of labor composed of or at least dominated by relatively stable, identifiable specializations like those that were organized at various points in history as guilds, crafts, and professions. In such a form, each specialization controls the work for which it is competent, negotiates its boundaries with other specializations, and by that method determines how the entire division of labor is organized and coordinated. The actual performance of that work is, of course, carried out and controlled by individual members of the occupation. *This occupationally controlled division of labor is an essential part of professionalism.*

A related conception of a division of labor essentially organized and controlled by the workers themselves has been presented recently by Barley and his collaborators (Barley and Orr 1997a) Unlike visions of the future of the industrial proletariat, however, theirs is explicitly concerned with the divisions of labor in which modern-day technicians are found – computer technicians, quality control, science and medical laboratory technicians, emergency medical technicians, and the like. Emphasizing the critical importance of the growing number of technicians in the productive enterprises of our time, and of practical and working rather than formal knowledge in their work, they suggest that the vertically organized division of labor characteristic of bureaucracy needs to be replaced by a "horizontal division of labor" in which different specialists work together as equals, assisted if not directed by a "coordinator" (see especially Zabusky 1997: 151–2). There are certainly some instances in which this could occur, but as I shall show, when occupations control a division of labor, even if bureaucratic modes of control are absent, hierarchy is not.

The Occupational Division of Labor

Under conditions of perfectly free competition, consumers are sovereign. It is they who have the money or goods upon which the worker depends for a living and who, in the absence of any constraint on their choices, can therefore decide what goods and services to demand, whose labor to employ for producing them, and what they are willing to pay. The content and structure of the division of labor that produces those goods and services are created by the competitive enterprise of workers seeking to gain a living by satisfying consumer demand. In a bureaucratically controlled division of labor, on the other hand, a directing authority and support staff decide what work shall be done and how it shall be divided among jobs. Distinctly different from those is an occupationally controlled division of labor. Specializations are stabilized as distinct occupations whose members have the exclusive right to perform the tasks connected with them. Functionally related occupations negotiate with each other the boundaries or jurisdictions of the specializations that their members are allowed to offer and perform, often with some ambiguity when tasks overlap. Should consumers or managers wish to have the tasks connected with those specializations performed, they are not free to employ any willing worker, or to themselves train workers for the purpose. Instead, they must use bona fide members of the occupation. The occupations themselves determine what qualifications are required to perform particular tasks and they control the criteria for licensing or credentialling procedures that are enforced by the state. An occupationally controlled division of labor can have a horizontal structure of cooperating occupations working parallel to each other at related tasks, and a vertical structure in which some occupations have authority over others, or both, depending on the special productive goals of a particular division of labor which establish technical or functional limits, however loose, around what is possible. Ideal typically, the authority of one occupation over others is based not on economic or administrative status but rather on the content and character of its expertise and the functional relationship of that expertise to that of the others.

Jurisdictions are negotiated among occupations whose work is interrelated in a particular industry or economic sector. Some negotiations concern only the particular task each will have the right to perform and control – whether it is a dental surgeon or an oral surgeon, for example, who has the right to perform a particular procedure in the mouth, or whether a barrister or a solicitor has the right to argue before the Bar of particular English courts. Since the outcome has an impact on the amount of work available to the members of the contesting occupations, it is understandably a matter of importance to them. Another issue in the negotiation of jurisdictions lies in establishing priorities in a joint production process – which tasks are central and take priority over others, the order in which different tasks are to be performed, and the like. Sometimes this may involve the legal right of members of one occupation to direct and supervise others in a division of labor, even to the point of the state requiring that no work be performed without authorization by a member of a superordinate occupation. For example, under most circumstances in the United States today, neither nurse nor pharmacist may legally dispense a medication regulated by the state in the absence of a physician's order. The medical profession dominates the health division of labor (Freidson 1970) notwithstanding the growth of non-medical or "alternative" practitioners (Saks 1995) and the proliferation of stratified paraprofessional health workers (see, for example, Althauser and Appel 1996). Indeed, the vertically or hierarchically organized division of labor dominated by a single directing occupation can become quite complex, as is graphically demonstrated by Peneff's analysis (1997) of the concrete manual work performed by open heart surgeons and the variety of specialized occupations they direct both in the operating room and in post-operative care facilities.

The organization of the occupationally controlled division of labor that results from such negotiations will have considerably more definite vertical structure than we can expect to find developing from the perfectly free exchanges between individual workers and consumers, and it will also be much less likely to change rapidly. As Weber observed about the exercise of collegial authority, when decisions must be negotiated among a number of interested parties, they are likely to take longer than would be the case in a bureaucratically organized division of labor where they can be made by authoritative fiat. While innovation and change can take place in an occupational division of labor, it may be more often at the boundaries of jurisdictions, and sometimes in grudging but necessary reaction to the development of new knowledge, skill, or technology (Abbot 1988).

Given the complexities of negotiation among occupations, and in the absence of any decisive action by some prime authority, the degree of the division of labor, and the number of specializations organized as occupations, are likely to be smaller than would be the case in either a free market or a bureaucratically organized division of labor, and movement of workers to and from different occupations considerably more restricted. Strang and Baron's finding (1990: 479–95) that craft and professionally organized workers tend to be classified under fewer job titles than other kinds of workers accords with this expectation. *Within* the boundaries of complex occupations, however, it is possible for a great deal of differentiation to exist in the form of specialties and sub-specialties, together with considerable internal struggle and negotiation over jurisdiction.[12]

Occupational organization of the division of labor in a political economy as a whole, what Marx called the social division of labor, may be visualized as a number of parallel industrial groupings of cooperating and interdependent occupations, with little movement of workers between them. As Machlup (1962: 45–6) suggested, rather than hold jobs in conventional multi-occupational firms organized by an administrative authority, the members of occupations could work in occupational firms.[13] Such occupational firms would cluster into sets of interdependent producers as do, for example, carpenters, glaziers, metalworkers, plumbers, electricians, masons, and the like who cooperate in working on a common construction.[14] This could also be the case for physicians in various specialties, nurses, dietitians, aides, and a variety of technicians who collaborate in working on a common medical case in a hospital: it is possible that each of these specialists can be members of occupational firms which then contract with hospitals to supply their skills, where they coordinate their work with members of other occupations supplied from different occupational firms. Something resembling this seems to be emerging from the increasing practice of "out-sourcing" in some industries. There also emerge agencies which take the responsibility for finding and

12   For a case study of such a historic struggle within medicine, see Gritzer and Arluke 1985; for more general discussion, see Bucher and Strauss 1961; for jurisdictional negotiations of the division of labor between occupations and specialties in concrete work-settings, see Strauss 1985.

13   In the United States, some occupational firms have assumed the legal form of the professional corporation. For a brief description of its characteristics, see Freidson 1986: 126–8. Partnerships, of course, represent another legal form. Abbott's discussion (1991a: 23–4) of organizations as "divisions of expert labor" distinguishes occupational firms from firms with a "mixed" or heteronomous division of expert labor.

14   The classic portrayal of this is Stinchcombe's paper (1959), though he is less concerned with the division of labor than with the organization of a labor market.

temporarily "placing" people with particular skills into temporary but highly specialized positions, as Bielby and Bielby (1999) show for talent agencies in the moving picture industry.

Finally, I suggest that the "shape" of the occupationally organized division of labor is likely to differ from the shapes of those organized by other means. Occupational hierarchies will be flatter and less differentiated, with a narrower span of control than is likely to be found in an ideal-typical bureaucratic division of labor. The basis for legitimizing hierarchy among occupations will be putatively functional and based on specialized knowledge and skill, with superordinate occupations thought to have specialized knowledge and skill that is of central importance to a productive goal shared by all (Freidson 1970: 127–64). In perfectly free competition among workers, by contrast, both stable hierarchies and firmly established jurisdictions are absent.

The Occupational Division of Labor of Professionalism

In this chapter I have shown that the human division of labor is by its nature socially organized through the exercise of power, and that variation in the basis[15] for controlling that organization – that is to say, who or what controls it – influences the number of specializations (or the degree of the division of labor in the terminology of the social ecologists), the type of specializations, the task content of specializations, their relative permanence over time, and the overall structure of the division of labor in a political economy as a whole, in its different industrial sectors, and in individual workplaces. I demonstrated this by comparing three ideal-typical bases for organizing and controlling a division of labor: control by free interaction among individual workers and consumers, by monocratic and specifically rational-legal authority, and by occupation. The content and outcome of the struggle for jurisdiction depends on which of those three bases is dominant.

Occupational control of the division of labor is a central element

---

15 It should be noted that I have been dealing with the *immediate* basis of control for constituting a division of labor. The *ultimate* basis is the sovereign power of a society, most commonly, today, the state. It is the state that supports the conditions required for something resembling free competition, that charters organizations which create bureaucratic divisions of labor, and that empowers occupations to establish and maintain secure jurisdictions. I will discuss the role of the state in creating and sustaining professionalism at greater length in chapter 6.

of ideal-typical professionalism. It involves direct control by specialized workers themselves of the terms, conditions, goals, and content of their particular work. The content and, since relationships with others are intrinsic to specialization, the boundaries of specializations are established, maintained, and changed by the negotiation of jurisdictions, which establish the basis for coordinating their work. This negotiated order also establishes the functional and hierarchical relations among the occupations that cooperate in the joint production of a particular product or service. The major consequences of this mode of organizing a division of labor are summarized and compared with those of the other modes in table 2.1.

Table 2.1   Differences in the division of labor by basis of control

Basis of control	*Proportion of different occupations*	*Permanence of occupations*	*Degree of differentiation*	*Predominant type of specialization*
Free market	High	Low	Low	Everyday
Bureaucracy	Medium	Medium	High	Mechanical
Occupational	Low	High	Medium	Discretionary

3

Labor Markets
and Careers

In order to develop the concept of the division of labor as a social organization of tasks I have had to discuss the three different forms of organization abstractly, almost as a set of purely technical arrangements designed to accomplish some productive end. But that is an inordinately artificial view because productive human activities require exchange relations for their survival. No one can make a living performing specialized work without others who provide the resources for a making a living. It is labor markets that provide the resources for sustaining and organizing divisions of labor by bringing together workers and labor consumers. Intimately connected with the ideal-typical modes of organizing divisions of labor that I discussed in the last chapter, therefore, are labor markets that organize the exchange relationships between workers and labor consumers. And as in the case of the division of labor, there are a number of ways by which markets can be organized and controlled. In this chapter I will expand on the three logically distinct ideal-typical methods for organizing the division of labor so as to include the labor markets that are in reality intertwined with them, distinguishing a free labor market, a bureaucratic market, and an occupational market.

These days the word "market" is found on virtually every influential lip in the worlds of business, politics, and the academy. For some it has come to represent a magic solution to all the ills of advanced industrial societies. Unfortunately, even within the relatively disciplined usage of economics, let alone in the considerably less disciplined sphere of everyday public life, it is a word that can refer to many different things. Within economics, as Steiner

(1968) has noted, it can and does refer to a geographic area, the conditions under which exchanges take place, the outcome of a process of exchange, the products or commodities involved in exchange, the buyers or sellers in an exchange, the rules by which an exchange is governed, and the time when goods are to be exchanged. Here, where I am addressing work and the way it can be organized, my focus is on the labor market, or employment relations.

Distinguishing Labor Markets

As it happens, the past twenty-five years have seen an explosion cof interest in labor markets.[1] Some scholars examine the occupations or jobs held by the members of the national labor force and compare them to those of their parents in order to measure intergenerational mobility. Others trace the movements of workers from one job to another in order to determine their social mobility during the course of their working lives. Still others compare the educational, racial, gender, and other characteristics of those who hold poorly paying jobs and those who hold well-paying jobs. Most of that work conceives of the labor market on a national scale, though in order to explain the differential distribution of wages and different kinds of mobility the national labor market may be divided into "sectors," or "segments." Those sectors or segments can themselves be treated as labor markets and defined by the particular kind of industries (for example, clothing manufacture, food service, health, and agriculture) that characterize them. Thus, it is not uncommon for the scope of labor markets to be delineated both nationally and, less broadly, as an industrial or economic sector of a national economy.

Labor markets are also pictured more narrowly and concretely as organizations or firms, a conception that emerges in the distinction between internal and external labor markets. Doeringer and Piore defined the *"internal labor market* [as] an administrative unit, such as a manufacturing plant, within which the pricing and allocation of labor is governed by a set of administrative rules and procedures. This internal labor market, governed by administrative rules, is to be distinguished from the *external labor market* of conventional economic theory where pricing, allocating, and train-

---

1   For recent reviews of the development and likely future direction of such work, see Peck 1996, Kalleberg and Sørenson 1979, and especially Kalleberg 1996.

ing procedures are controlled directly by economic variables" (1971: 1–2, italics in original). It should be understood that a union hiring hall is by that definition as much an internal labor market as is a manufacturing plant. The value of the distinction is that it forces recognition that hierarchically organized firms (and worker-organized associations) regulate the way work is obtained and compensated by methods that are quite different from those assumed to operate in the open market of freely negotiated exchanges between individuals from which classical and neoclassical economists (including Adam Smith and Karl Marx) reason.

Taking that distinction as given, it is nonetheless only a beginning. Many analysts have suggested more refined typologies, but most are essentially pragmatic, attempting to simplify the variety of empirical forms without reducing them to theoretically derived or at least logically exclusive alternatives.[2] While each makes some sense, there are no authoritative criteria by which to choose from among them. Still, in one way or another all recognize the importance and empirical existence of three mutually exclusive circumstances that parallel those I have already suggested for the division of labor: one in which a labor market operates without organized constraints and is controlled by the individual decisions of its participants, a second organized hierarchically and controlled by administrative authority, and a third organized and controlled by those offering their specialized labor.

Careers in the Free Labor Market

The *free labor market* need not be discussed at length both because of its familiarity and because of my discussion in chapter 2. It is, in logical or conceptual terms, perfectly free.[3] As Kerr (1950: 279) put it, it

> exists as a result of free entry and exit, complete knowledge, a sufficiency of relatively small and undifferentiated buyers and sellers, and the absence of collusion. Perfection is achieved if the product

2   An outstanding exception is Althauser and Kalleberg 1981.
3   Here, as elsewhere, I insist on using the "pure" model of perfectly free competition without introducing the qualifying imperfections and externalities that economic theorists have been forced to deal with in order to apply the model to the real world. By the same token, I employ pure models of bureaucracy and professionalism, both of which also require qualification in light of empirical reality.

market also displays these characteristics; and the consumer reigns supreme in the allocation of resources and the determination of rewards to individuals. . . . The single price [that is, wage for labor] prevails and the market is cleared.

As Parnes (1968: 482) notes, for such a market to exist in reality one must imagine an island in which there is no immigration or emigration and neither workers' organizations nor employers' associations, while all workers are equally skilled and efficient, employers are indifferent to the personal characteristics of those they hire, and workers have complete knowledge of the pay rates prevailing for different work, choosing work solely on the basis of what it pays.

Obviously, the conditions for such a market never exist, so that empirical examples are impossible to find.[4] (For insightful discussion of the dubious intellectual value of the perfectly free market model, see Offe 1985: 10–97, and especially Polanyi 1944.) As I indicated in chapter 2, it is incompatible with both a complex and a stable division of labor. Indeed, it seems no accident that the only empirical examples of something resembling a free labor market exist in what Caplow (1954: 172–5) describes as the organization of the market for common labor, which demands little or no skill and draws on a casual labor force, and in what Block (1990: 76–7) calls a "spot market" for labor. What Fisher (1953) describes as the "structureless market" for harvest labor in California in the 1940s before unionization, also resembled a free labor market.[5] It no doubt exists also in some sectors of the informal market that lie outside the official economy. Where it does exist, working conditions are likely to be poor, wages low, and the required skills minimal. According to Marsden (1986: 244–5), "Casual markets can work with relatively little regulation because of the small degree of investment in skill that is required and the low technical specification of vacancies."[6]

In such relatively free markets, therefore, we should expect little investment in specialized training prior to entering the labor market, workers relying instead on native wit and everyday knowledge. Once employed in the labor market, of course,

4 These circumstances are almost as utopian as those dreamt of by Marx, where one could hunt, fish, raise cattle, and philosophize without ever having to settle on one form of work.

5 For the considerably more structured agricultural labor market in California in more recent times, see Gonzales 1985.

6 But for evidence of structure even in casual labor markets, see Stymeist 1979.

they have the opportunity to accumulate the working knowledge that goes with experience at performing particular tasks, though they cannot be assured of either continuous demand for those tasks or an attractive wage. My guess is that versatility in performing a variety of tasks, none of which requires more than everyday knowledge (and whatever formal knowledge which that routinely includes) is most conducive to success in relatively free markets. Such versatility may be cumulative, based on practical experience in a variety of jobs, but it seems likely that for a large proportion of workers there will be no stable specialization and little public or official recognition of their work as distinct occupations.

The series of tasks or jobs performed over the course of a working life in a perfectly free labor market – the career-line of workers – thus has no consistency or direction. Movement from one job to another is determined solely by competitive wage rates and in so far as there are many labor markets, each being open to all and free of constraint (influence by nepotism, prejudice, and personal networks having been miraculously abolished), random accident may be the most powerful source of opportunity for upward mobility.

What I suggest, of course, is an exercise in imagination, for of the three ways of organizing work, the perfectly free market has the weakest link with empirical reality. As most economists agree, the conditions for a perfectly free labor market are virtually impossible to find in all but minor and marginal segments of modern economies. The information available to both workers and labor consumers about available work and available workers is always flawed (see Rees 1966; Granovetter 1974; Spence 1974), and the capacity to move from place to place to take better-paying jobs is lessened by a variety of practical and sentimental human factors. Recognizing the instability, if not impossibility, of the conditions for a perfect market, Kerr (1950: 280–2) suggests a kind of natural history in the course of which ostensibly free markets develop into institutionalized markets. Like Adam Smith before him, he notes that in what he calls "the natural market" (the flawed empirical version of the purely theoretical perfect free market) employers possess intrinsic resources that, even in the absence of collusion, give them a distinct advantage over prospective employees. This produces a situation that limits mobility and competition for particular jobs and that structures wage levels. He goes on to note that since employers and workers eventually organize themselves and negotiate with each other, the natural market is displaced by an "institutional market" which is governed by formal rules and policies.

Kerr's concept of the institutional market, considerably expanded in a later paper (1954), is based on distinguishing from the perfectly free market *any* market governed by rules, no matter what agency is responsible for establishing them. His typology is expressed as a continuum from the perfectly free market at one extreme to the completely managed market at the other. Thus, he is concerned with the *degree* to which constraint is exercised and not the *source* or basis of constraint. But surely the rules themselves will vary as the source varies: the particular rules employed to structure the labor market are likely to be different when workers create them than when employers do so. Instead of opposing the extreme of the "managed" market to the perfect market as Kerr did, and as do most present-day contrasts between external and internal (or firm) labor markets, I will contrast the perfect market with two other modes of managing it – a bureaucratic or managed labor market, or in Williamson's (1975) terms, hierarchy, and an occupationally controlled labor market. Both managers and workers introduce structure to markets, but each group has a different purpose and each structure has different characteristics and consequences.

Careers in the Bureaucratic Labor Market

In the purest sense, one must designate the control of labor markets by managers as a monocratic labor market, a pyramidally organized market subject to the ultimate authority of a single agent. But as Max Weber has shown, there is more than one kind of authority, and each kind tends to create a different administrative apparatus for controlling an enterprise. This has been true in the annals of political history from which Weber drew his data, and more recently in the annals of industrial history from which Edwards (1979), for example, drew the data upon which he based his typology of the progression of authority structures created over time by the owners and managers of manufacturing firms. Because it is more directly relevant to the organization of labor markets in modern times than other variants, however, it seems appropriate to delineate the ideal type of control by managers more narrowly as bureaucratic rather than as hierarchical or monocratic, and by doing so to mean what Weber analyzed as rational-legal bureaucracy, an ideal type involving the intersection of rational-legal authority with an administrative form based on officials. The hierarchically administered or *bureaucratic labor market* created and controlled by managers or administrators is a type that is compatible with what Caplow (1954: 149–55) described in the same words, and what others have described as "administered" (Form and Huber 1976: 760–2) or "industrial" (Osterman 1984: 167). It is a refined case of a more general form of monocratic administration that includes within it the simpler, sometimes less orderly forms that Williamson (1975: 49–56) discusses as simple hierarchies and Edwards (1979) as organizations exercising "direct" control.

While only one variant of monocratic administration, Weber's discussion of the greater efficiency and stability of *rational-legal* rather than traditional or charismatic administration is sufficiently persuasive to adopt as a basic model for organizing and controlling work. In virtually all the discussion of labor markets I have cited, however, the term "bureaucratic" is generally used to refer to particular productive organizations, or firms. These are conceptualized as internal labor markets which workers enter, initially hired to hold particular jobs or positions, then gain raises in salary, and promotions and transfers to other positions within the firm. However, it is not difficult to expand the scope of a rational-legal bureaucratic labor market by using it to characterize the labor market outside the individual firm as well. Planned economies such as existed in eastern Europe until recently could be analyzed as bureaucratic external labor markets. The same may be true for some industrial sectors of contemporary economies, as in the case of public power, water, and transportation authorities and, if we can consider it a sector in itself, state civil service (for the US civil service, see DiPrete 1989).

The ideal-typical bureaucratic labor market is created and administered neither by consumers nor by workers. It is created by staff members of a hierarchy, specialists in personnel management, design, and planning who are responsible to the ultimate authorities of the bureaucratized state, industrial sector, or firm rather than to the producers or consumers of their products.[7] Their duty is to advance the policies of their superiors, whatever they may be. The obligation of those who produce the goods or services of the bureaucratic market is to carry out the duties assigned them

---

7 This is not to say that firms do not try to guess or to learn what consumers want, or what are acceptable working conditions for their employees. Rather, once management has made a decision to produce some service or good, it, rather than workers or consumers, controls both personnel and production policies.

in the production plan, duties (or specializations) which can be abolished or rearranged at will, but by orderly means.

Since there is now a massive literature in political science, management, sociology, and (to a lesser extent) economics that reflects the substance of the ideal type, I need not elaborate on it here. Its essential features are that it is monocratic in structure, with a systematic division of labor composed of positions or jobs whose tasks are defined by written rules and which are arranged hierarchically (or vertically) as well as functionally (or horizontally). Access to those positions or jobs, as well as to transfer and promotion between them, is determined by specified impersonal criteria of competence as well as by other formal personnel policies.[8] Wages or salaries are graded by position in the hierarchy and except for increments based on tenure tend to be uniform for all within each position and therefore may be seen as in equilibrium.

This bureaucratic form of labor market is easily observed on every level of modern industrial societies. On the national level it is represented as a centrally planned market, with the division of labor and labor force planned, and wages specified for each officially established and recognized category of worker. Empirically, a planned labor market for a large nation is much less likely to resemble the ideal type than are markets planned for smaller political and industrial units, for it depends upon having virtually complete information about (or control over) consumer demand and, considerably more difficult, about how the market is performing. The free flow of information up through bureaucratic channels is difficult to maintain on a large scale so the participants in a very large, hierarchically planned system develop their own informal or "underground" market designed to serve their own interests. As Kerr's natural history assumes, a similar tendency to circumvent policy occurs in free markets when privileged participants undertake to control the indeterminacies of freedom by establishing their own private understandings and conspiracies.

When such labor markets exist in particular industries, and even more so in particular firms surrounded by a turbulent or disorganized economic environment, they cannot be expected to remain

8 This is an ideal-typical statement, for as Rosenbaum's (1984) study shows, competence or ability is difficult to determine, and in considering promotion, superiors are virtually forced to use evidence that cannot be formally stated in personnel policies. Where seniority, additional formal training, and the passing of a succession of written tests constitute the norm, as in some civil service systems, however, the requirements of the ideal type are more closely approximated.

completely bureaucratic and survive. As Caplow (1954: 155) notes, "it is probably impossible for a bureaucracy to maintain a consistent internal structure and at the same time establish parity with a market based on short-run supply and demand factors." And indeed, throughout the advanced industrial world some firms are changing their organizational characteristics by reducing the ranks of both middle management and production workers and reorganizing the responsibilities and tasks of both. Over the past decade or two, a number of analysts have observed that tendency and speculated about the development of forms of organization which deviate so greatly from ideal-typical bureaucracy (which is characterized as "hierarchy") as to represent something generically different. Nonetheless, hierarchies of authority remain, as do systematic methods of classifying jobs, specifying the qualifications of training and experience required of candidates for them, and evaluating performance. This includes ranking jobs by authority, training, and experience and specifying differential wages that follow the rank order (Caplow 1954: 153).

This mode of controlling work has quite distinct consequences for the pattern of training, entering the labor market, and the career-line involved in moving through it. Prospective workers are likely to seek specialized training designed to qualify them in advance of actually seeking work. The prior training they seek would vary by the level of authority as well as the specialized nature of the entrance jobs they aspire to, for bureaucratic labor markets are organized both hierarchically and functionally. The hierarchical dimension implies job ladders[9] whereby someone entering the firm at the bottom can hope for the opportunity to be promoted to higher positions of pay and status. The functional dimension refers to different kinds of work requiring different qualifications and perhaps involving separate job ladders.

Furthermore, job ladders in bureaucratic labor markets are rarely, if ever, formulated to allow entrance at the bottom with continuous promotion up to the highest executive position. Movement from factory hand or stock clerk to CEO is far from common. Rather, each ladder has its own entry level and its own ceiling. Some, such as those called administrative or staff jobs, begin at a

---

9 Althauser (1989: 179) quite correctly notes that in many cases workers move across (or transfer) to a different job ladder with better pay and prospects. In light of the existence of multiple job ladders, and the possibility of moving across them, he suggests that the image of a lattice rather than a ladder or separate ladders is more faithful to reality.

fairly high level of authority, status, and pay in the firm and extend to near the highest position; others, such as "clerical" and "production" or "line" jobs,[10] begin at a very low level of authority, status, and pay, and are blocked from extending past middle levels of the firm.

The ports of entry to the bureaucratic labor market, therefore, are open to those who have already obtained the prior training and status required for various positions, something that varies with the position. To be hired in the lowest positions, as dual labor market writers note, may require little more than the everyday knowledge provided by primary and secondary education. For others, the formal knowledge and cultural capital presumed to be provided by post-secondary, higher education may be required, and for still others the specialized working knowledge provided by both working- and middle-class vocational programs. Prior work experience may also serve as a qualification for entry, though in the case of civil service jobs, passing an examination may be sufficient.[11]

However, for a number of reasons – the absence of training programs outside the firm that teach the knowledge and skill that is specifically designed for particular positions, the importance of first-hand, working knowledge for particular jobs, and the like – firms may have their own internal training programs and recruit individuals less on the basis of prior training than on assessment of their capacity to learn the proper skills once they become members of the organization.[12] As Ryan (1984) found, though, firms are more likely to invest in training for firm-specific skills –

10   For a lengthy analysis of the historical development of the distinction between "clerical" and "administrative" jobs and job ladders in the US federal civil service, see DiPrete 1989. He is especially concerned with their bearing on blocked mobility for women and members of minorities, an important issue which I do not address in this book. In that context, Strang and Baron (1990: 481) observed that the theoretically unexpected proliferation of professional job titles in the California civil service system was initiated by white male lawyers who wanted to distinguish themselves from female and non-white colleagues so as to receive better rewards and privileges.

11   Naturally, I gloss over empirical variation, though there are few studies to draw on in any case. See DiPrete on the civil service (1989) and Rosenbaum (1984). Spilerman (1986) suggests three different "rule-structures."

12   Knoke and Kalleberg (1994) find that firms have been increasing their internal training programs, though apparently only for employees they expect to be permanent. If trends in the downsizing of firms and "outsourcing" continue, however, it is hard to see how internal training programs can increase. Quite the reverse: the importance of external training and credentials is likely to increase.

that is to say, in the specialized knowledge and skill that is useful solely within the firm and not for jobs in other firms. If they train employees in generalizable skills they can very well lose their investment if employees then use these new skills to qualify for better positions elsewhere. On the whole, it seems plausible that within a firm the jobs at the bottom of the hierarchy are unskilled, or semi-skilled at best, and require only everyday knowledge: in some sense, therefore, they are generalizable in so far as they can be performed in a number of workplaces. On the other hand, those in the middle ranks may be more likely to have firm-specific skills and to seek advancement within their firm. Those in the professional, technical, and sometimes managerial ranks, however, are likely to have gained generalizable skills from training received before entering the firm, which makes movement upwards through the ranks of a single firm only one career possibility among many.

Contrary to the assumption of long-term careers moving up the lattice of the bureaucratic firm, many recent analysts see a fundamental change in both the organization of production and the staffing of latter-day firms which precludes lifelong, one-firm careers. (See Littek and Charles 1995; Sabel 1995; and Weick and Berlinger 1989 for examples of such literature; and Kalleberg 1996 for a clear summary of trends.) First, they note a shrinking of the size of middle management, which does reduce the number of levels of authority though not the existence of managerial authority itself. Second, they see the demise of the traditional detailed division of labor that employs workers to perform semi-skilled, repetitive tasks, and its replacement by teams of specialists whose skills are flexible enough to be shifted from one productive task to another and who can exercise a certain degree of discretion in organizing and apportioning tasks. This practice does not abolish specialization so much as reorganize it. Third, they point to a tendency in large firms to reduce long-term investment in a self-sufficient process of production (that is, vertical integration) and to rely instead on outside contractors to produce some of what is needed for the final product. Instead of producing all the parts of a computer, for example, a firm may merely assemble the parts provided by other firms, then test, sell, and service them. It can change outside contractors at will, and itself operate with a considerably smaller set of employees than would be the case if it were organized to produce all parts of the final product. Under such circumstances, firms can operate with a considerably reduced permanent staff of their own and be part of a loose, adaptable network of firms. Some see in this the development of a new form of organization which is neither a bureaucracy nor an external market but rather a network. (See Powell 1990, and Podolny and Page's 1998 review of the recent literature on network organizations.)

Even if these trends continue, it is probable that the work careers of the small permanent staff of firms will remain typical of bureaucracy. They may still be able to assume that they will have permanent employment in a single firm over their work-life and to count on a progressively larger income, if not necessarily greater authority and responsibility. Other workers, however, must assume either that their career will be spent moving from one firm to another or that they will become relatively permanent members of firms which supply specialized employees on a temporary basis to other firms or produce specialized products or services for other firms. Such a career will be distinctly different from that in the large, bureaucratic firm, one which Sabel (1995) confusingly calls a "spiral career" taking place in an "open" labor market. I suggest that these putatively new kinds of careers are empirical variants of what one might expect in the ideal-typical occupational labor market characteristic of the third logic, professionalism.

The Occupationally Controlled Labor Market

While a great deal of attention has been given to the free market and the bureaucratic market in the literature, considerably less has been given to occupational labor markets. This is not because such markets do not exist today, for virtually every student of labor markets has noted the existence of craft markets that have different characteristics from others. Althauser and Kalleberg (1981) took occupational control as a major axis by which to differentiate labor markets. Stinchcombe (1959) argued that the entire construction industry was organized into craft or "professional" markets. I did an extensive analysis of the special institutions organizing the markets in which professions work (Freidson 1986). Recognizing their existence, Williamson (1975: 41–9) explicitly recognized the possibility that independent worker "peer groups" could function efficiently. In all, there can be little doubt that it is both empirically and logically useful to conceive of a third type of market that is structured by occupation rather than by consumers or by management.

The heart of occupational control is the determination of qualification for particular kinds of work (and thus of the definition of the work) by the occupation itself. Its members, or their organization, become "an agency external to the hiring firm or consumer . . . [that establishes its own] *permanent labor market status*, [which] is not to be confused with permanent firm status" (Stinchcombe 1959: 168). The mode of structuring the labor market that results is distinctly different from that of bureaucratic management in that the former substitutes "professional [*sic*] training of . . . workers for detailed centralized planning of work" (1959: 175). Furthermore, "ejection from the market is controlled by the [occupational group] . . . An employer can discharge a man from a specific job but not from the market" (Kerr 1954: 98).

This worker-controlled labor market is by definition one in which organized occupational groups have the exclusive right to determine the qualification for particular jobs and the nature of the tasks to be performed by individuals in those jobs. Their jurisdiction is established by the outcome of direct negotiations or struggles with other occupational groups that may claim to be able to perform the same or contiguous and perhaps overlapping tasks in a division of labor. Alternatively, jurisdiction can be unilaterally established by the state, no doubt informed by consultation with the interested parties. But since work takes place within a market from which a living is gained, there must also be negotiation with the consumers of labor – with individual clients, the general public, or employers in firms. Labor consumers must be required to pay only for bona fide members of the occupation to perform a specified set of tasks; potentially competing occupational groups must be contained within non-competing jurisdictions or driven out of the market entirely.

In the ideal-typical occupationally controlled labor market of professionalism, the obligation to employ only those qualified by the occupation is made mandatory by law, thereby preventing the employment of anyone without the qualifications determined by the occupational group. Similarly, in theory but rarely in practice, the workers control their own numbers so that they can maximize their *average* income in light of demand. As Caplow (1954: 167–8) notes, the equalization of the distribution of income among all members of the occupation (which is analogous to the equilibrium of a common wage rate in the perfectly free market and the uniformity of wages in particular jobs in a bureaucratic labor market) is likely to be possible only if the occupation itself is the agency through which labor consumers must go in order to obtain the workers they wish. In effect, the occupation establishes an internal labor market. In other circumstances, income or wage differences can be minimized by devices such as establishing minimum fees and rules against competitive bidding. By such means, within the social closure or market shelter of the occupational group, movement is toward the "equilibrium" of equal income for all. On the other hand, wage differentials between occupational groups in an occupational labor market are set neither by a directing administrative authority nor by the calculating transactions of individuals in a perfectly free market: they are established by negotiations between organized occupational groups and between them and their labor consumers.

From these conditions we can infer the typical career-line of those in occupational labor markets. First, before entering the labor market as a full-fledged member of the occupation,[13] all must obtain the training that qualifies them to be employed. Labor consumers cannot use anyone who does not have that training. This requirement shapes the way employers must constitute the jobs and division of labor of their firm: they are not free to design jobs themselves.[14] As Maurice and his colleagues (1986: 67) point out in their comparison of French and German firms,

> theoretically, a firm can organize its work system in one of two ways: it can define jobs according to its own criteria and require workers to adapt or train them to fit the job definition, or it can take account of the existing qualifications of the work force and design jobs around the capabilities of the workers. In the first case, job demands determine the worker's profile. In the second case, the worker's profile exerts an influence upon the job definition.

They go on to note that the German educational system of the time contained a strong vocational apprentice program linking schools with industry. This provided authoritative formal qualifications to workers on the basis of which the firms of an industry designed their jobs. The French educational system, on the other hand, more

---

13 Formal schooling in advance of entrance is only one way by which a worker can become qualified. Apprenticeship – which is to say gaining practical knowledge and experience at work and holding a special tutelary status while being instructed and supervised by fully qualified workers – is certainly the more ancient and ubiquitous method, though more difficult to control and ultimately, as I shall argue in the next chapter, less effective.

14 In this context, see Littek and Heisig 1991 for German white-collar workers in industry. For a more recent comparison of the United States, Japan, Germany, and France, see Fligstein and Byrkjeflot 1996.

often than not provided prospective workers with a general rather than a narrow vocational education, leaving firms free to design their own jobs and expect workers to adapt to them. The former case, in which workers are certified for particular skills, leaves them more free to move from job to job in different firms, the career-line being one of a considerable amount of mobility and less dependence on any single firm or locale.[15]

The occupational labor market can be organized in several different ways. First, it can be divided into a number of occupational firms that produce goods or services for others. As firms, they can be organized bureaucratically, but they are distinguished from ideal-typical bureaucracies by virtue of the requirement that both the executive head and those who perform the central work be bona fide members of the occupation. Such firms can also be organized as partnerships or as collectives, governed collegially if they are relatively small or by the collective delegation of authority to executive officers if they are large. These are all free-standing organizations to which consumers must turn if they wish to obtain the services or products for which they have exclusive license. Empirical versions of this are to be found in large American law and accounting firms and some medical groups or health maintenance organizations.

Second, occupational labor markets can be organized by gaining the exclusive right of the members of an occupation to hold particular "professional" positions in firms which are ultimately controlled by bureaucratic authority, firms which are, from the occupation's point of view, heteronomous. Legal departments in large firms, medical and nursing staff in investor-owned hospitals, and technician and craft positions in firms are all empirical examples of this form.

Finally, occupational labor markets can be organized as autonomous, self-employed practices, in which individual members of the occupation offer their specialized skills in the marketplace. Self-employment, however, is the typical status of workers in a free market in which they have no special privilege and are highly vulnerable (see Aronson 1991). Only in an occupational labor market are practitioners protected by an exclusive license which

---

15 Between jobs, of course, they are technically unemployed. This would show up in official statistics as a higher unemployment rate. Haller et al. (1985) found this for craft workers in Austria compared to France, and it was observed about craft workers by Spilerman (1986: 70).

allows self-employment to be a relatively secure and attractive option.

Variations in Career-Line

Given these varied possibilities, while the typical career in an occupationally controlled labor market is one in which one remains in the same occupation for all one's work-life, the particular shape of work careers is more variable than in the bureaucratic labor market. In that workers remain in the same occupation, they all share what Zabusky and Barley (1996: 58) called a "horizontal" as opposed to a "vertical" career. The latter is characteristic of the bureaucratic labor market, where mobility involves promotion up a firm's hierarchy in "careers of advancement." "Horizontal"[16] careers, on the other hand, are "careers of achievement." Mobility need not involve any increase in bureaucratic authority but involves instead an increase in reputation or prestige based on expertise. The term "horizontal career" also suggests the mobility from one firm to another that is characteristic of the occupationally controlled labor market. It can also entail moving one's practice as a consultant or contractor from one place to another.

A characteristic career dilemma posed to workers in an occupationally controlled market, one which is found most often among engineers but which professionals of all kinds may face, is the cost of obtaining effective bureaucratic authority. With the exception of those who are self-employed, all professionals working in organizations face two parallel lines of upward mobility: one entails continuing to practice one's craft and over time gaining increments in title and sometimes the right to supervise the work of less senior workers, but never gaining more than minor degrees of bureaucratic authority in the firm; the other entails essentially forsaking the practice of one's occupation and moving across the firm's lattice to a staff position in which one gains authority, then up that hierarchy, sometimes to become the chief executive of the firm but no longer able to practice one's craft. This is a choice that often troubles those who identify strongly with their craft, who enjoy its

---

16 "A horizontal career's syntax could be specified as a movement toward a more central position in a social network located at a specific level of a stratification system. Vertical careers are therefore more likely to trace increments in formal authority, whereas horizontal careers are more likely to encode increments in prestige or expertise" (Zabusky and Barley 1996: 58).

practice, and who wish to advance it. Colleagues who continue to work at their discipline often regard such movement as selling out.

I have already commented briefly on the belief of some scholars that changes in the organization of work are creating entirely new forms of organization and work career. Sabel (1995) insists that present-day changes are new, that an "open labor market" is developing which is distinctly different from what he calls craft or firm labor market. This allegedly new form is the outcome of methods of production that employ workers who have flexible skills and can adapt rapidly to changing production needs. He rejects the craft labor market as a model because distinct sets of fixed, jurisdictionally bounded skills, however complex and discretionary in character, are no longer relevant. This ignores, of course, the dynamic character of jurisdictional boundaries and skills in both historic professions and crafts, but it is worth considering in my effort to conceptualize occupational labor markets.

Casey provides a rationale for Sabel's view:

> The transformation of occupation in the corporation and the emergence of post-occupational work in corporate practices of team and "family" groupings is affecting the composition of a post-industrial self and will affect the forms of social solidarity in society after industrialism. . . . Furthermore, we can observe the amalgamation of other skilled occupations . . . into generalist pan-occupational jobs known by their company-specific designation, such as "customer test interface controller." . . . The integration of knowledge and function . . . has rendered specialization obsolete and generalization the new uniform requirement. (Casey 1995: 186–7)

Apart from Casey's inappropriate dismissal of specialization, there is the matter of the prerequisites for career mobility. The title "customer test interface controller" of course delineates a particular specialization. The basic question is whether or not it is firm-specific. If it is a set of duties which can be performed only in that employing organization, then the incumbent's future career is limited to that firm. But if fewer and fewer workers can hope to be permanent employees of particular firms, then in order to be employed by others they must have generalizable skills and job titles which are recognized by and transferable to other firms. The trend toward temporary employment, therefore, *increases* rather than decreases the importance of occupation as a source of horizontal inter-firm careers in the labor market, whether it is an open market or not. Occupational title and occupation become even more essential market signals than was the case before such changes.

Labor Market Shelters

The professional labor market is typically structured by what Weber called "social closures" (Weber 1978: 339–48; Parkin 1979: 44–73; Murphy 1988). Remembering that this labor force is composed largely of non-competing groups, and that most of those who are excluded are neither struggling to enter nor necessarily without equally valuable options, it is appropriate to take the perspective of the protected rather than of the potentially excluded, and to use Marcia Freedman's (1976: 114–16) apt term, "labor market shelter," to characterize the closure. Her term serves as a useful counterbalance to the covert assumption of the virtues of a free labor market on the part of most writers on occupational or class mobility, a point to which I shall return in chapter 9. In the empirical circumstances of the imperfectly free labor market, shelters are the successful result of workers' efforts to gain some security in the face of the intrinsically greater power of employers (see, for example, Elbaum 1984). They also result from the efforts of managers to develop a stable and reliable workforce in at least the primary sector of firm internal labor markets. Sheltered jobs and occupations are intrinsic to both bureaucratic and occupationally controlled markets, but they are created and controlled in different ways, for different purposes, and with different consequences.

In professionalism, sheltered labor markets for particular jurisdictions in a division of labor are created on the basis of a claim to be able to perform a defined set of discretionary tasks satisfactorily. They are not justified by asserting a right to have a secure position, which is characteristic of the bureaucratic labor market. Individual recruits are selected on the basis of what is believed to be their capacity to learn how to perform those tasks. Their training is conducted by members of the occupational group. Upon completion of their training, they are provided with a credential that serves as evidence of their now trained capacity to perform those tasks, a credential that serves as qualification for entry into the labor market. In the ideal-typical occupational labor market the credential is a labor market signal based on a formal system of training that is controlled directly or indirectly by representatives of the occupation and sustained by force of law or strong custom.

Credentialism and Labor Market Signals

Information is the critical element that influences how both worker and consumer are brought together – information to the prospective worker about available work and what will be paid for its performance, and information to the prospective consumer about available workers, the tasks they can perform, and the pay they will accept. Information shapes both supply and demand in labor markets, and it is often highly problematic. It is least problematic for labor consumers when the work that is required has been reduced to a mechanical specialization: most prospective workers could be expected to be able to perform it, and one can evaluate their performance without much difficulty. The requirement of discretionary specializations, however, and most particularly those based on esoteric, abstract theory, poses a serious problem to prospective labor consumers. How are they to judge whether a prospective worker is able to perform tasks adequately?

In a free labor market, workers would compete with each other for the consumer's custom by claiming competence and leaving the consumer to evaluate their claims and consider the attractiveness of their wage demands. In a bureaucratically organized labor market, the consumer's choice must be between firms or organizations in the external labor market, each claiming to be able to provide the desired good or service at an attractive price by virtue of its method of bringing competent workers together and supervising their work. Once chosen, the firm is responsible for satisfying demand. Thus, in exchanges in the free labor market, individual workers are the nominally responsible parties about whom consumers would seek information; in the bureaucratically organized labor market organizations are the responsible parties about which consumers would seek information. In the occupationally controlled labor market, however, the occupation is the responsible party. The consumer must first choose the desired product or service, then choose someone who is a member in good standing of the occupation that has exclusive right to provide it. The occupation's exclusive jurisdiction represents a double monopoly: over the performance of a particular set of tasks and over the information required by the consumer who must choose someone to perform those tasks. That information comes in the form of an occupationally approved credential.

Credentials and Labor Market Signals

Spence's (1974) concept of labor market signal is more general than the concept of credential, and may be used to encompass all those devices that are employed to contend with the ever-present problem of information in the marketplace. How do people find work? (For a now classic review and study, see Granovetter 1974.) How do people find workers? What kind of information is available to aid the choice of both prospective workers and prospective consumers of their labor? To employ someone on trial and suffer the consequences of possible error is generally expensive of time and other resources. Trial use may not be possible anyway because, as Rosenbaum's study (1984: 265) suggests, performance is difficult to assess and ability even more so. In addition to direct testing of an individual's performance of an actual task, some kind of indirect or inferential information must be used if one is to avoid essentially random selection. All indirect and inferential forms of information can be called, generically, labor market signals.

Labor market signals, displayed consciously or unconsciously by those offering their labor, and interpreted or "read" consciously or unconsciously by those seeking someone to perform work for (or on) them, cover a very broad range of phenomena. The biological and physical characteristics of a prospective worker may – rightly or wrongly – represent signals to a prospective consumer. Gender, for example, may be used as a signal for probable competence to care for a young child, or to sell cosmetics or hardware. Age, too, can be used. Such physical characteristics as height, weight, or muscularity may be a signal, or even the capacity to catch an apple thrown into a crowd of job applicants (Jacoby 1984: 25). And of course race, ethnic background, and religion have been used as signals. Beyond such characteristics, a variety of others reflect schooled competence and prior performance at work. Past work experience, whether specified verbally in an interview, or written on a job application, or embodied in a resume, is often used as a signal. So, too, are letters of recommendation written by former employers or clients, or by those who claim to have taught the applicant the skills necessary for the desired work. And so, too, are test scores.

These are all indirect forms of testimony and must be taken on faith. Furthermore, in none of these cases can the prospective labor consumer know what is false in the information submitted or what is omitted. How complete and accurate is the job history or résumé provided by the applicant, for example, and what kind of work of what quality was in fact expected and performed in those prior jobs? How many dissatisfied employers or associates would not write positive testimonials? How many former teachers were unwilling to write a letter of recommendation? In the face of such uncertainties, the prospective consumer is likely to seek other kinds of signals to help evaluate the information provided by the applicant: the status or prominence of prior employers may be appraised as a signal, as may the status or prominence of those who write the testimonials or letters of recommendation.

It is important to emphasize the indirectness of those signals. Rarely is it possible to examine the actual work that people have done before investing the time and money required to hire them and gain a direct assessment of their performance. When the work itself is especially complex, specialized, and discretionary, a considerable amount of time and money may be expended before one can reach a secure judgment about the way in which it has been performed. Indeed, one may never reach a truly secure judgment about the performance of some kinds of work. It is in part for that reason, and in part for the reason that few if any empirical labor markets are much like Parnes' little island where full information exists, that labor market signals are essential, and that formal credentials are ubiquitous in contemporary industrial societies. Collins' (1979) distaste notwithstanding, it is hard to see how they could be dispensed with. Indeed, since the formal credential is ostensibly achieved rather than ascribed, many informal signals, not to speak of personal judgments, are ruled out of bounds as unfair and even discriminatory. And when the problem is to engage the labor of someone just entering the labor market without prior work experience, the formal credential testifying to successful training is the most likely primary signal for employment even though its connection with performance on the job is questionable. In the ideal-typical occupational labor market of professionalism, however, the formal credential is the *mandatory* key to entry. It is an official signal that labor consumers have no choice but to accept if they want the work it represents performed, for no one but those possessing it is allowed to perform it.

Professionalism and Schooling

In this chapter I have shown how labor markets vary in scope and source of control, and I have distinguished the occupationally controlled labor market that is typical of professionalism from the free labor market and the bureaucratic labor market. Additionally, I analyzed how each kind of market creates different career-lines. Finally, I discussed the labor market shelter that is the typical outcome of occupational control. Table 3.1 summarizes the differences in labor market participation for each of the ideal types.

Table 3.1 Variations in labor market participation by type of market

Type of market	Port of entry	Requirements for entry	Typical career-line	Predominant knowlege
Free	Open	Consumer choice	Disorderly, irregular	Everyday
Bureaucratic	Personnel office	Formal job description varying by position	Regular, vertical within firm	Variable by position but firm-specific
Occupational	Practice institution	Training credential	Horizontal across firms	Discretionary, transferable

The key to creating and gaining access to occupationally controlled shelters is the credential that serves as the prime, indeed, the mandatory market signal for consumers. The training credential is the hinge between two major institutional complexes – those organizing the performance of work and those organizing training for that performance. I turn now to training institutions.

4

Training Programs

I have been describing and analyzing the essential institutions of the ideal type, professionalism, in part by contrasting them with those organized by the free market and the bureaucratic firm. The prerequisite for all other institutions of professionalism is official recognition that the occupation uses in its work a complex body of formal knowledge and skill that commands abstract concepts or theories and requires the exercise of a considerable amount of discretion. The general public's views of that occupation can facilitate and support such recognition, as can the views of some influential elite, but recognition and support from the state or some other paramount power is essential. When so recognized, an occupation is in a position to control its own work rather than be controlled by consumers or managers.

One facet of that control is exercised in the choice of how tasks are organized and divided among workers – the division of labor. In discussing that I made a systematic comparison of the logic of occupational control with that of the perfectly free market and rational-legal bureaucracy. I outlined the different consequences of each source of control for such things as the transience of particular occupations and jobs and the degree of occupational differentiation, or specialization. I then turned to an analysis of how each logic had systematic consequences for the organization of labor markets, pointing out that occupational differentiation, career-lines, and the terms, conditions, and goals of work all vary systematically as the source and nature of control varies.

Occupational control of work depends on the establishment of a labor market shelter for members, a shelter which provides a monopoly over particular kinds of specialized work and over the right to supervise and evaluate such work. When work takes place in a formal, complex organization, occupational control requires that some members of the occupation become supervisors or managers. Under such circumstances, the occupation becomes stratified by administrative authority. As we shall see in this chapter, the ideal-typical method of maintaining control over training creates a second source of internal stratification, namely, cognitive authority. Thus, leaving aside internal differentiation by sub-specializations in knowledge and skill, an intrinsic consequence of the occupational control of work is internal division between practitioners, administrators or managers, and cognitive authorities.

The key to the occupational control of work is the creation of a training credential that becomes a prerequisite for entering a labor market and performing a defined set of tasks. In the empirical world, there is more than one source of training credentials and many different ways of organizing training. In the case of ideal-typical professionalism, however, the credential testifies to successful training in a specialized, relatively exclusive school associated with a university.

Professional schooling is an indispensable component of the ideal type, but this is not solely because it produces the credential. It does much more than that. As an institution, it is also responsible for formalizing the particular kind of knowledge and skill claimed by an occupation and for providing an intellectual basis for its jurisdictional claims and its relation to other occupations. It is the factory that produces new knowledge and skill and, to some degree, tests and approves it. It is the authoritative source establishing the legitimacy of the practical work activities of the occupation's members, and it is the primary source of the status of its members and their personal, public, and official identities. It also contributes to the development of commitment to the occupation as a life career and to a shared identity, a feeling of community or solidarity among all those who have passed through it.

The Larger Educational System

When I discussed the nature of specialized work in my first chapter, I distinguished the kind of task that any competent adult could be expected to perform reasonably well from the kind that could be performed well only by those who had undertaken a special course of training. I noted that in pre-industrial societies few if any special courses of training existed. Most children were trained informally by their elders in household and community. Even in the greatest civilizations preceding the Industrial Revolution, only a small number of people attended special schools, were formally tutored, or were apprenticed to a specialist. With industrialization, however, came the development everywhere of formal educational institutions which children were required to attend for a number of years.[1] Green (1992: 309) concluded from his comparative study of France, the UK, and the USA that the major impetus for developing their educational systems was the "need to provide the state with trained administrators, engineers, and military personnel; to spread national cultures and inculcate popular ideologies of nationhood; and so to forge the political and cultural unity of burgeoning nation states, and cement the cultural hegemony of their dominant classes."

The first or primary level of schooling, lasting six to eight years and aimed at inculcating elementary literacy, numeracy, and information (if not also state-approved values) became a virtually universal requirement.[2] It is almost entirely general rather than vocational in character, designed to establish the elementary competencies and values expected of ordinary adults,[3] and required for what is officially classified in the United States as unskilled labor. More affluent nations extend the requirement of formal schooling to a secondary level lasting an additional four to six years. Like primary education, secondary education devotes itself to inculcating a basic stock of general knowledge and skill, though on a more advanced level. Unlike primary schools, however, it is common for secondary schools also to provide opportunities for acquiring specialized knowledge and skill. Taken together, the education provided informally in the household and community along with the general education provided by formal primary and secondary schools constitutes the core qualification for most work

1 For an important effort to explain the development of primary and secondary education, with considerable material on its history in Russia, Denmark, France, and England, see Archer 1979.
2 There is a surprising similarity in primary school curricula throughout the world even though nations and national cultures vary in many important ways. See Benavot et al. 1991.
3 Similarities of substance aside, for an interesting discussion of how the emphases of elementary curricula vary in societies with differing political ideologies, see Wallace 1961. Such variation has distinct consequences for the ideologies supporting or challenging professionalism.

that is officially classified as semi-skilled in the United States. National variation in the relation of vocational training to the educational system and to the labor market has significant consequences for the organization of industrial work and industry itself, as Maurice and his colleagues (1986) show in their comparative study of France and Germany, differences confirmed by many subsequent researchers. (For a brief review of the literature on differences in national educational systems and their implications for work careers, see Kerckhoff 1996.)

In addition to this minimal formal training, all industrialized nations have developed tertiary educational institutions designed to provide further education to a proportionately small but growing segment of their populations. This is where professional training is located. Admission to all such institutions requires successful completion of primary and secondary schooling, and often passing a special examination as well (for an international comparison of examinations, see Eckstein and Noah 1993). Those tertiary educational institutions are everywhere divided into technical or vocational institutions often labeled "institutes," and institutions of higher education, often labeled "universities."[4] The former have a specifically vocational orientation while the latter have a dual concern: they want to extend the socializing function of primary and secondary schools by providing their students with an advanced general education thought to deepen and broaden their knowledge, skills, and cultural sophistication, and they want to qualify their graduates for desirable, middle-class jobs by providing specialized vocational programs. Professional training is explicitly vocational in character but presupposes the advanced general education connected with the university. It is in fact characteristically attached to the university, which distinguishes it from the training of technicians that goes on in technical institutes and training on the job that is practiced by the crafts.

Finally, it seems appropriate to note that vocational training is

---

4 I avoid the term "college" because its usage in other times and places is quite variable, having been used originally for associations or organizations that perform no formal educational functions, and subsequently for certain secondary schools in England, France, and elsewhere. In the United States it is usually applied to post-secondary institutions offering either two- or four-year degrees. For the former, see Belitsky 1969, Brint and Karabel 1989, and Litt 1969. There is of course a huge literature on universities, a good introduction to which are the comparative studies in B. Clark (1985) dealing with the relationships between secondary and tertiary institutions.

by no means an exclusive prerogative of the state. A good part of the everyday knowledge and skill involved in work is learned informally by people in the household and local community, and the state has little direct influence on it. Similarly, the state has little influence on the vocational training that is carried on informally in small trades and businesses. Even a craft apprentice system of vocational training can be operated on an informal basis quite independently of the state. The state is involved only when a training system depends for its success on official recognition of the credentials it produces, and, even more, on official enforcement of the use of those credentials as a social closure, or labor market shelter. Such recognition requires official approval of the institution that produces the credential as well as whatever examination is employed.

Ideal-Typical Models of Training

Of the three ideal-typical models of the control of work that I have been discussing in the past chapters, only occupational control has unambiguous consequences for training. Under the conditions of the perfectly free labor market, it is possible to conceive of some people serving as self-employed teachers of particular skills – their practice more like that of a tutor than a schoolteacher. In a free market, however, demand is so fluid that it is difficult to imagine many workers investing in training for specialized skills before entering the market. Thus, schooling in preparation for work is likely to be modest and general in character, providing little more than such basic skills as literacy and numeracy: perhaps that was what Adam Smith had in mind when he urged the support of educational programs for workers.

The character of schooling is much clearer for ideal-typical bureaucracy, but more complex. As I observed in discussing the way the bureaucratic labor market is organized and the hierarchical shape of its division of labor, a number of specialties are required and on a number of levels of skill and authority. It is unlikely that any firm could itself train everyone for every position it requires. Its existence depends upon an external system of education organized, administered, and paid for by others. A bureaucratic organization would base its own requirements for the positions it wishes to fill largely on what it can expect from external educational programs, relying as little as possible on the expense of mounting its own training program, but it would certainly try to influence educational policy so as to have prospective workers trained to suit its own needs.

There are different strategies for this. Compared to France and the United States, which tend to provide relatively unspecialized education, the traditional German policy ties education closely to industry and creates well-defined craft qualifications which allow the creation of occupational labor markets. This policy leads Marsden to observe that

> occupational labour markets have a number of key features. First, there is the establishment of standards of the mix of skills and the level of attainment offered by people trained in a particular occupation. Secondly, there is some standardization of the form of training. And thirdly, there is some standardization in job slots or job descriptions across organizations. Together these help assure a high degree of transferability of skills which is the prime characteristic of occupational labour markets.... Employers using occupational markets need fairly standardized job slots into which such workers can fit. (Marsden 1986: 234)

Those job slots are in essence produced by occupational training programs. There is, however, more than one kind of program for training workers to exercise relatively complex skills requiring more than average discretion. By reviewing these possibilities it is possible to clarify the distinctiveness of ideal-typical professional training.

Three Patterns of Specialized Training

The empirical crafts have usually been considered weaker than the professions. To explain this, a number of reasons are often advanced – the virtually universal stigma of manual labor, the class origins of their members, the greater power of employers, and the character of the knowledge and skill to which they lay claim.[5] Apart from those factors there is, I believe, another: the way they have institutionalized the training of their members.

Empirically, three different occupational categories are commonly associated with fairly complex specialized knowledge – those called in English crafts, technicians, and professions. While

---

5　A recent study of the craft guilds claims that they were far more successful than reputed, and that they "failed" in Europe primarily because they were abolished by the state. It also contains a superb bibliography. See Epstein 1998.

the particular names for those categories, the occupations they include, and some of the characteristics of their training institutions all vary historically and from nation to nation, the variation is not so great that I cannot abstract three distinctly different forms of training, with technicians providing the weakest version of the occupational control of training and professions the strongest.

Recruits to the *crafts* have traditionally received their training on the job, whether that is the shop of a self-employed craft worker or the site of a project at which craft work is performed for others. Training takes place *within* the labor market, and so is contingent on the demands of production as well as of those who finance it.[6] Trainees have apprentice status at a reduced salary and learn their craft as they work on the job with a full-fledged member of the trade who serves as teacher and supervisor. The craft is learned as a practical, vocational enterprise in which the working knowledge and tacit skills required are learned as work is being performed. Patently, however, what can be learned is contingent upon what work happens to be performed during the course of training. Some may not require use of the full range of knowledge and skill over which the craft has jurisdiction. What can be learned may also be contingent on the work required by the employer or client at the time of training, which affects the amount of practice and supervision that can exist. Furthermore, the particular craft workers who engage in training and supervising novices may differ in their proficiency, their effectiveness as instructors, and their conscientiousness. Finally, since training takes place in practical circumstances that require the continuous performance of productive work, there may be no opportunity to engage in discursive instruction that conveys abstract concepts and formal theories. In all, there is very real danger that on-the-job training will be perfunctory and exploitative, its substance sacrificed in favor of gaining the benefit of cheap apprentice labor. And since both jobs and work-sites vary, as well as the capacity and motivation of those who provide the training, it is difficult to standardize training: one cannot readily assume that all who have successfully completed their training are roughly equal in competence. Craft programs which include certification, however, do attempt to control those difficulties.

6 For employers, the investment cost of in-house training is an important consideration for determining their personnel policies; see the discussion in Ryan 1984. See Eurich 1985 for an overview of training within firms, as well as Knoke and Kalleberg 1994 for the finding that in-house training in large firms is increasing.

Technicians receive a different kind of formal training. Unlike many of the crafts, whose identity and organization have deep historical roots that extend even further back in history than most of the professions, technicians developed as entirely new occupations during and after the Industrial Revolution. The term itself did not appear until the nineteenth century. Technicians are now increasing in number and variety as advanced economies exploit new technologies and expand services, and no doubt they will continue to increase in number and variety well into the twenty-first century. Their position in the labor force is ambiguous and unstable, however, and in the United States, at least, unlike the crafts, they have no tradition of collective action. Some, particularly those working in the medical division of labor, require credentials to work and have more or less exclusive rights over their work though, like nurses, they are in subordinate positions in the division of labor. Others with technician job titles are in a considerably more ambiguous position: in their analysis of a variety of workers with the title, Whalley and Barley (1997) describe one instance in which originally classified "operatives" were reclassified as "technicians" in an effort to forestall their eligibility for unionization. It may very well be that the occupational category itself is too new to permit generalization. The occupations themselves are often very new and have a variety of origins. Few of them have become stable and well established as occupations in a division of labor, most of them being still in an early stage of development. In the future some individual occupations in the technician category may gain professional status, others become semi-professions (Etzioni 1969),[7] others simply disappear as their skills are made redundant by new technology, and still others become members of the occupationally anonymous semi-skilled worker category.[8]

7 If one can stretch the method a bit and create an ideal type for an impure or incomplete social form like semi-profession, one might call it an occupation that has gained a jurisdiction in a division of labor, as well as a labor market shelter and control over its own training, credentialling, and supervision, but that has not established sufficient cognitive authority to dominate either the division of labor in which its jurisdiction is located or public discourse concerning its work. A crude measure of this weak economic and cultural authority is its relatively low but by no means ignominious social status. When studied historically and transnationally, secondary school teachers are quite interesting in this context, for the *Gymnasium* and *lycée* teachers of nineteenth-century France and Germany come fairly close to professionalism, while today they and especially high school teachers of the United States, are closer to semi-professionalism.

8 See Kraft 1977 on programmers, and also Wright and Jacobs 1994. It is quite

A critical index of those that are collectively mobile and on the road to professional or semi-professional status is the successful association of their training programs with a university and the development of a curriculum that emphasizes new or syncretic theory which intellectualizes their work. Historically, many of the institutes created to train technicians and "mechanics" during the nineteenth century in Europe and North America had, by the twentieth century gained university status – witness the German *technische Hochschule*, the red-brick universities of the UK, the land grant colleges and normal schools of the United States, and more recently, the polytechnics of the UK. All of them were originally designed to provide up-to-date technical training to students of modest background who could be expected to serve the practical needs of the commercial, industrial, and agricultural communities. The faculties of those institutes sought and finally gained university status by advancing theory and research in their curricula and claiming professional (or semi-professional) credentials for their matriculants.[9]

Unlike training for the crafts, the basic training of technicians is not commonly gained on the job or as an apprentice though, like all workers after they enter the labor market, they gain additional training and experience on the job in the form of working knowledge. Their training typically takes place in para-secondary and post-secondary institutions that are sometimes called technical institutes.[10] In the United States they are most often community

---

possible that some of those who are traditionally called professionals, rank-and-file engineers being the most obvious example, might fall to the status of technician in the future. Apart from specialties of high status connected with public works and military affairs before the Industrial Revolution, engineering grew out of subordinate service positions in industry from which it has not been able to extricate itself in most nations. For a brief account of its struggle to join the ranks of the professions in nineteenth-century Germany, see Torstendahl 1993. For a broad but brief comparative history see Lundgreen 1990. I discuss engineers at greater length in chapter 7.

9   Faculties are independent sources of pressure for gaining university status. However, it is important to keep in mind also that *prospective* members of the profession themselves press for credentials based on higher education, both for the prestige they provide and for the higher authority they are thought to have. Burrage (1993) notes how in the UK it was *students* who were most responsible for seeking university law and engineering degrees, not practitioners. Practitioners have often resisted the control of training by a faculty. Indeed, I suspect that only elite practitioners are likely to be prominent in efforts to establish formal professional schooling.

10   As Kerckhoff (1996: 49) observed, our knowledge of "vocational post-secondary institutions" is very poor. For one empirical source, see Geer 1972.

colleges offering two-year post-secondary degrees. And unlike the crafts, while the content of their training is largely practical in character, they are taught some theory and abstract concepts. Thinking of them as an intuitively coherent occupational category, they represent a comparatively weak set of occupations that are not able to control their own training because, unlike both crafts and professions, they do not create their own body of knowledge and skill. The content of their training is largely synthetic, derived from both technical and theoretical knowledge and skill produced and controlled by other occupations. Nor are they often trained solely by members of their own occupation. And while the knowledge and skill they learn is not typically limited to specific work-sites – like that of crafts and professions, it is transferable rather than firm-specific – it is fitted into a division of labor that is dominated by either lay managers or professionals. Their status in the labor market may be quite favorable in times of high demand and short supply, but since their work is often highly vulnerable to rationalization and obsolescence, and their training programs open and often accessible to many, they are in an intrinsically vulnerable position in the labor market (see Keefe and Potosky 1997 for one set of technicians). It remains to be seen whether their training institutes will, like those of the past, assume university status in the future.

In *ideal-typical professionalism*, the training of recruits is, like the other elements of the ideal type, fully under the control of the occupation. Unlike craft training, it largely takes place outside the labor market. Like technical training, it takes place in a school, but unlike it, the school is attached to institutions of higher education. Like the crafts, training is controlled and conducted by members of the occupation, but unlike the crafts, those who do the training are more or less full-time teachers who are not obliged to gain their income from work in the labor market outside the school and the educational system. And finally, in contrast to those involved in both craft and technician training, the faculty of the ideal-typical professional school is expected not only to teach, but also to be active in the codification, refinement, and expansion of the occupation's body of knowledge and skill by both theorizing and doing research. Taken together, these characteristics have a number of important implications for the status and organization of an ideal-typical profession. My analysis of the differences between the vocational training of ideal typical crafts, technicians, and professions can be seen in table 4.1.

Table 4.1 Characteristics of training by type of occupation

Characteristics of training	Craft	Technician	Profession
Proportion of training in school	Low	Significant	High
Teachers members of the occupation	Always	Not always	Always
Primary training on the job	Always	Sometimes	Seldom
Full-time teachers	Rarely	Sometimes	Usually
Teachers do research	No	No	Yes
University affiliation	No	No	Yes

Professional Control of Supply

The labor market shelter characteristic of professionalism protects professionals from competition by other occupations. In order to be truly effective, however, it must also protect its members from each other – that is, protect itself from unrestrained competition among members that would seriously threaten its cohesion as an occupation. Obviously, severe internal competition can occur when there is a considerable excess of practitioners over consumer demand. This is likely to result in both a low average income for the profession as a whole, and divisiveness created by significant differences between the lowest and highest income of colleagues. A major source of protection from this possibility lies in restricting the supply of practitioners, for when supply is not out of line with demand, virtually all practitioners can be expected to gain a satisfactory, if not fully equal, income. The restriction of numbers is an important part of what Larson (1977: 9–18) called the profes- sions' "market project" and is central to Abel's effort to establish a conceptual framework for the comparative study of lawyers (Abel 1989).[11]

11 The same result can be obtained by increasing demand. Professions can increase demand by inventing new services that are attractive to consumers and by purporting to discover heretofore unrecognized consumer needs that only the profession can satisfy. As I shall note, professional schools institutionalize the process of systematic research and innovation by which new demand can be created. A quite different method of increasing demand lies in legislation or

Some of the devices designed to control the supply of services and stimulate demand for them are to be found in local labor markets, where practitioners may collude to limit the number of colleagues who may offer services in their locality. They may also try to fix minimum fees or "the going wage" and ostracize or otherwise punish colleagues willing to settle for less. They may forbid competitive bidding or the advertising of competitive prices or fees in their labor market. They may succeed in gaining legal privileges that *require* consumers to employ them or otherwise use their services even when consumers do not feel the need to do so. These devices do not distinguish them from the historic crafts apart from the greater tendency of the latter to undertake strikes. What *is* distinctive about the professional market project, however, is the inherent conflict between the practitioners' collective interest in limiting supply and the countervailing interest in increasing supply created by the institutionalization of formal schooling.

An essential characteristic of professionalism lies in controlling the number of practitioners entering the labor market by imposing stringent standards on admission to professional school and requiring candidates to pass some sort of examination in order to obtain their qualifying credential. Such control cannot be *too* stringent, however, because of the need of professional schools and their faculties for students. Even when practitioners control training by using an apprentice system, restricting the number of trainees is difficult. In the crafts, masters could and did take on more apprentices than could find work later as journeymen because they gained cheap labor from apprentices. So, too, have professional schools a tendency to take on more students than proper control of supply would demand: in some cases they need cheap labor for the faculty's teaching, projects, or practices, but most important is the expansion of their training programs and increase of their resources.[12] Furthermore, since professionalized occupations offer prestige and attractive careers, the press of applicants creates political support for expanding the professional school and increasing admissions. What may be to the benefit of

administrative rules that require consumers to use professional services. "Medicalization" is one of the most notorious methods of expanding demand, though as Lowenberg and Davis (1994) make clear, it would be inaccurate to ascribe it solely to imperialistic or entrepreneurial impulses of the medical profession.

12   A good empirical example of formal professional schools whose admission policies, curriculum, and standards for graduation were strongly influenced by economic self-interest is provided by the proprietary medical and law schools that existed during part of the nineteenth century in the United States.

professional schools, however, conflicts with the practitioners' interest in restricting supply.[13] This is one inherent source of tension between practitioners and the faculty of professional schools.

The Professional Curriculum

While professional training, like that of the crafts, is vocationally oriented, it is not merely practical in substance. Theory and first principles are taught formally in school, where students and teachers are insulated from the immediate practical demands of everyday work. Professional training may even eschew practical training entirely, assuming (sometimes requiring) that students obtain their working knowledge after they leave school. Above all else, the ideology supporting professional training emphasizes theory and abstract concepts. This is justified by claiming that whatever practitioners must do at work may require extensive exercise of discretionary judgment rather than the choice and routine application of a limited number of mechanical techniques. Hence, it is more important to have a firm grounding in basic theory and concepts to guide discretionary judgment than to gain practice in what can only be a selection from among all the concrete practical and working knowledge that particular work-settings may require.

The particular theoretical knowledge thought to be appropriate to professional training varies, of course, according to time, place, and occupation. Ideology is inevitably an element in the curriculum, whether this be ethics in liberal democracy or "the principle of community morality" in the training of Soviet engineers (see Zborovskiy and Karpova 1984). The organization of that training also varies. Although it is far less common today, even now some professions in some nations do not require formal attendance in professional schools, instead training their members as apprentices on the job, as in the crafts. This shares the handicaps of craft training, since the large variety of work-sites and the differences inherent in a scattered group of practitioner-instructors make it difficult to standardize the outcome. But even when apprenticeship instead of schooling has been used for professional training,

---

13 Thus, I would argue that unless the state exercises control over the number of applicants admitted, it is empirically unlikely for market projects to be successful. In chapter 7 I introduce the state as an essential contingency for the ideal type.

apprenticed professionals are also required to be exposed to book learning in the academic or liberal studies of the ideas, theories, and works treasured by the cultivated elite. Such book learning is not only necessary for the social status desired by professionals, but also claimed to be a necessary intellectual foundation for the capacity to learn and perform the complexities of professional work. While the crafts can exist without any connections with the higher educational system (and high culture) of a society, this has not been true of the empirical professions, nor is it true of ideal-typical professionalism. The connection of training with the high culture valued by the elite and often respected by the masses, even when training does not take place in schools, establishes an essential part of the ideological foundation for the occupation's status. It provides a foundation for the claim to be more than narrow technical specialists.

The Control of Knowledge

The fact that the training of professions ideal-typically takes place outside the labor market and in formal training institutions rather than in scattered practices or work-sites has important consequences for the control of knowledge and technique. Since it is carried on independently of the lay consumers of their discipline, it escapes any immediate influence from them and can be wholly controlled by the faculty. Since it is carried on by faculties in formally organized institutions rather than by individual practitioners coping with a variety of work contingencies at the same time as they try to teach, the school can plausibly claim standardization and reliability for the credentials it produces. Finally, perhaps the most important difference from the historic crafts lies in the fact that ideal-typical professional training institutions do not merely recruit, train, and certify students. What gives them and the profession of which they are a part the capacity to preserve and even expand their jurisdiction is the fact that in addition to teaching, their faculties can devote themselves to systematizing, refining, and expanding the body of knowledge and skill over which the profession claims jurisdiction. This institutionalized capacity to innovate and adapt facilitates a more flexible response to technical and social change than is possible for the crafts.

The faculty of the professional school is a distinctive element of the ideal type in that it represents one of the major structural sources for sustaining professionalism. Historically, professional training has not always taken place in schools or in organized programs of formal instruction with full-time teachers. It is true that from the very beginning on the European continent, law, medicine, and theology were taught in universities – indeed, the first universities were established to prepare people for those very vocations. But in England and later in the United States, the common law and, to a lesser degree, medicine, were taught by less formal means – for example, by maintaining a presence in one of the Inns of Court, or by clerking with a practicing lawyer or judge. Only during the twentieth century did professional schools emerge in the United States as the dominant form of training, and in England they were still not dominant in law and engineering, though things were moving in that direction.[14] Some of the newer professions, such as engineering and accounting, initially conducted their training on the job, then slowly developed their own schools, first as vocational institutes and only later as schools or faculties within universities or as institutes with university status.[15] Even now, training for the newer professions in many countries is not firmly institutionalized in schools associated with higher learning – the lower ranks of engineering in England, for example, receive their training on the job rather than in a school (McCormick 1988).

For the ideal type, a primary source of the theoretical importance of formal schools associated with higher education lies in their faculty as well as their standardizable, theoretically based curriculum. Ideal-typically, the faculty is not composed of part-time teachers, though empirically teachers who spend most of their time in practice were the rule in some times and places. Ideal-typically, the faculty is composed of credentialled members of the profession who devote themselves on a full-time basis to teaching up-to-date knowledge and skill, engaging in research and scholarship designed to codify and refine what is already known, and innovating and experimenting in an effort to develop new knowledge and technique and extend the old.

14 For brief reviews of the development of professional schools in Russia, Germany, the UK, and the United States, see Engel 1983: 293–305, McClelland 1983: 306–20, Timberlake 1983: 321–44, Light 1983: 345–65, and Halpern 1987. For recent comparisons of the development of professional schools for law, medicine, and engineering in France, the UK, and the USA that stress the resistance of practitioners, see Burrage 1984, 1993.
15 For engineers in the United States, see Calvert 1967. For somewhat different circumstances in France and Germany, see Crawford 1989, Shinn 1978, 1980, Gispen 1989, and Torstendahl 1993.

These duties sharply distinguish the training institutions of professions from those of the crafts. The practical and working knowledge of craft workers are refined and enhanced in the course of work. Innovation certainly exists, but is at best part-time and is seldom systematically pursued. It is not intellectualized and formally codified but instead is communicated by word of mouth and practical demonstration (see Epstein 1998). By contrast, the faculty of the professional school is free to engage routinely in the pursuit of new knowledge as a normal part of its duties without having to gain a living by dealing with the practical, everyday problems posed by consumers or employers. The consumers of its work are academic or scientific colleagues within the discipline rather than those in the outside lay world. Freed from the demands of lay consumers, it can pursue abstract, logically derived problems.[16] This freedom can lead to theorizing that is partially free of the concrete times and places of practical activities.

Such a configuration of training corresponds to what Stinch-combe (1990: 300–1) calls "institutionalized reason" in which "people are trained as practitioners in an area in schools in which both the role of teacher and the role of student are differentiated from the roles in the practical work of the institution; in the highest development the role of teacher itself carries an obligation to contribute to the rationalization of the body of culture by writing textbooks or technical monographs, and students learn the paradigms separately from practice rather than only by doing progressively more complex jobs." The formal institutionalization of teaching and research provides professions with a powerful resource by which to maintain and expand a defensible jurisdiction, a resource that encourages the systematic refinement, growth, and legitimation of their discipline. It has been different for the crafts which, historically, tried to protect their monopolies by attempting to keep their specialized techniques as "mysteries," swearing apprentices to secrecy. But secrecy is difficult to sustain indefinitely even when invention of an equally useful technique by competitors does not occur. Furthermore, it does not provide systematic encouragement to the development of new techniques to supplant those which have become obsolete, commodified,

16 It should not be forgotten that the faculties of professional schools have much different economic prospects than those of most of the arts and sciences, whose living depends primarily on the academic marketplace. Professional school faculties have skills of considerable value in the ordinary marketplace, which is why they generally receive a higher income than their colleagues in the arts and sciences and why they are a threat to practitioners.

mechanized, or otherwise fallen into disuse.[17] In addition to efforts at secrecy, the historic crafts have defended their jurisdictions by taking collective action against the use of new machinery or of less skilled workers, and while they have survived far longer than many had predicted, they remain more vulnerable than professions to the loss of their jurisdictions and shelters because they lack an institutionalized means of developing new knowledge and skill and adapting successfully to new technological developments.

In contrast to the defensive craft techniques of secrecy and collective labor action, the professional school with its full-time faculty has much more flexible and powerful resources with which to control its labor market. It institutionalizes the cognitive authority of the profession by rooting it in the officially recognized authority of higher education itself. And in so far as its faculty is able to devote itself to teaching and research on a full-time basis, it stimulates the continuous creation of new knowledge and skill that can increase consumer demand. Should the general population or other occupations gain command over important segments of the profession's current knowledge and technique, new knowledge and technique not yet known to competitors or consumers can compensate for the loss. Many of the possibilities that outsiders might otherwise discover and exploit can be pre-empted. And when relevant new knowledge, skill, and technology are developed by other occupations or by firms, unlike practitioners the faculty has the leisure to study and gain command over them so as to be able, at the very least, to claim the capacity to collaborate in their use rather than submit to direction by outsiders.

Intrinsic to a faculty that devotes itself full-time to training and research, and intrinsic to the continued codification if not also expansion of its knowledge that such a full-time faculty implies, is its development of special intellectual perspectives and interests that are different from those of the practitioners it trains. The faculty can focus on abstract concepts, theories, and principles as well as highly esoteric procedures and techniques because it is insulated from the everyday demands of consumers and the variety of work settings, each of which has its own contingencies bearing on what work must be done and limiting how it can be done. Its protected circumstances also encourage it to create stan-

---

17 Not being a specialist, I can only repeat the conventional view of the crafts, which is a useful foil to ideal-typical professionalism. Epstein (1998) would probably take exception, but as the historian Louis Gottschalk once said, "Se non è vero, è ben trovato" (Even if it isn't true, it's a great story).

dards for work performance that emphasize the ideal and demean the improvisations required of colleagues who must adapt to the confusion and impurity of practical affairs where knowledge is incomplete and resources finite. It is understandable, then, that practitioners are likely to resent the intellectual authority of the faculty, not only because it provides economic advantage to faculty practitioners who may compete with them, but especially because it advances more stringent and up-to-date standards for practice than most are able or even willing to meet in light of settled habit and the demands of practice. When we remember that the interest of the faculty also lies in increasing the number of students who will become, after being credentialled, competitors of those already in practice, we can see that two important sources of tension and conflict are intrinsic to the division of labor between formal schooling and practice that is typical of professionalism.[18]

Encouraging Occupational Solidarity

In sum, the institutionalization of training in schools associated with universities creates the conditions for the relatively secure establishment, refinement, and expansion (in current jargon, the "manufacture" or "construction") of the specialized knowledge and skill of professions. Furthermore, it provides such training with the prestige of higher, rather than merely technical, education. This accomplishment sustains the occupation as a whole, its reputation, its jurisdiction, and its practicing discipline. But when we consider the process of schooling itself, we can see how it also creates the foundation for a strong sense of occupational community. First, all who enter have aspired to that occupation and have chosen in advance to undertake any special course or examination required for admission to training. Second, students are trained in batches or cohorts, unlike those trained individually as apprentices. Third, they are separated from students in other schools of the university and undergo training over a sustained period of time. Fourth, they must all take the same basic courses

---

18 This tension is ubiquitous in time and place for the empirical professions. See, for example, Auerbach 1971 and W. R. Johnson 1978 for law, Kendall 1965 for medicine in the United States, Pring 1992 for schoolteachers in the UK, and Burrage's focus (1993) on the struggle for control of training between practitioners and faculties elsewhere.

and assignments that initiate training and they must all brave the demands of their sometimes unpleasant faculty.[19]

In all, it is reasonable to assume that one consequence of ideal-typical professional schooling is to strengthen the students' commitment to and identification with the occupation. Another is to create a degree of solidarity with other students who have gone through the same process and who share the prescribed body of knowledge and skill, or discipline, that their schooling was designed to teach. Once they leave school and enter the labor market, however, the contingencies of practice are almost certain to temper their use of formal knowledge. In some cases they will ignore it and replace it with practical knowledge, and in other cases they will adapt it, developing their own pragmatic methods of coping. Of course, the *particular* contingencies of practice vary from one setting to another, but they hold enough in common that when practitioners meet, they invariably trade anecdotes about how to cope with the practical difficulties of practice and about new techniques that facilitate their work. The sense of community, or solidarity, among those trained at professional schools is strengthened by the common problems they confront in the course of their work, and both together encourage an inclination to form societies or associations in which they can come together to talk shop, trade war stories, and share new knowledge and techniques. Their common interests stimulate the formation at the very least of small, local groups in which shared problems of work and new developments in knowledge and techniques are discussed. Historically, such local "scientific societies" or "journal clubs" were far more ubiquitous than formal associations.

Stratified Career-Lines

An ideal-typical career-line for professionals is based on the commitment that is created by professional training. Aspirants to the profession must devote a considerable period of time and effort to the demanding secondary (and sometimes tertiary) education that qualifies them for admission to professional school. In itself, the "sunk cost" or "side bet" (Becker 1970: 261–73) of time and loss of earnings that is required to qualify for admission establishes a

---

19 For some empirical studies of the experience of professional schooling in the United States, see Becker et al. 1960 and Hafferty 1971 for medicine, and Granfield 1992 for law.

high degree of commitment to a career in the profession, a commitment that is increased quantitatively and qualitatively by the relatively long and demanding period of professional training. The training is likely to socialize the student into a distinct occupational culture that is shared with fellow-students, reinforced and elaborated first by the faculty and later by colleagues in practice. The course of training is also likely to foster a deep interest in the specialized knowledge and skill upon which it is focused. This commitment, in conjunction with a fairly stable and rich occupational culture, a distinct social identity, and a privileged official identity supports the inclination to make their work a lifetime career.[20]

But several different career-lines are possible by virtue of the very organization of ideal-typical professional institutions. On the one hand, one can become a practitioner, which can mean, depending upon the particular profession and the specialties it contains, building an individual practice, moving up through the ranks of a professional or other organization, or moving from professional positions in one work-setting to those of another, in each case performing much the same kind of work. On the other hand, the profession can be organized in such a way that early choice among quite different specialties and careers is required which sharply divides professional identities and commitments – the choice of a judicial or prosecutorial career in law as opposed to that of an advocate in many European nations being one such example. In any profession, a major divergence of career-lines occurs when a faculty or administrative position is chosen, a choice that leads to interests and commitments which are intrinsically in conflict with those of practitioners. Still, whatever the choice among alternatives, the ideal-typical circumstances of professionalism that are organized by formal schooling lead to lifelong membership in and commitment to a profession and to fairly orderly and stable careers.

Professional Schooling, Status, and the State

Finally, I must note the importance of professional schooling in shaping the economic and cultural status of professionals, the former referring to income and the latter to prestige. Empirically,

---

20 For empirical comparative information that raises questions about this tendency for some American occupations, see Evans and Laumann 1983.

the two are only modestly correlated, for two professions can have equally high prestige but markedly different levels of income. It is only high *cultural* status, or prestige, that characterizes ideal-typical professionalism, and a career-line that includes a relatively secure, but by no means necessarily high income. The prestige that distinguishes the professions from the crafts stems from the connection of their training with higher education. And this in turn, I suspect, stems from the connection of higher education with service to the elite. Historically, institutions of higher education long predated all other formal modes of schooling, and were closely associated with service to the rulers of high civilizations. The rulers and the aristocracy received private tutoring as children and, with some exceptions, did not attend formal schools. Formal schooling was for the functionaries and scribes who managed and recorded the affairs of both state and religious institutions, and in some cases it was organized for aspirants to the occupations of law, medicine, and the priesthood that served the personal needs of both sovereign and aristocracy. In Europe, as Torstendahl reminds us, the university was established to train the specialized servants of elite needs:

> Much rhetoric to the contrary notwithstanding, university objectives were professional in learning from the very beginning. They were designed to assure that groups of people would be given a training which would enable them to cope with problems of certain defined fields of practice of particular concern to princes and churches. Thus, bluntly put, universities were called upon to provide the manpower needed for the purposes of [the] mental and bodily welfare [of the elite]. Of course, this was not their sole duty, but it was certainly one of their principal tasks, and one which was favoured by many worldly and spiritual powers. (Torstendahl 1993: 111)

Thus, in applying Foucault's analysis of the development of "governmentality" to the professions, it is correct to emphasize the importance to the modern state of the rise of intellectual disciplines in western Europe from the eighteenth century on, but it is not accurate to consider this a new role for the professions. Their service to the elite goes back to their very origins.[21]

---

21 We must never forget that there is often an informal or underground economy of services to the elite that competes with respectable "learned" occupations. Witness the recurrent vogue of irregular practitioners among the elite throughout history; recall the notorious example of the role of Rasputin in the Romanoff court

Seen in this light, I suspect that the prestige attached to professions stems less from the social origin of their members than from the fact of their attending institutions of higher education that are respected by the elite, and from their service to elite interests. Aristocratic origins have not been characteristic of those drawn into the professions: even when eighteenth-century sovereigns attempted to literally force the aristocracy into university study so as to make them competent to be the politically reliable functionaries required by their expanding administrations, the vast majority understandably preferred the pleasures of the court and estate.[22] During the course of the great expansion of university studies and professional schools in the nineteenth century, members of the aristocracy constituted a very small minority of students. The middle class filled that vacuum and gained prestige beyond their origins by connecting their vocational training to universities. That connection provides one significant resource for the ideology of professionalism.

---

and the role of Nancy Reagan's astrologer. And of course the general population has always had its share of officially unrecognized practitioners.

22 Things were of course more complicated than that. See the comparison of the Prussian and English aristocracies in the seventeenth and eighteenth centuries in Mueller 1984: 83–5, 108–9, and note the stringent efforts in Russia during the same period to draw the aristocracy into the formal education believed to qualify them to be competent bureaucrats discussed in, for example, Alston 1969: 3–30. An interesting exception to the rule of the nobility's indifference to professional careers is provided by Konttinen 1991, for when Russia conquered Finland in 1809, it disbanded the Finnish army, leaving the nobility no acceptable careers other than in the law and state bureaucracy.

5

Ideologies

The formal institutions of professionalism establish the economic and social conditions which allow those with a specialized body of knowledge and skill to control their own work. They are objective in that it is possible to determine empirically whether or not they exist by examining charters, official classifications, licensing laws, tables of organization, and the like. However, at their root are other elements which are rather less tangible, but which are no less essential, for they justify the institutions of professionalism: the claims, values, and ideas that provide the rationale for these institutions of professionalism. I shall use the word "ideology" to refer to those elements. Unlike some writers (for reviews of usage, see Lichtheim 1967; Larrain 1979; McLellan 1986), I do not use the term to imply either empirical falsity or deliberate efforts to mask group, class, or institutional interests. Some elements of an ideology can be empirically true in some times and places, and false in others; some may conflict with the immediate interests of their proponents while others may consciously defend and advance them. Ideologies can be and often are fervently believed by those who advance them.

Ideology is the primary tool available to disciplines for gaining the political and economic resources needed to establish and maintain their status. Neither political nor economic power is intrinsic to bodies of knowledge and skill. Their generic resource is *persuasion*, which Lindblom asserts stands alongside exchange and authority as one of the "three elementary mechanisms for social control that all politico-economic systems employ" (Lindblom 1977: 11).

Persuasion is central and fundamental in all social systems. It does not, however, play in any existing politico-economic system the distinctive role that exchange plays in markets or authority plays in government. Nevertheless, it is a ubiquitous form of social control and is of special importance in the analysis of politico-economic systems on three counts. In the form of ideological instruction and propaganda, persuasion is a major method of elite control of masses, much more so in communist systems than in liberal democratic ones. In the form of commercial advertising, it is a major instrument of corporate control of masses of consumers in market societies. In the form of mutual persuasion in "free" societies – that is, in the form of "free competition of ideas" – it is fundamental to liberal democracy (Lindblom 1977: 13)

The ideal-typical ideology of professionalism is concerned with justifying the privileged position of the institutions of an occupation in a political economy as well as the authority and status of its members. To do so it must neutralize or at least effectively counter the opposing ideologies which provide the rationale for the control of work by the market on the one hand, and by bureaucracy on the other. I shall call the ideology of market control *consumerism*, that of bureaucratic control *managerialism*, and elaborate the character of the ideology of professionalism by contrasting it with the others.[1] There are many issues embedded in those ideologies, one of the most fundamental being the meaning and purpose of work, both in general and to those who perform it. A more narrow but nonetheless critical issue lies in the value of specialized work, most particularly the type of specialization ascribed to professionals and the authority over their own work and affairs related to it that they can properly claim. The issues raised by the ideology of professionalism go well beyond the organization of work. At their center is the question of the proper role of knowledge in political and social life.

---

1   For a rather different analysis of professional ideology, see Larson 1977: 208–44. Given the breadth of what I discuss here, some might think it better called the culture of professionalism (see Bledstein 1976), but "culture" is more often than not a formless catch-all term which can refer to almost anything. By contrast, "ideology" can be used more precisely to designate elements of culture which are thought to provide authoritative explanation and justification for a particular set of institutions like professionalism.

Commitment to Work

In chapter 1, I discussed the way work is classified according to the conceptions of the knowledge and skill required to do it. The assignment of position and ranking in the official labor force is based upon those conceptions. That position can be treated as an objective datum because, being official, it has the force of the state behind it. But conceptions of knowledge and skill are themselves qualified by broader ideas and values which have considerable impact on the degree to which work is privileged. The most general are those surrounding the meaning and value of work.

Several useful surveys of the meanings imputed to work in the Western world are available to us. Tilgher (1958) was concerned primarily with the intellectual and theological positions to be found in the writings of ancient and near-modern classical authorities. Applebaum (1992), on the other hand, was more concerned with connecting those positions to the different political economies in which they were formulated, and Meakin (1976) with the positions of literary figures over the past two or three centuries (see also Anthony 1977). As varied as are the intentions of those surveys, two basic issues run through them all – the value or meaning of work in and of itself, and the value of different *kinds* of work.

Taking as a given that human work is generically connected to biological survival or, in a more indirect way in most societies, to gaining a living, the question is whether necessity is its sole value. Weber's classic analysis of the role of Protestantism in motivating the activities of entrepreneurs and workers during the development of capitalism and the Industrial Revolution suggested that work can have ends that go beyond economic consumption. Even when it is arduous and unpleasant, it can be performed for its spiritual as well as its economic value. Karl Marx, drawing upon Hegel, was a major voice among those who argued that work was valuable not merely because it provided workers with a living, but also because in some of its forms it could express the essence of being human – "species-being."

Throughout discussions of work runs a basic distinction between work performed solely in order to gain a living, and work that is performed more for the pleasure or self-fulfillment it provides than for the living it yields. This distinction is one of those used by Haworth (1977) to delineate alternatives to a life of toil, one of which is to develop work not as a means but as "part of the end for which we live" (1977: 43). He calls that alternative "professional," implying, correctly enough, that one important element of the ideal-typical ideology of professionalism is the claim that members of professions work more for the satisfaction gained in performing their work well than for its role in providing them with a good living. He is not invoking a work ethic which asserts that there is value in *any* kind of work because working is in itself virtuous, nor that it is valuable because it serves the interests of labor consumers, whether individual customers in the market or the managers of bureaucracies (see Anthony 1977; Rodgers 1978). Rather, satisfaction is intrinsic to the performance of work that is interesting and challenging because it is complex and requires the exercise of discretion. Commitment to that kind of work is part of what C. Wright Mills (1951: 220–3) called "the ethic of craftsmanship," and what such people as William Morris and the Arts and Crafts movement (see Stansky 1985; Boris 1986) argued for in the nineteenth century. Professional work can thus be a secular calling, a modern source of meaning and identity that Goldman (1988) believes Max Weber advanced as an answer to the increasing rationalization of contemporary life.[2] Such a calling includes concern that it be performed as well as possible (Carr-Saunders and Wilson 1933: 284), interest in elaborating, refining, and extending a body of knowledge and skill underlying it, and belief in its value both in and of itself and for serving the needs of others. In ideal-typical professionalism, work is more than a commodity in the marketplace (Gordon 1988).

By contrast, in the ideal-typical ideologies of consumerism in markets and managerialism in bureaucracies, work is valued primarily as a means to gain a living or hold a job. Consumerism assumes that workers are motivated primarily by their desire to maximize their income, the particular work they do being second-

---

2 I take some liberties with Goldman's analysis, for he explicitly states that "the calling is not primarily a source of self-satisfaction or of the satisfaction of craftsmanly desires, nor is it seen as the fulfillment of talents or of satisfying involvement with an activity that they love. Instead, it serves the needs of self-definition, self-justification, and identity through devotion to a higher ideal through service" (Goldman 1988: 110). I believe that the "service ethic" is indeed an important element of the professional ideology, but because it is difficult to invoke for the practice of disciplines having no immediate practical benefit to any person or institution it must be assigned a supplementary rather than central role in the idea of calling.

ary. It also assumes that any kind of work is intrinsically unpleasant and that satisfaction is to be found in the consumption of goods and in leisure rather than in work. In the case of managerialism, work is the means by which a production plan can be realized, workers being motivated more by their desire to hold on to their jobs and their prospects within the organization than by their commitment to any particular kind of work. Since tasks and positions in firms are subject to change as productive ends and means change, commitment by workers to any particular job and body of knowledge and skill is obstructive and therefore undesirable.

Specialization and Productivity

The ideological core of professionalism is its claim to a discretionary specialization. Quite apart from questions about the efficacy of particular specializations, there is a long history of discussion and debate about the value of specialization itself. There seems, however, to be no controversy about its technical or functional value. Adam Smith introduced his treatise with praise for specialization because it led to the greater productivity that would create "universal opulence," which is to say, more goods available to all by virtue of their quantity, variety, and lower price. In his words, specialization "occasions, in every art, a proportionate increase of the productive powers of labor" (1976a: 9). In the case of the pinmakers' specializations, Smith argued that productivity is maximized because the worker's dexterity is increased "by making this operation the sole employment of his life" (p. 11). Smith went on to note that specialization in *intellectual* work has also led to greater productivity, observing that "philosophy, or speculation becomes, like every other employment, the principal or sole trade and occupation of a particular class of citizens. Like every employment, it is subdivided into a great number of different branches.... Each individual becomes more expert in his own peculiar branch, more work is done upon the whole, and the quantity of science is considerably increased by it" (p. 14). When any body of knowledge and skill becomes very complex, with many ramifications, specialization in just a segment of it makes exploration more manageable by limiting breadth and permitting depth and possibly innovation. It is reasonable to assume, therefore, that specialization is more often than not connected with productivity – with an increase in the *quantity* of production, both of consumer goods and services, and of scientific (Price 1961) and humanistic knowledge.

Productivity, however, must be distinguished from efficiency. The former refers to the quantity and quality of the outcome of work activities in their relationship to cost. In so far as there is consensus on the definition of quality, it can be used in a wholly descriptive fashion. But the notion of efficiency is instrumental rather than substantive, referring to means toward an unspecified end. Rueschemeyer (1986: 44) defines it as "the economical use of means in the pursuit of specific goals," and goes on to note that the choice of goals and the evaluation of the cost of using alternative means, including what one takes into account as a cost, are critical variables in defining efficiency.[3] Thus, he is quite right to deny that efficiency is necessarily associated with specialization and to assert that quite arbitrary values and ideologies are involved in selecting the criteria for it.[4] Power plays the determinative role in choosing the goals and the means of production as well as the particular costs that are to be taken into account when assessing efficiency. It is reasonable, therefore, to ascribe productivity to specialization, but it is considerably more arbitrary to ascribe efficiency to it.

It is still less certain that we may assume that specialization always results in an increase in the quality of goods, services, and knowledge. There is general agreement that people who do not devote all their working time to performing a particular task or set of tasks cannot develop the proficiency to produce work of quality equal to the work of those who do. This is one of the implications of the term "amateur."[5] Adam Smith assumed that in the part-time specialization to be found in "barbarous" societies lacking a complex division of labor, "Every man has a considerable degree of knowledge, ingenuity, and invention; *but scarce any man has a great degree*" (Smith 1976b: 304, italics added). To follow out Smith's logic, one might wrongly assume that specialists necessarily pro-

---

3 Oberschall and Leifer (1986) provide us with even more evidence on the concealed ideological assumptions and social forces underlying the use of the concept of efficiency.

4 Unfortunately, Rueschemeyer does not seem to distinguish between efficiency and productivity (1986: 16–21).

5 The exact substance of the notion of "amateur" has varied in time and place. In the late Victorian period the "gentlemanly" conception of the amateur stressed the absence of remuneration more than principled incompetence (see Wilkinson 1964: 64–79).

duce work of higher quality than non-specialists. But while there is every reason to agree with Smith's connection of specialization with productivity, once we distinguish mechanical from discretionary specialization it becomes necessary to distinguish between the quantity and quality of the products of work. If we assume that the whole task of pinmaking is a craft, there is no reason to think that the quality of pins will necessarily be better when created by mechanically specialized workers rather than by an experienced worker who performs the whole task from beginning to end – more *uniform*, yes, but not necessarily better. For example, hand-crafted pottery is often valued more highly than more efficient production-line ceramics. The ideal-typical ideology of professionalism stresses the lack of uniformity in the problems its work must contend with, therefore emphasizing the need for discretion. This is essential if practitioners are to vary their products to the needs of individual consumers or circumstances.[6] They do custom work which must be, by the very nature of the case, more costly and less productive than standardized work. This is a critical characteristic claimed for both professional and craft work.[7] In the ideology of professionalism, the quantity and cost of work defer to quality. Thus, in the broadest sense, the ideology of professionalism claims that its specialization is fitted to individual tasks rather than standardized production. It claims that the work of a trained and experienced specialist is superior to that of an amateur; in a narrower sense, it claims that the work of a specialist with professionally controlled training is both superior to and more reliable than that of someone who may have experience but lacks training.

The Value of Specialization

The productivity of mechanical specialization lies in its capacity to produce quantities of goods and services, while that of discretionary specialization by definition lies in its capacity to be flexible

6 One cannot doubt that practitioners of all discretionary specializations more often than not develop and use routine methods. The presumption, however, is that they are prepared to recognize and deal appropriately with individual circumstances for which routine is inappropriate.
7 One can of course have a "custom product" assembled out of different mixes of standard parts or modules rather than parts made entirely to order. This has become common practice in some industries today.

and adaptive in dealing with qualitative differences among individual tasks. However, there is considerable debate about the effect of different kinds of specialization on the workers who perform it. In relatively complex, stratified human societies, all do not work: those with the highest status do not perform any productive labor at all. Getting their living from goods and services produced by others, they often view work with disdain if not contempt. This is the case not only for manual labor, but for any kind of specialization. Disdain for specialists is justified in a number of different ways. Hereditary aristocracies, for example, avoid any specialized proficiency. As Barrington Moore (1966: 488–9) put it,

> because aristocratic status was supposed to indicate a qualitatively superior form of being, whose qualities were hereditary rather than the fruit of individually acquired merits, the aristocrat was not expected to put forth too prolonged or too earnest an effort in any single direction. He might excel, but not just in one activity as a consequence of prolonged training; that would be plebeian. . . . Similarly, the critical stance toward the technician as the dessicated brain at the service of any master derives from the aristocratic conception of the amateur.

The aristocrat's rejection of specialization is based on status, but another, more intellectually important rejection is based on a philosophy that demands the full cultivation of human potential. We are all familiar with the idea of the polymath, the Renaissance Man who is capable of the accomplished performance of a wide variety of complex skills. A contrast is often drawn between such a person and a specialist who does only one thing and no other in whom only one talent is developed. Implicit in such a comparison is admiration of versatility rather than specialization. It has probably received its most elaborate development in the work of Hegel and most particularly Karl Marx (Rattansi 1982: 1; Meakin 1976: 12–13). For both, work or labor represented the essence of humanity and the major source for human liberation and development. Although they were most hostile to the kind of specialization performed by Adam Smith's pinmakers, they attacked the very *principle* of specialization. They regarded exclusive commitment to any specialization as deplorable because it prevents the realization of other potentials. Neither those who make fine cabinets nor those who fasten the heads on pins have the opportunity to do as great a variety of work as their human capacities allow (see Ollman 1976–7: 22–4). All specialists, whether sculptors, chemists, sociologists, violinists, or cabinet-makers, manifest what Marx called "craft-idiocy" (1963: 144).[8]

In a more pragmatic context, others relegate specialists to the narrow domain of their specialties. They are not "whole persons" but limited and narrow. Whitehead (1963) described their capacity as "the restraint of serious thought within a groove. The remainder of life is treated superficially, with the imperfect categories of thought derived from one profession." And although he was writing of bureaucrats, Merton (1957: 197–8) discussed similar conceptions of the intellectual limitations of specialists, such as Veblen's "trained incapacity," Dewey's "occupational psychosis," and Warnotte's "professional deformation."

Still other writers have concerned themselves less with the vices of specialization than with its consequences for relations *among* specialists. They point to intellectual fragmentation and social divisiveness. Ellul (1964: 132), for example, claims that "specialization prevents mutual understanding. . . . The man of today is no longer able to understand his neighbor because his profession is his whole life, and the technical specialization of his life has forced him to live in a closed universe." And Geertz, in an allusion to the nineteenth-century ideal of liberal learning, notes the absence of a common culture and language that can join together all specialists, going on to say that

> the hard dying hope that there can again be (assuming there ever was) an integrated high culture, anchored in the educated classes and setting the general intellectual norm for the society as a whole, has to be abandoned in favor of the much more modest sort of ambition that scholars, artists, scientists, professionals, and (dare we hope?) administrators who are radically different . . . in the very foundations of their experience, can begin to find something circumstantial to say to one another again . . . that we can devise a way to gain access to one another's vocational lives. (Geertz 1983a: 60)

While Durkheim assumed that the functional interdependence of specialists would draw them together, he did acknowledge (for example, for science, 1964: 356–7) that there were pathological forms of specialization which created fragmentation and isolation rather than the solidarity he celebrated.

Nonetheless, some writers have found distinct virtues in special-

---

8 For especially cogent criticism of Marx's views on work, see Arendt 1959: 79–153 and Haworth 1977: 114–19.

ization. They associate it not only with greater productivity in a quantitative sense, but also with the production of goods and services of a superior quality. As we saw in the passage quoted in chapter 1, Xenophon assumed that the specialist did better work than the non-specialist. So did his contemporary Plato. The invidious words "dilettante," "amateur," and "dabbler" all refer to people who do not devote themselves wholeheartedly to cultivating proficiency in some particular activity: they are scorned for the relatively poor, "amateurish" quality of the tasks they perform. Yet creativity is the ideal underlying the arguments of a number of writers who have seen in lifelong devotion to a particular specialized task the opportunity to focus one's life around the continual perfection of skill, insight, and knowledge – to produce fine goods of a high artistic order, to make new discoveries in science, and to develop new insights into some phenomenon of value. Implicitly attacking the ideal of *culture générale* (see Ringer 1992: 303–7), Émile Durkheim asked, "Why would there be more dignity in being complete and mediocre, rather than in living a more specialized, but more intense life?," going on to argue that "far from being trammeled by the progress of specialization, individual personality develops with the division of labor ... for individual natures, while specializing, become more complex" (Durkheim 1964: 403–4). Preoccupied with the issue of the moral cohesion of society, and his notion of an "organic solidarity" created by the division of labor, Durkheim even asserts specialization as a duty:

> Since the division of labor becomes the chief source of social solidarity, it becomes, at the same time, the foundation of the moral order. We can then say that, in higher societies, our duty is not to spread our activity over a large surface, but to concentrate and specialize it. We must contract our horizon, choose a definite task and immerse ourselves in it completely, instead of trying to make ourselves a sort of creative masterpiece, quite complete, which contains its worth in itself and not in the services that it renders. (Durkheim 1964: 401)

Given these opposing valuations of specialization, it follows that there will be opposing conceptions of the social and political prerogatives of specialists. How much control should they have over the work they do, and over its application to human affairs; how much in the human affairs that lie beyond their specialty? That issue was raised, for example, in the remarks of Ferdinand Brunetière in 1898, who claimed he could not accept the pro-

Dreyfus position of professors at the New Sorbonne because their understanding was "shrunk and narrowed by their specializations ... I do not see how a professor of Tibetan has the qualifications to govern his fellows, nor how knowledge of the properties of quinine ... confers rights to the obedience and respect of other men" (Ringer 1992: 222). The anti-Dreyfusard Agathon attacked Durkheim (as one of the Dreyfusards) for preaching the virtues of specialization (Ringer 1992: 241). At bottom, the question revolves around the tension between specialized knowledge and general knowledge and experience. Generically, specialization represents what Talcott Parsons characterized as "functional specificity," one of the major attributes of his delineation of the professional role. The command, "Shoemaker, stick to your last!" limits authority to the immediate body of knowledge and skill connected with specialization, making necessary the exercise of some broader authority to guide, coordinate, and evaluate performance.

Generalism and Specialization

Critical views of specialization all imply that a generalist is to be preferred over a specialist.[9] Those who perform executive and management functions in both political and economic institutions exercise specialized skills of a more general sort than subordinates doing the productive work, and while they lack the particular knowledge, skill, and experience to perform that work, they claim competence to command.[10] This is characteristic of managerialism. And it is characteristic of consumerism in the perfectly free market that individual consumers who cannot themselves perform the work that produces the goods and services they desire nonetheless claim competence to choose those to perform work for them, determine what tasks they will perform, and judge the results. Contrary to the professional's claim that only the specialists who can do the work are able to evaluate and control it properly, both managerialism and consumerism claim a *general* kind of knowl-

9 There is a double standard embedded in this notion which depends on the work one has in mind. Since an infinite number of different mechanical specializations can be performed by those with only minimal *general* education and training, they are in some sense generalists rather than specialists. The debate over general/specialized education implicitly assumes the necessity of elaborate preparation for skilled work of one kind or another.
10 This was Veblen's major complaint about "captains of industry" (Veblen 1983).

edge superior to specialized expertise that can direct and evaluate it. Each ideology asserts a somewhat different kind of generalism.

The ideology of consumerism contests the authority of specialists by asserting what might be called *populist generalism*. Populist generalism is deeply embedded in the assumptions of liberal economics and closely related to those of liberal democracy.[11] Essentially, it asserts that average people with ordinary human abilities are capable of learning and knowing all that is necessary in order to make economic and political choices that will serve their own best interest without specialists to choose on their behalf. The neo-liberal economic creed holds that the marketplace should be free of any constraint on consumer choice, just as in liberal democratic political thought the polity should permit free and open debate and choice of policy by all, independent of the authority of experts.[12] The ideology of populist generalism underlies a number of political, economic, and legal institutions in both liberal democracies and collectivist political economies, though issues of representation by "professional" politicians and "vanguard parties" do complicate matters. The customer is always right, and the people are always right. Specialized knowledge must serve rather than command in both the market and the polity.

The ideology of managerialism presents a rather different basis for resistance to specialized knowledge and skill – the celebration of what can be called *elite generalism*. Like populist generalism, it does not defer to the authority of specialized knowledge, instead claiming authority over it. However, it goes beyond populist generalism by claiming the authority to command, organize, guide, and supervise both the choices of consumers[13] and the productive

11　My distinctions do not sit well beside Lindblom's, who treats revolutionary China, for example, as a "preceptorial" society whose ruling party is engaged in persuading its population to behave according to plan. But he does note "its antagonism toward specialization" (Lindblom 1977: 278). See also the extensive discussion of the "Red and Expert" debate in Schurmann 1968, and see Fisher 1986. For the Soviet Union see Guroff 1983.

12　"Technocracy" is the epithet used to characterize circumstances in which policy decisions are made by credentialled experts. For a recent review and evaluation of the historic development of the theory and practice of technocracy, along with discussion of how technical decisions can be participatory in nature, see Fischer 1990.

13　While the ideology of managerialism is often accompanied by the claim that it is merely a passive servant of consumer demand, consumer desires may be taken into account in a production plan only within the constraints of the established resources and structure of the organization or agency. Furthermore, work of specialists. It denies authority to expertise by claiming a form of general knowledge that is superior to specialization because it can organize it rationally and efficiently. Unlike populist generalism, it does not claim merely ordinary human qualities informed by everyday knowledge and skill and the capacity to learn whatever is necessary to make economic or political decisions. Rather, even when it eschews the common claim of elites that they are endowed with superior qualities by virtue of lineage, innate ability, or character, it can fall back on its own special kind of preparation for positions of leadership – an advanced but general formal education that equips them to direct or lead specialists, consumers, and citizens.[14]

Education and Ideology

Adam Smith notes that "in the barbarous societies ... the varied occupations of every man oblige every man to exert his capacity. ... Invention is kept alive, and the mind is not suffered to fall into ... drowsy stupidity" (1976b: 302–4). However,

the man whose whole life is spent in performing a few simple operations, of which the effects too are, perhaps, always the same, or very nearly the same, has no occasion to exert his understanding, or to exercise his invention in finding out expedients for removing difficulties which never occur. ... His dexterity at his own particular trade seems, in this manner, to be acquired at the expence [sic] of his intellectual, social, and martial virtues. (1976b: 302–3)

Though hardly concerned with the educational prerequisites for citizenship, since workers were not enfranchised at the time, Smith did consider their position as British subjects, and went on to

---

organizations often try to create or manipulate consumer demand to suit what they are equipped or prepared to supply. Thus, the organization or agency only sometimes serves consumers passively; otherwise it creates, manipulates, or constrains their choices. Perhaps the critical difference between managers and entrepreneurs is that managers limit their energies to using existing organizations as efficiently as possible while entrepreneurs perceive an unsatisfied or latent demand and create new enterprises explicitly designed to serve it.

14 In its political form it may not claim advanced *formal* education, but instead privileged knowledge of the general goals and principles by which to direct the work of specialists. This was exemplified by the claims of Communist Party leaders in various state socialist nations, and of leaders of theocratic states like Iran.

suggest that in a "civilized and commercial society," the state should be concerned that "the common people" be taught to read, write, and "account" (1976b: 309).

With these comments, Smith introduces the critical factor of formal education as a major source of the knowledge and skill embodied in work and its control, and in civil dialogue. The content of that education reflects both conceptions of the kind of work for which people are prepared, and of the roles they are expected to be able to play as members of society. It was the latter that Adam Smith had in mind when he argued the political usefulness (if not the moral obligation) of providing a basic general education to counteract the effects of performing mechanical specializations. He might have added some consideration of the kind of education that ordinary people need in order to be able to act as the rational, well-informed consumers hypothesized as essential actors in the perfect market, but my guess is that he did not imagine common people playing the role of rational consumers in his perfect market, let alone participating in political affairs. The writings of liberal economists down to this day portray consumers as the mirror-image of their own calculating middle-class selves, or at least as the way they would like to think of themselves.

Until the Enlightenment in the West, most of the debate about education was concerned with the elite, whether privileged citizens of the Athenian _polis_, rulers, or political leaders.[15] On the whole, we need only remember parts 7 and 8 of Plato's _Republic_ to distill the general thrust of debate about elite education even today: while Socrates hardly ignores the substantive knowledge connected with specialized work, asserting the wisdom of deferring to the judgment of such specialists as the physician and the ship's

15 It would not do to endow most aristocrats of any historical period with intellectual interests. While Rothblatt (1976) argues that in the eighteenth century the English, unlike the German, aristocracy came to appreciate the value of education, most devoted themselves solely to hunting and the other doggedly unintellectual pleasures afforded by their country estates. Illustrating that tendency is the story that Paul (1985: 287) tells of the Duke of Gloucester who, on receiving the second volume of _Decline and Fall of the Roman Empire_ from the author said, "another damned, thick, square book! Always scribble, scribble, scribble! Eh, Mr. Gibbon?". Perkin (1983: 213) notes this to be the case for the old landed gentry in the nineteenth century as well, summarizing his anecdotes by noting that "education was mainly valued for the group unity and social superiority it brought, including the ability to understand the Latin tags in parliamentary speeches, but this was more a product of the great public schools than of the ancient universities, which were 'optional extras'. As for the modern universities, they were objects of charity for the lower orders."

navigator, it is breadth of knowledge and understanding that he stresses for the elite, and the capacity to think critically, whether as a philosopher qualified to become the ruler of the republic, or as a person qualified to represent and make decisions on behalf of the citizenry. Much of the discussion of this conception of education can be organized around the changing meaning of "liberal education" over the millennia, and while Kimball's semantic history (1986) separated that meaning into two distinctly different threads, the term has always seemed to involve avoiding a purely practical or specialized education. For the education of ordinary people the aim has been to instill the religious, cultural, and political values deemed proper by the elite, as well as some knowledge of tradition or history, while also preparing them for their specialized vocations. On the other hand, the education designed for those likely to become members of the political and economic elite is *advanced* in character, more general and less specialized, and ranges over a broader terrain (see Rothblatt 1993).

Debates about education always seem to involve a struggle between generalism and vocational specialization, and the history of any industrial nation over the past two centuries cycles back and forth between the two. Those who champion a broad liberal arts curriculum assert the ideal of the well-rounded person who has gained knowledge of a wide variety of topics that are deeply embedded in the traditional high culture favored by the elite. Such a notion has historic kinship to earlier ideas of learning that were stressed in notions of *Bildung* in German universities,[16] *culture générale* in France (see Ringer 1979: 6–12), perhaps *nauk* in Russia, and liberal education in England (Rothblatt 1976) and the United States (see e.g. Haskell 1984; Persons 1973; Kimball 1986). It was what Max Weber (1946b: 426), in discussing Confucian education, called a "pedagogy of cultivation." Until the twentieth century such education was required to qualify Germans, English, French, and others to become higher civil servants and political executives (though not always executives of private firms). It formed the foundation of elite generalism,[17] legitimizing the exercise of control over political and economic enterprises. As Ringer

16 There has been much sophisticated and interesting discussion of the concept of *Bildung* among historians, an excellent recent example of which is Liedman 1993.
17 Aside from the issues of status or prestige, which in my opinion have been overemphasized by many analysts, it could be argued plausibly that "specialized knowledge may become obsolete; general qualities of mind cannot" (Wilkinson 1964: 71).

(1979: 21) put it, "The ability to do without any special competence was clearly honorific. It suggested the power to direct others, as against having to be useful and usable oneself.... This social advantage became associated with the cultural ideal of the educated man as rationally autonomous, self-directed, unspecialized, fully human."

Elite generalism is embodied in the idea of versatility or generalized skills, something that Suleiman (1977: 63) claimed was taught in actuality at the French *grandes écoles* rather than the highly technical and specialized training for which the schools were reputed. In an address to Cambridge University students in 1912, university graduates were described as "prepared for all jobs by being specially prepared for none" (Rothblatt 1968: 297). Elite generalism is implied by the idea expressed by contemporary French engineers (Crawford 1989: 71–4) that "polyvalence" or general skills were a more important outcome of their professional education than its specialized curriculum, that it was polyvalence which separated them from technicians. And it is also implicit in the position exemplified by Harold Laski's eloquent Fabian tract, *The Limitations of the Expert* (1931), in which he rejects the notion that the expert's judgment should be the final source of political decisions. He states that "*expertise* consists in such an analytic comprehension of a special realm of facts that the power to see that realm in the perspective of totality is lost. Such analytic comprehension is purchased at the cost of the kind of wisdom essential to the conduct of affairs" (1931: 9). The proper statesman, by contrast, preserves both a sense of the whole and the common sense of "the plain man," and so is better suited to make final political decisions.

Today it is often the expectation that the managerial and political elite obtain specialized training in the form of business management, accounting, political science, law, or engineering rather than merely a general education. However, none of those specialized degree-granting programs, including those in business or management schools, has succeeded in obtaining a monopoly over executive positions in the labor market for their graduates. After almost a century of effort in the United States, business schools have not managed to make the MBA a binding prerequisite for management positions as an MD degree, for example, is prerequisite for performing surgery. And even when they possess advanced degrees, I doubt that managers would invoke them as qualification for their positions. Rather, they are likely to invoke a capacity to rise above specialization: as Laski (1931: 11) put it "A great Minister ... must have the power to see things in a big way, to simplify, to coordinate, to generalise."

Beyond Specialization and Service

How does the ideology of professionalism, which is generically rooted in specialization, contend with the challenge of populist generalism advanced by consumerism, and elite generalism advanced by managerialism? The components of the ideology of professionalism that can successfully do so stem from the kind of education at the foundation of expertise. Against populist generalism it counterposes knowledge and skill based on cultural or scientific concepts that it claims are, at best, only touched on in general public education, and that are too esoteric and complex to be understood spontaneously or to be learned quickly by the average person. Against elite generalism it asserts that its knowledge and skill are too complex and esoteric to be managed by those who have only general knowledge and skills, however advanced. But equal in importance to the complexity of its specialized knowledge is its claim to *general knowledge*. The ideology of professionalism claims that its qualifications go beyond specialization. Unlike a purely technical education, ideal-typical professional training provides or requires prior exposure to high culture in the form of advanced general education.

The ideology of professionalism asserts knowledge that is not merely the narrow depth of a technician, or the shallow breadth of a generalist, but rather a wedding of the two in a unique marriage. This wedding of liberal education to specialized training qualifies professionals to be more than mere technicians. It qualifies them to serve in managerial positions where they can establish policy as well as organize and control their own work and the work of their colleagues independently of both managers and consumers. By grounding a functionally specific specialization in the advanced, elite generalism that provides executives and politicians with a mandate to command consumers, subjects, and citizens, the professional ideology creates a basis for claiming legitimacy that goes beyond the technical. It is on that basis that the Dreyfusard professor of Tibetan can claim something more than linguistic authority.

Professionalism and its Goal

Ideal-typical professionalism is always dependent on the direct support of the state and some degree of tolerance of its position by both consumers and managers. Such support cannot be gained by relying solely on what many writers have emphasized about professions – their ideology of service. Many other kinds of occupations also claim to serve – merchants their customers, politicians their constituencies, and, most appositely, technicians their patrons. But those who merely serve are subordinates. Specialists who are mere technicians (as I define them here) serve their patrons as freelances or hired guns (to employ both ancient and modern terms for mercenaries): their loyalties lie only with those who pay them. They accept the choices of their patrons and serve them loyally as best they can. In light of their specialized knowledge such servants may advise their patrons to qualify or modify their choices, but they do not claim the right to make choices *for* their patrons, to be independent of them, even to violate their wishes. That, however, is the kind of independence claimed by professionalism.

The professional ideology of service goes beyond serving others' choices. Rather, it claims devotion to a transcendent value which infuses its specialization with a larger and putatively higher goal which may reach beyond that of those they are supposed to serve. Each body of professional knowledge and skill is attached to such a value, one sometimes shared by several disciplines. Part of the struggle that can occur between occupations (and between specialties within occupations) can be over which one may legitimately claim custody of a particular value. Such values as Justice, Salvation, Beauty, Truth, Health, and Prosperity are large, abstract, and on the face of it indisputably desirable, the devil, of course, being in the details.[18] Nonetheless it is because they claim to be a secular priesthood that serves such transcendent and self-evidently desirable values (see, for example, La Vopa 1988: 348) that professionals can claim independence of judgment and freedom of action rather than mere faithful service. The assertion of such independence is more ritual than not in ordinary times, faithful and reliable service being the normal claim. Lying behind that, however, separate from individual conscience, is the ideological claim of collective

18 See, for example, the contending positions surrounding "the duty to do justice" in American law (Carle 1999).

devotion to that transcendent value and, more importantly, *the right to serve it independently* when the practical demands of patrons and clients stifle it.

Once established, the institutions of professionalism themselves support and encourage the ideal of independent service even though they are always under some pressure to serve the needs of the state and the ruling class. This is because the formal professional school supports a faculty whose task is to codify, refine, and extend the profession's body of knowledge and skill, and also elaborate and clarify the values served by their discipline. The professional school is where ethics is elaborated as well as taught and where that can be done somewhat independently of the market and the polity. Indeed, the very organization of academic disciplines encourages critical thought rather than acceptance of received ideas and methods and practical compromises, for that is how its practitioners make their mark. Thus, ideal-typical professions may be part of a service class, but they cannot be described as belonging to a servant class. Their service is to the differing substantive goals appropriate to their specialized disciplines.

Part II

The Contingencies of Professionalism

6

States and Associations

I discussed in the five chapters of part I what I consider to be the interdependent elements of the ideal type, professionalism. They are:

1 specialized work in the officially recognized economy that is believed to be grounded in a body of theoretically based, discretionary knowledge and skill and that is accordingly given special status in the labor force;
2 exclusive jurisdiction in a particular division of labor created and controlled by occupational negotiation;
3 a sheltered position in both external and internal labor markets that is based on qualifying credentials created by the occupation;
4 a formal training program lying outside the labor market that produces the qualifying credentials, which is controlled by the occupation and associated with higher education; and
5 an ideology that asserts greater commitment to doing good work than to economic gain and to the quality rather than the economic efficiency of work.

The ideology claims both specialized knowledge that is authoritative in a functional or cognitive sense and commitment to a transcendent value that guides and adjudicates the way that knowledge is employed.

Ideal-typical professionalism is of course an intellectual construct and not a portrayal of any real occupation. It is intended to serve as a stable standard by which to appraise and analyze

Portions of this chapter have been published previously in Freidson 1999a.

historic occupations whose characteristics vary in time and place. Some occupations may come to closely resemble that ideal type in some places at some moments of history, the process by which this occurs being called professionalization. In other places, or at other moments of history, that resemblance may diminish during the course of what has been called deprofessionalization. Many of the historic studies I have cited in this book have been devoted to analyzing the professionalization of such occupations as medicine, law, engineering, science, and university teaching during the nineteenth and early twentieth centuries, Larson's (1977) being the most sweeping and influential. But in light of changes in the political economies of industrial nations that affected the status of professions during the latter part of the twentieth century, the emphasis of many recent analysts has been instead on the process of deprofessionalization. The problem facing those dealing with both processes is to understand the forces which support or impede the development and maintenance of professionalism.

The prime contingency of professionalism is the state and its policies. I use the term loosely to refer to the sovereign political authority which has the power to grant occupations special status in an official economy. In earlier times, the authority was the sovereign. Later it became the nation-state. Now, it may very well be becoming some transnational authority, as in Europe, where the European Union moves toward "harmonizing" the labor and trade policies of its component nations. Some even see the emergence of a global international authority (see Evetts 1999). Keeping this broad usage in mind, we can say that none of the ideal-typical institutions of professionalism could exist without the support of the state. It is the state that has the power: (1) to officially define and classify particular kinds of work in the labor force; (2) to permit and support the occupational constitution of a division of labor and adjudicate jurisdictional disputes within it; (3) to defend labor market shelters against both labor consumers and would-be competitors; (4) to legitimate the connection of vocational training with officially classified higher education and to accept and support the credentials it produces; and (5) to give credence to the professional ideology. Furthermore, the state creates and maintains the general educational system which provides the foundation for professional schooling. In sum, it is the key force required for the creation, maintenance, and enforcement of ideal typical professionalism.[1]

1   For a recent review of the literature on the nature of the state's relationship to professions, with some comparative material, see Macdonald 1995: 66–123.

Whether or not it does so depends upon its own organization and agenda, which varies in time and space. And how it does so has critical consequences for the degree to which all the institutions of ideal-typical professionalism are realized, as we can see by examining some extreme cases.

The State and Deprofessionalization

There is not much doubt that the empirical professions are and have been vulnerable to deprofessionalization by the actions of the state.[2] Perhaps the most extreme empirical examples are provided by ideologically driven totalitarian regimes like Nazi Germany and the Soviet Union. In those states no associations were permitted but the ones that were politically acceptable, and both their officers and those of their members serving as functionaries in state agencies had above all to be loyal to the regime and provide at least public lip-service to its ideology. Their members received additional rewards when they were active in the regimes' parties, and what they could do in their practice was restricted to what was officially approved. Jarausch (1990) declared many professions to be "deprofessionalized" in Nazi Germany, as did Field (1957) for medicine in the Soviet Union.

I believe that there are good grounds to consider "deprofessionalization" as well as "proletarianization" and "corporatization" to be more often hyperbole than analytically sound description (Freidson 1994b: 30–45; 106–46). For those terms to be analytically accurate, a previously professionalized occupation would have to lose its special status in the official labor market and its control of its jurisdiction in a division of labor, be no longer protected by a labor market shelter or control the training and certification of its members. Loss of those institutions of professionalism did occur briefly following the French and Russian revolutions (though there is some doubt that they ever existed in anything like a strong form in Imperial Russia before the Bolshevik revolution)[3] but the reconstitution of many of the institutions of professionalism followed quickly. With few exceptions, they were not destroyed. The

2 Activist ideology and political power are of course not the only possible sources of deprofessionalization, as those who properly emphasize the power and direction of investment capital show. The most sweeping recent appraisal is Krause 1996.

3 With Cold War perspectives considerably weakened, the view one has of the degree of professionalization permitted in tsarist Russia before the revolution is markedly tempered by the studies reported in Balzer 1996.

emphasis of some disciplines was changed in order to conform to the ideology of the state, the most vulnerable being history, philosophy, law, and the social rather than natural sciences, though in both Soviet Russia and Nazi Germany genetics was subject to ideological control. The Soviet regime lasted long enough for policies to change over time, sometimes attempting to force disciplines to adapt to state ideology (as in the case of genetics and Lysenkoism) and sometimes relaxing the grip of ideology when it interfered with practical goals, as when it withdrew its planned condemnation of idealism in Western physics upon learning of its importance for creating an atomic bomb (Josephson 1992: 603, and, more generally, Josephson 1988).[4]

While deprofessionalization was claimed in both cases, there is good evidence that most professionals merely adapted superficially to the ideological requirements of their regimes and otherwise were free to go about their ordinary work with reasonable success. If we regard a profession as a purely technical pursuit, and professionalism as merely the institutions which grant and protect a special position in the political economy, then neither politics nor ideology is likely to deprofessionalize it if it does not abolish those institutions. Without question the institutions of professionalism for most disciplines were maintained, even protected by monopolizing positions in such states as the Soviet Union and Nazi Germany. Furthermore, we must remember that even though there may be a "mainstream" orthodoxy, disciplines are more often than not heterodox, containing a number of different theories and points of view. Thus, an authoritarian regime need not abolish or deprofessionalize a discipline; it need only choose a school within it that is compatible with its aims, taking up a previously minor school of thought in a discipline and advancing it over others. This was done, for example, when public health and community medicine were advanced over conventional medical practice in some post-revolutionary societies.[5]

In considering this possibility Jarausch (1990: 199) asks,

> did the Third Reich, by design or default, "enormously advance professionalization?" Undoubtedly doctors gained greater dominance over patients, psychologists and psychotherapists "established

4 For science, see Macrakis 1993, Graham 1967, and Vucinich 1984.
5 For a study of the history of Cuba's health system both before and after its 1959 revolution which is sensitive to internal divisions within the profession and changes in the influence of physicians of various persuasions on state policy, see Danielson 1979.

professional and institutional status," and engineers obtained more
social esteem and influence. The impetus toward professionalization
continued in some careers (e.g., primary school pedagogues), while
specific Nazi policies, such as the reduction of the sickness funds,
the creation of a diploma in psychology, or the public honors for
technology favored useful expert groups. . . . [But] a broader and
more morally sensitive perspective suggests that Hitler's rule led to
deprofessionalization instead. Although experts were essential to the
Third Reich, they were instrumentalized for inhuman ends, eventually losing many of their prized privileges as well as their autonomy
and *Berufsethos*, which formed the core of their professional self-
esteem. From being essential partners [with the state], lawyers were
reduced to being minor cogs in an administration of injustice. From
imparting knowledge, philologues were restricted to indoctrinating
in a school system that "educated" pupils in anti-intellectualism.
From advancing human welfare through technology, engineers were
redirected toward designing machines for mass maiming and killing.
The Nazi war . . . fundamentally subverted the ethical purposes of
professionalism.

What Jarausch is saying is that professionalism is more than the
economic and political institutions which protect and empower the
practice of a technical specialty. It is also, and most critically, an
ideology, a set of values rooted in the profession itself that directs
the economic and political institutions of practice independently of
the state. Such values are implied by notions of "social trustee
professionalism" (Brint 1994) and "civic professionalism" (Halliday 1987), as well as in notions of serving the public interest, the
public good, or the people. Of course, there is no state today that
does not claim to serve the public interest or the people, so a
critical question is whether a profession can be considered to serve
the public interest by serving the state, or whether it can (arro-
gantly in populist eyes, subversively in the eyes of the state) adopt
a position independent of the state and attempt to serve the people
according to its own lights.

The poignancy of this issue is exemplified by efforts to reform
health policy in Russia shortly before the First World War, when
zemstvo (community) physicians who formed the Pirigov Society
were seeking corporate power independent of the tsarist state.
They were opposed by Dr G. E. Rein, a prominent academic
physician who sincerely advanced an ethic of state service rather
than professional independence. He led a commission charged by
the Imperial government with reorganizing health services in

Russia which issued recommendations to establish "a powerful [centralized health] ministry committed to the expansion of medical research, the improvement of medical education, and the maintenance of professional standards in the healing arts, headed by a physician with a distinguished record of professional accomplishment" (Hutchinson 1996: 109). It is difficult to take issue with the committee's recommendations on disciplinary grounds, for as Hutchinson observed, Rein's recommendations were firmly grounded in legitimate scientific medicine. However, "what separated him from the community physicians [of the Pirigov Society] was that he saw no inherent conflict between the authority of knowledge and the authority of office." He did not conceive of medicine as a profession which chooses its own goals and is independent of the state; rather, he saw medicine as a profession which serves the state and in the course of doing so, serves the common good.[6] The onset of the First World War and the Bolshevik revolution following it prevented the option of Rein's plan to reform and consolidate the organization of medical care, though the Soviet regime ultimately created a state-controlled health system which, according to Field, deprofessionalized medicine.

In the historic cases represented by Field and Jarausch, the central issue is less the technical independence of the professions than their ethical independence. They were more or less in control of their division of labor, labor markets, and training institutions, but they did not have an independent voice in how and for what purpose they should employ their knowledge and skill. However, if as occupations they cannot control the uses to which their discipline is put but at the same time the state claims to serve the public good, can it be said that service to the state is unprofessional even though all other institutions of professionalism are relatively strong? Is the freedom to assert an autonomous occupational ethic, or *Berufsethos*, so essential to professionalism that its absence may be taken to negate the importance of other institutions of the ideal type? Patently, in the kind of state represented by Nazi Germany and the Soviet Union professions are not free to define the public good in their own way, asserting their own occupational ethic or *Berufsethos*. However, this power can and does exist to some degree, though never absolutely, in other kinds of state.

6 Once we no longer take the liberal profession to be prototypical, it is not impossible to imagine career civil servants to be professionals. See Caplan's (1990) stimulating discussion of the *höhere Beamte* or higher civil servants in nineteenth-century Germany.

What is the State?

It is traditional to consider the state to be the ultimate or sovereign source of coercive power.[7] This sharply distinguishes it from civil society, which includes professions and other institutions and which I consider separate from and subordinate to it. That is how I treated the relationship between state and profession in an earlier study that analyzed the institutions of professionalism in the United States (Freidson 1986). In discussing that relationship, I noted that while professions, unlike other kinds of occupations, control their own work and thus can be considered autonomous in a division of labor and in their labor markets, they are dependent on the coercive power of the state to support such autonomy. They are autonomous in their own economic sector but not in society at large because they depend on the state for their empowerment.

In recent writing that seems to turn away from his earlier (Johnson 1972) treatment of the state as a distinctly separate agent mediating between professions and their clients, Johnson (1995) argues that the separation of state from profession is misconceived. He argues that the modern professions are *part* of the apparatus that constitutes the state, and are therefore inseparable from it. Using Foucault's conception of "governmentality," he argues that while in premodern times coercion, even terror, was the essential resource of state power, in modern times the state uses the professional disciplines to create a docile population. The state, then, is not separate from professions, but in intimate interaction with them because the professions provide the tools by which populations are made docile and use the delegated power of the state to administer them.[8]

> The concept of the state that emerges from this discussion includes, then, that multiplicity of regulatory mechanisms and instrumentalities that give effect to government. This state itself emerges out of a complex interplay of political activities, including the struggle for occupational jurisdictions. . . . It is in the context of such processes

7 For a now-classic review of the concept of power, see Wrong 1988. For a less conventional, highly influential conception, see Lukes 1974.

8 In an interesting paper, Porter 1996 points out that the Foucauldian view obscures the structural determinants of power differentials and makes it impossible to differentiate between different degrees of power; he also produces empirical data to show that in the last analysis, power in institutions is exercised by those on site, rather than those at a distance.

that expertise in the form of professionalism has become part of the state. (Johnson 1995: 23)

In essence, Johnson seems to deny the value of distinguishing state and profession as analytically separate agents. Certainly it is true that the two are intimately connected. In the West, if not necessarily everywhere else, the professions have always had a special relationship with the sovereign or the state, a relationship that differs from that of other kinds of occupations. But while we should not forget that state and profession interpenetrate, if we do not treat the state *as if* it were an entity separate from professions in particular and civil society in general, we are awash in a fog-bound sea of ambiguity. Furthermore, we risk forgetting that the ideal-typical ideology of professionalism is one that denies the sovereignty of both the state and lesser clients, asserting independence in serving some transcendent value. So long as we do not mistake a strategy of analysis for reality, we can make our analysis more systematic and concrete, and therefore more subject to logical and empirical challenge, by treating the state as an entity in itself. It can be seen to have objectives of its own that are separate from those of the professions, objectives which it implements by Johnson's "multiplicity of regulatory mechanisms and instrumentalities." Should members of the population fail to be docile, it is the state, not the professions (or at least not most professions) that can employ the power to impose coercive penalties. The prime coercive and regulatory mechanisms of the state are expressed in law and codes of procedure, and its instrumentalities are to be found in state ministries and agencies, and in administrative, civil, and criminal courts. With some exceptions, those instrumentalities may be conceptualized as formal organizations, and more particularly bureaucracies that are separate from whatever form of organization professions may adopt. The empirical professions depend upon the state's instrumentalities to organize and exercise the power that creates and maintains the essential elements of professionalism, but since at least some of them may not be supported, may even be suppressed, as we saw in the cases of Nazi Germany and Soviet Russia, we must therefore think of the state as a contingency for professionalism. Only some kinds of state will support it.

How States Vary

Patently, all states are not the same. Some have a very elaborate set of ministries and agencies which assume extensive responsibility for directing the affairs of a political economy, while others have a comparatively simple structure and undertake rather few directive activities. Heidenheimer (1989) is one of a number of analysts who have found it useful to distinguish among states by the degree of their "stateness," which is to say, the degree to which state institutions are centralized, formally coordinated, and clearly distinguished from the institutions of civil society, as well as the degree to which they exercise direct control over a comparatively wide range of political, economic, and social affairs. Thus, it is not uncommon to claim that France is high in stateness, while the United States is low. However, such a sweeping distinction is problematic because a state may be strong in some areas and weak in others.[9] Rough as it is, it points to the necessity of considering how variations in state organization and policy affect the professionalization or deprofessionalization of occupations and the role their members and associations play in organizing and administering the practice of their disciplines.

Until there is a generally recognized conception of the entire range of economic, political, social, and cultural activities over which the state can exercise control,[10] any distinction is likely to be only partial. At present, there is more than one way of distinguishing among states, choice depending on the focal concern of the analyst. Dahl (1956: 133), for example, is concerned with the way interests are represented in state actions, and distinguishes between polyarchy and dictatorship as government actions influenced by a wide variety of civil interest groups in contrast to government by one or a small number. Lindblom (1977: 161) discusses polyarchy as a political system controlled by rules guaranteeing political freedom and joins it to economic systems. He contrasts states that are polyarchal and market-oriented with dic-

9 The visual arts, for example, were stringently controlled by the state in Nazi Germany, controlled to a lesser extent in fascist Italy, even less in fascist Spain, and not at all in fascist Portugal (Hinz 1979: unpaginated foreword). For fascist Italy, see Berezin 1991.
10 An interesting study by Campbell and Lindberg (1990) shows how the United States government, usually regarded as a passive or weak state, exercises considerable influence on the economy by manipulating property rights – an area of state activity ignored in other studies.

tatorships that exercise centralized authority over the economy, the former predicated on the logic of the market and the latter on that of bureaucracy. In delineating two polar models for the organization and control of state actions, he describes one based on the conviction that the social world is too complex and the human intellect too fallible to permit the discovery of a single correct solution to societal problems so that individuals and civic groups should be left the latitude necessary for solving their own problems. In the other it is argued that it is possible to learn enough about the social world to be able to plan and exercise guidance over it (Lindblom 1977: 247–60).[11]

These distinctions are logical, or ideal-typical, of course, designed to allow simplifying the detail of actual historic states by singling out strategic characteristics of importance. For my purpose, which is to delineate differences between states that bear on the establishment and maintenance or the dissolution of professionalism, it is essential to be able to conceptualize variation in the constitution and mode of operation of the state – its regulations and instrumentalities. This variation is implied in the strong/weak, polyarchal/authoritarian, free market economy/centrally planned economy distinctions. I believe that Damaška (1986) provides a more useful set of distinctions, one that not only delineates two basic methods of organizing government itself, but also two basic orientations of state policy. The two dimensions he distinguishes allow us to discriminate quite different kinds of strong and weak states. In the case of organizing and staffing state agencies, he delineates one structure that

> essentially corresponds to conceptions of classical bureaucracy. It is characterized by a professional corps of officials, organized into a hierarchy which makes decisions according to technical standards. The other structure has no readily recognizable analog in established theory. It is defined by a body of nonprofessional decision makers, organized into a single level of authority which makes decisions by applying undifferentiated community standards. The first structure I shall call the *hierarchical* ideal or vision of officialdom, and the second I shall term the *coordinate* ideal. (Damaška 1986: 17)

---

11 I refer here to Lindblom's discussion of the first two of what he holds to be the "three elementary mechanisms for social control that all political-economic systems employ – exchange, authority, and persuasion" (1977: 11–12). I have already had occasion to refer to his discussion of persuasion in chapter 5.

We may presume that Heidenheimer's high stateness is closely related to the hierarchical ideal, and low stateness to the coordinate ideal. However, while the distinction identifies the way state agencies are staffed and organized, it does not suggest the kind of policies they adopt and the degree of state activity invested in advancing them. Damaška's second basic distinction enriches analysis considerably by distinguishing between "two contrasting dispositions of government: the disposition to manage society and the disposition merely to provide a framework for social interaction" (1986: 71). The former he terms the activist state; the latter the reactive state:[12]

> The task of the *reactive state* is limited to providing a supporting framework within which its citizens pursue their chosen goals. Its instruments must set free spontaneous forces of social self-management. The state contemplates no notion of separate interest apart from social and individual (private) interests: there are no inherent state problems, only social and individual problems. (Damaška 1986: 73, italics added)[13]

By contrast, at the other end of the continuum is the activist state:

> It espouses or strives toward a comprehensive theory of the good life and tries to use it as a basis for a conceptually all-encompassing program of material and moral betterment of its citizens. . . . Existing social institutions and social practice command little deference: as it exists, society is defective and in need of improvement. With civil society stripped of legitimacy, projects and perspectives that arise spontaneously among citizens are suspect, for they may clash with those favored by the government, may weaken commitment to state goals, and sap confidence in its actions. Accordingly, voluntary associations should either be dismantled or placed under supervision . . . civic associations, even if superficially independent, become annexes of state agencies. (Damaška 1986: 80–1)

---

12   This distinction is similar to Lindblom's (1977: 249–51) between two models of the role of intellect in state policy – one assuming that it is possible for the human intellect to produce a comprehensive theory to guide state policy, the other arguing that it is not possible, and that transient human preferences and volition must be relied on instead.

13   It is important to emphasize Damaška's observation that "there is no necessary connection among the reactive posture, capitalism, and individualism. The ideal of the minimal state constitutes part of an important socialist tradition: its anarcho-syndicalist variant envisages a society composed of *mutualiste* associations in the context of an 'abstentionist' form of government" (1986: 74).

Without doing serious damage to Damaška's logic, a simple 2 × 2 table can be created to portray the four ideal-typical states and suggest how interaction between the ideology guiding state policy-making and the way state administration is constituted influences variation in the agents who are empowered to formulate and implement policy toward the establishment and maintenance of professionalism.[14]

Table 6.1 Agents of policy by variations in state policy orientation and implementation

Policy orientation	Policy implementation	
	Hierarchical	Coordinate
Reactive	State agencies establish and protect professionalism as agent of professions	State agencies protect power of private associations to establish and maintain professionalism
Activist	State agency formulates and implements professional institutions	State-approved labor groups formulate and implement policy toward professions

State Variation and Professionalism

Damaška's classificatory scheme was explicitly designed to ident-ify axes that would be useful for an analysis of variation in state systems of justice. While it is not uncommon for systems of justice to be staffed by professionals who perform prosecutorial, judicial, and advocacy functions, Damaška's concern was less with vari-ation in the place of professionals in such systems than with variation in the patterns of legal procedure they employ. My concern, on the other hand, is with showing how variation in the

14 For both empirical and logical reasons, a complete analysis would consider circumstances in which the state and its agencies are so disorganized as to be frozen, inefficient, or incompetent, able to settle neither on policy nor on how it is to be implemented, when, as Halliday (1987: 355) put it, the state suffers "crippling ungovernability." This would add an "Indeterminate" mode of implementation, and an "Ambivalent" policy orientation.

policy orientation and organization of different ideal-typical state institutions influences the way the basic elements of professionalism are established and maintained. Damaška's typology is useful for that purpose as well, for in table 6.1 I indicate the outcome for professionalism of different configurations of the state.

Before discussing how different kinds of state administration and policy affect professionalism, it is important to observe that state and profession are necessarily in interaction even when state actions appear to be unilateral. While power is generic to the state, the specialized knowledge required to shape that power into concrete administrative actions and regulations classifying and governing occupations and their work is not generic to the state. When state agencies ratify arrangements established in civil society by occupations to establish professionalism, they rely by default on the competence and legitimacy of those who created those arrangements. If they choose to favor one competing occupation over another, they must rely on its claims and the particular body of knowledge it represents to legitimize that action. If, on the other hand, state agencies themselves create a division of labor, labor market shelters, and training institutions for particular occupations, they must either themselves be staffed by properly trained specialists from those occupations who can deal with such technical issues – that is, civil servants who are bona fide members of the occupation – or rely heavily on the advice of legitimately qualified outside consultants. Dependence on qualified members of a profession (or experts) for the very exercise of state power stems from the fact that what is at issue is the institutionalization of a body of knowledge and skill – however tentative or flawed, but authoritative in its time – that has developed well beyond everyday knowledge and is mastered by a limited number of people. Thus, in one way or another, only authoritative representatives of the profession can provide the critical *substance* of state policy actions bearing on its work and its place in the political economy, no matter what the administrative organization and policy orientation of the state. The only way to avoid reliance on experts is to deny any authority at all to specialized knowledge, to invoke populist or elite generalism, which literally deprofessionalizes the labor force, the labor market, and the organization of work.

Keeping in mind this interactive relationship between state and profession, the *reactive-coordinate* state represents the familiar circumstance of officially recognized "private" or "free" interest groups exercising powers delegated to them by the state. Most of the Anglo-American literature on the professions takes something resembling this arrangement to be the typical environment of professionalism, implicitly employing a model of pluralism in a liberal democracy in which occupations organize themselves and their affairs and come to gain recognition and support from the state while remaining independent of it. Here, state agencies ratify and enforce policies created by favored occupations, but otherwise leave them free to control their own affairs. There is minimal state intervention in those affairs, not only because of a laissez-faire philosophy, but also because state agencies are small, with few resources, and staffed by people who are essentially amateurs. Because of their lack of specialized training and their modest resources, they are dependent on the knowledge and advice of outside groups and consultants for their administrative actions.

The *reactive-hierarchical* cell suggests a different way by which policies establishing and maintaining professionalism can be formulated and implemented, namely, by bureaucratically organized state ministries and agencies staffed by professionally trained officials who themselves establish and administer regulations and institutions designed to serve the interests of chosen occupations. While ostensibly concerned with advancing the interests of professions, however, a rational, bureaucratic framework for administration must be established and conflicts between different groups adjudicated, so that some tension between professions and the state bureaucracy is inevitable. A reasonably close empirical example of such a state might be drawn from Germany, whose policies include one version of corporatism, a mode of organizing interests that I shall discuss later in this chapter.

When we consider the *activist-hierarchical* state, of which the Soviet Union and Nazi Germany are examples, we find a strong state that officially recognizes and supports only those civil groups which advance its own activist goals, controlling them ultimately by bureaucratically organized state agencies. Such professions as medicine, law, and engineering, which are thought to be essential to the state, gain support, though generous support is given only to those segments of disciplines that are believed useful in serving the state's activist goals. Disciplines and individuals with the potential to challenge the dominant ideology of the state are suppressed, and the power to organize, administer, and supervise the work of professions is carefully restricted to officials and professionals who are considered politically reliable.

Finally, I may note the difficulty of visualizing a stable state which employs the *activist-coordinate mode* of formulating and implementing policy. While committed to a vision of actively creating society, it eschews the use of stable, rationally organized administrative machinery for doing so. It relies instead on the actions of ideologically acceptable civil groups or communities to formulate and administer policy. But even though we can conceive of a mode of administering *justice*[15] compatible with such a state, it is difficult to conceive of the administration of other activities presupposing technical expertise. In fact, such a state seems likely to wish to dissolve specialist groups into larger community groups which make decisions collectively on the basis of the official ideology. Empirical examples of such state-organized policy-making seem to be found only in the transient moments following ostensibly egalitarian revolutions, when prior differences in status and function are dissolved and all are taken to be equals in the common task of constructing a new society. The Russian and French revolutions provide us with the best-documented cases of such enterprises, though the more recent Chinese revolution should not be ignored. All such efforts were quickly transformed, institutionalized as activist/hierarchical state administrations permeated with suspicion of self-organized civil groups that might threaten their ideology and their direct control of the population.

The Composition of Professions

In my discussion of how (and whether) the elements of ideal-typical professionalism can be established in different kinds of states I focused on the actions of state agencies more than on those of the occupations that are candidates for professionalization. My emphasis is appropriate because the ultimate power to establish professionalism is held by the state, but as I have already noted, the specialized knowledge required to shape the power of the state into concrete administrative actions, rules, and regulations governing the organization of work stems from those who are qualified to do the work. While the way the power of the state is organized and directed represents a critical contingency for the development of professionalism, therefore, so also does the way occupations themselves are organized and represented. Most studies of the

15 In the case of the administration of justice, neither specially trained judges nor lawyers would be considered necessary to gain state ends, "people's" or community courts being sufficient, and ideological commitment to the activist goals of the state being sufficient qualification for those administering justice. In the case of health affairs, folk or "people's" practitioners might be considered sufficient.

professions attend to the efforts of formally constituted associations to gain a charter from the state and the power to control their own affairs, but in light of history it is important to go beyond that and consider the sources of professional influence that extend beyond the formal association. It is for that reason that in my discussion thus far I have been careful to refer both to qualified members of a profession and to professional associations as significant actors. I treat "a" profession as all those who have received the same qualifying vocational training. They need not be members of an association, and an association need not be taken to represent them even when, as in some nations, membership is required by law. More ubiquitous and inclusive than an association is the core "community" of workers created by shared training and work experience (see Goode 1957). Such a community of interest exists, even if sometimes in an attenuated and transient form, among all who perform much the same work, no matter what it is, but it is palpably more important among those performing specialized work for a lifetime (see Mackenzie 1973). It is even stronger among those whose specialization is discretionary, complex, and intellectualized, requiring a relatively long period of training segregated from the ordinary marketplace.

Formal professional associations[16] based on a truly inclusive community of interest do not often exist in reality, however. Many include only elite, unusually successful and distinguished practitioners, in some cases by virtue of deliberate restriction of membership and in others by the inability of lesser practitioners to bear the cost in time and money that membership requires. Assuming that an association represents primarily what its active members perceive to be their interests, we can also assume that the desires of the members of exclusive associations are probably not likely to reflect those of the entire professional community. Their standards are likely to be more demanding and narrow than those of others. My impression is that in the *early* stages of the development of professional associations the active membership (which is not the same as all who practice the discipline) is composed largely of elite practitioners. Their concern is less to raise their status by a "collective mobility project" (Larson 1977) than to preserve and solidify their official and public status, in part by gaining state recognition and support, and in part by preventing the decline in status that

---

16 I know of no general source on professional associations. However, even though dated and limited to the UK, the work of Millerson 1964 and Carr-Saunders and Wilson 1933 provides important resources.

might occur if practitioners of more humble origins become members.[17] From the very beginning, the broad community of practitioners is divided by status differences of some consequence stemming from different social backgrounds and different clientele. However, during the course of development, differences in social origins become less important than cognitive and functional differences.

Halliday (1987: 60, 347–76) expands on the consequences of the important distinction between the *formative* period of establishing the institutions of professionalism, when the struggle is to gain official privilege and control of jurisdictions, labor market shelters, and training, from what might be called the *established* period, which begins once those institutions are secured. Once established, professions are less preoccupied with defending their jurisdictions from interlopers than with extending the application of their disciplines, he suggests. Internal growth and differentiation[18] through technical specialization and varied practice settings develop within the protective shelter of the profession's position in the official political economy. Curiously enough, within that shelter there seems to be a reversion to the *status quo ante*, when a variety of uncredentialled occupations contended with each other for jurisdiction in the unsheltered marketplace.[19] Once privilege is gained, contention occurs between credentialled practitioners *within* the officially sheltered marketplace. It occurs through internal differentiation that is driven by the expansion of knowledge, skills and their applications, the invention of new skills, and the variety of practices which develop.

Differentiation takes place along several dimensions. Some extend and expand segments of the common corpus of knowledge and skill and, protected by the profession's labor market shelter, institutionalize those segments into specialties. Those specialties often compete with each other in dealing with the same kind of work problems by different means. To take an obvious example, in medicine, surgical and medical approaches to the same signs

17   The stated concern of the early Chicago Bar Association was to *maintain* rather than raise "the honor and dignity of the profession" (Halliday 1987: 63–4). For similar concern to maintain status by excluding or segregating lawyers of lesser status who serve lesser clientele, see Auerbach 1976. See Powell 1988 for an elite association and its democratization over time.
18   For a discussion of the parameters of differentiation, see Abbott 1988: 117–42.
19   For a marvelous analysis of the variety of contenders in the health-related marketplace of late eighteenth- and early nineteenth-century France, see Ramsey 1988.

and symptoms can be quite different, the former prescribing physical repair or removal and the latter medication. In addition to fragmentation by substantive specialization, the economic and social interests of the professional community can become differentiated by the particular institutions in which its members work, by whether they are employed or self-employed, by their different clientele (Heinz and Laumann 1982), and by whether they perform managerial or supervisory rather than research, pedagogical, or direct service tasks. And quite apart from socioeconomic and specialty differentiation, from the very beginning of a recognizable profession some members become prominent and influential as individuals by virtue of their reputation for unusual acumen or skill, or by personally serving and gaining the trust and respect of the political, economic, or social elite. Others become cognitive authorities by virtue of their development of concepts and theories which strengthen the body of knowledge and skill, and by their discovery, invention, and practice of new evidence, approaches, and techniques.

Once we recognize internal differentiation of professions[20] to include markedly different cognitive and practice positions as well as celebrated individuals and professional associations all seeking influence, a profession cannot easily be seen as a single community of interest. Established professions come to be composed of a number of highly differentiated sub-communities loosely held together by a common occupational title, a jurisdiction in the larger division of labor within which its members struggle over subjurisdictions, and a broad labor market shelter for different kinds of practice that can have conflicting economic and social interests. Most important, some of these differentiated orientations and practices within the profession as a whole are in conflict with each other, so that by the nature of the case the profession contains a number of varied, sometimes contradictory disciplinary and policy positions. But because they are all positions within the profession, they are legitimate even when they contradict each other.

If, then, there is often no single professional orthodoxy, how is it possible to discriminate between state actions sustaining professionalism and those that attack it? The answer to that question, I believe, can only be a permissive one that defines legitimacy by whether the source of the position lies within a *profession*, but not

---

20 The classic paper of Bucher and Strauss (1961) used the term "segment" to distinguish different schools of thought within a specialty, rather than differentiation within a profession as a whole.

necessarily within the program of its *association*. It is true that by definition the establishment of the institutions of professionalism and their maintenance require the use of occupationally generated policies, but such policies need not be generated by a professional association to be "professional." They can as well be generated by a distinguished member of the profession, by a committee of members of the profession who advise the state and its agencies, or by professionally qualified staff in state agencies. So long as legitimate professional criteria are used – and we must remember that a number of alternatives are legitimate – it is not important whether the representative of an association or some other creden- tialled authority advances it. The exact substance of the criteria that become established is a function of interaction between the particular agent or agents representing the profession and repre- sentatives of the state. As Siegrist (1990: 181) pointed out, in "continental Europe, the process of professionalization was initi- ated by kings, princes, patricians and states, who attempted to influence the behavior of barristers, clergymen and, to a lesser extent, also of medical practitioners, by issuing codes of ethical conduct." And Torstendahl (1993) notes that the professionaliza- tion of engineers in Germany began before there was an inclusive engineering association. Patently, private professional associations were not essential to the process.

Nonetheless, it must be assumed that while Peter the Great of Russia (see, for example, Alston 1969) and Frederick the Great of Prussia (see, for example, Mueller 1984: 84), took important initia- tives in encouraging professionalization, they did so with the advice of qualified consultants rather than on the basis of their personal knowledge. Unfortunately, in his provocative discussion of "state professions," Siegrist (1990), like many other historians of the professions in Europe, minimizes the role of professionals by treating the process of establishing such institutions as professional training programs as if statesmen or civil servants acted entirely independently of professional advice. This is quite unlikely, for even the leaders of the immediate post-revolutionary societies of France and Russia, for example, had their professional advisors. Adequate assessment of the limits on the state's role in establishing and governing professional institutions requires paying close attention to the technical or professionally qualified advisors who play a critical role in formulating the actual substance of state policy, much as the staff of administrative agencies plays a critical role in formulating the concrete ways by which legislation is implemented.

I believe that the importance of associations for the establishment of professionalism has been greatly exaggerated by theorists and that they are not essential for the initiation of institutions of professionalism. Nonetheless, the association is the generic mode of formal organization for professions and, for that matter, any occupation that has congealed into a "community" and seeks control over its own work. While the free market is composed solely of individuals pursuing their own interests and bureaucracy is a monocratic formal organization, an occupation in a position to exercise control over the work of its members is typically organized into an association or, in Ouchi's (1980) terms, a "clan." As Streeck and Schmitter (1985: 2) observe, the association is a "distinctive fourth institutional basis of order."[21] It is ideally characterized by "collegiality" (see Waters 1989; Sciulli 1990), which likely has historic roots in the guild ethic of "mutuality" or "brotherhood" (Black 1984: 13). Common economic and status interests, and common intellectual and practical interest in the work they do, join its members together into what was sometimes called a "college."

One cannot deny that professional associations and societies have played important roles in some historical circumstances, particularly in the English-speaking nations. But they rarely represent the entire profession, even when said to be "peak" or "umbrella" associations. The most comprehensive and structured form of representation to the state is corporatist[22] in character, when selected associations become formal participants in policy-making by state agencies or when they are created by those agencies for that purpose.

---

21 In addition to market, bureaucracy, and association, Streeck and Schmitter (1985) discuss "community" as another basis for order. I have already expressed my opinion that community, bound together by what Durkheim called "mechanical solidarity," is an inadequate basis for ordering anything beyond a simple division of labor – certainly not a complex division of labor composed of many different discretionary specializations. The broad community of shared occupational identity is not enough: it must ultimately be organized into associations for representation and negotiation.

22 For an extensive review of corporatist theory and comparison with interest-group theory, see Williamson 1989. The most influential conception is that of Schmitter 1979.

Corporatism

Few of those writing on corporatism have explicitly discussed the professions, most being concerned with the industrial sector of the economy and the role of trade unions.[23] Furthermore, as Williamson (1989: 140) noted, the relationship with the state is "the most problematic and unsatisfactory aspect of corporatist theory." Schmitter's definition of corporatism, while posing difficulties of its own, may be taken as a "strong" and graphic ideal type rather than as an empirical description:

> Corporatism may be defined as a system of interest representation in which the constituent units are organized into a limited number of singular, compulsory, noncompetitive, hierarchically ordered and functionally differentiated categories, recognized or licensed (if not created) by the state and granted a deliberate representational monopoly within their respective categories in exchange for observing certain controls on their selection of leaders and articulation of demands and support. (Schmitter 1979: 13)

In such circumstances, a professional association becomes the exclusive representative of a profession in dealing with the state. It can truly represent the profession as a whole because membership in it is compulsory, and the bargains struck with state agencies are binding on its members.

Crouch and Dore (1990: 22–4) elaborate on the concept of corporatism and point up some of its difficulties by noting that

> for an institution to be corporatist it must have power to *constrain and sanction*, either through its own resources or by effectively co-opting those of its constituent representative bodies.... But the power to constrain extends beyond discipline. Whenever an agency is responsible for administering its service it allocates resources, even if they are only intangible ones like recognition. It therefore decides who among its constituents should benefit. This automatically embodies constraints. Hence the importance of the distinction between representative bodies that merely consult as opposed to those that administer. Finally, to speak of corporatism we need some

---

23 But see Williamson 1989: 168–80. For an excellent discussion of the medical profession in the context of corporatism, see Frenk and Durán-Arenas 1993. For the legal profession, see Halliday 1989.

notion *of orientation to a public interest* ... This is bedevilled by the
fact that the public interest is such an elusive concept.

Crouch and Dore do not require compulsory membership in the
representing association, but in light of Schmitter's analysis and
the empirical examples of the German *Kammern*, the French *ordres*
and, for that matter, the integrated bars of some of the American
states, it seems an appropriate requirement. And while it is very
difficult to imagine the wholehearted support of the entire membership for any deals struck between state and association, in so
far as the association has a monopoly on representation and is
empowered to negotiate policy on behalf of the profession as a
whole, its members have little choice but to go along.

Corporatist arrangements seem compatible only with states
which have developed a fairly elaborate bureaucratic structure –
hierarchical states in Damaška's terms – so it is likely that corporatist arrangements will hold in the two different types of hierarchical state I have already discussed. Elaborating on the work of
Romanian and Portuguese writers, Schmitter (1979: 17–22) distinguished between *societal corporatism*, which emerges from civil
society pressure to establish some sort of order in its influence on
state policy, and *state corporatism*, in which the state itself unilaterally supports a system of exclusive representation in policy
decisions by associations it has either chosen or created. In the case
of the reactive/hierarchical state, societal corporatism may be one
method by which the elements of professionalism are established
and policies created that sustain them, though because the state is
reactive rather than activist, other arrangements are possible. State
corporatism, on the other hand, is likely to be found in activist/
hierarchical states which attempt to organize and control labor
around its special goals.

Once we recognize that when professional associations are active
in the process of establishing professionalism most cannot be
literally representative of "the" profession, and that their influence
on the state may stem as much from their members' social standing
as from their representativeness, we may wonder whether the
activism of associations is in fact a necessary condition for establishing professionalism and whether it is appropriate for them to
appear as a key element of the natural histories advanced by
Caplow (1954), Wilensky (1964), and Abbott (1991a). Private, self-
organized associations seem essential only when the state is reactive and invests very little in an administrative machinery of its

own. They may be positive handicaps when the state is activist in orientation and suspicious of potential resistance to its goals.

What, then, can be said about the role of associations in the establishment of professionalism, and in its maintenance and adaptation once it is established? In the broadest sense, one can say that it is "the" profession, and not associations as such, that is an essential element in all those processes. "The" profession can be represented only arbitrarily, in a number of different ways, which means that some of its distinguished members can as easily represent it in advising the state or state agencies as can an association. So can an agency staff which may draw on the authoritative advice of outside, credentialled consultants or may itself be composed of professionally qualified personnel. Furthermore, once professionalism has been established and many different specialties and perspectives develop, so may a variety of associations representing conflicting interests and cognitive orientations appear. The state then becomes the critical arbiter of influence by choosing one rather than another to represent the interests of "the" profession, as it did not long ago for medicine in France (Wilsford 1991). The state also has the power to make membership in that chosen association compulsory, and to make agreements between its staff and association representatives binding on the membership. As Streeck and Schmitter (1985: 256) note,

> Interest associations can usually govern the interests of their members only with some kind of state facilitation and authorization. At the very least, private interest government requires an *Ordnungspolitik* of deliberate abstention from [state] interference with the exercise of authority by powerful associations over their members.... An active role of the state is necessary in yet another respect ... the threat of the state to intervene directly if the group fails to adjust the behaviour of its members to the public interest. In this sense, the public use of private organized interests requires a strong rather than a weak state.

A Note on Class

It will not have escaped the attention of some readers that I have presented no sustained discussion of class, though I have connected professions with the middle class here and there in passing. I have no doubt that by and large professions are part of what can be crudely called the middle class, but I do doubt that such identification is very illuminating. It is true that the historic process by which empirical professions developed under capitalism during the nineteenth century, particularly in the English-speaking countries where they were often self-organized and sought support from the state, was one marked by efforts to raise or sustain their status by excluding from membership those from the working class, women, blacks, Catholics, Jews, and others considered equally disreputable. Where the profession was already composed of "respectable" members, exclusion of others was meant to preserve its status. Where the effort was instead to raise the status of a previously disreputable occupation, or to establish the status of a previously unrecognized occupation emerging from the informal economy, its organizers, themselves of the middle class, attempted to attract new members from respectable middle-class white males of the proper ethnic and religious background.

Such analysts as Larson (1977), Parry and Parry (1976), and Macdonald (1984) rightly described these as efforts at collective mobility, efforts to raise the occupation's status or prestige. This was clearly the case for nursing in nineteenth-century England, whose original practitioners were members of the servant class and whom Florence Nightingale attempted to replace with middle-class women. The process was (and is) not merely one involving an effort to increase an occupation's prestige, but also part of an effort to establish trust by the public and the ruling class, since respectable people are thought to be more trustworthy than those of lesser or uncertain background.[24] In professionalism, membership is characteristically drawn from the class that is, in the hierarchical scheme of things, superior to all but the ruling class. This, as much if not more than the certainties of their knowledge and skill, encourages sufficient trust by the ruling class to warrant their privilege and by clients to warrant their consultation. Occupations composed primarily of members of low class origins, such as bus drivers and nurse's aides, are more likely to be regulated than allowed to regulate themselves, even though their tasks require responsibility and discretion and would, if performed badly, endanger others.

From the very beginning of theorizing about class in the nineteenth century, professions have posed enough of an analytic

24 I hope I will not be misunderstood here or elsewhere in this book. I do not believe that such methods of establishing trustworthiness are desirable. I *am* arguing, however, that professionalism is attained and maintained by conforming to the prejudices of those who give professionals their power.

problem to lead thinkers to diametrically opposed conclusions. Professions have been seen as an anachronistic survival from pre-industrial times, as members or willing agents of the ruling class, and as a subordinate working class. They have been labeled part of the "new middle class" and part of the "new working class." (For a sample of the extensive literature, see Mills 1951; Crozier 1971; Bell 1976; Giddens 1975; Ehrenreich and Ehrenreich 1977a, 1977b; Gouldner 1979; Wright 1979; Freidson 1986; and Derber et al. 1990.) Goldthorpe treats them as part of a "service class," a class composed of occupations whose tasks involve the exercise of delegated authority in which sufficiently complex expertise is involved that direct and detailed control by nominal superordinates (or clients) is not thought possible. Its members are therefore given extensive discretion in performing their work, discretion which requires "an important measure of *trust*" (Goldthorpe 1982: 168). I suspect that the predominant class composition of those occupations, not merely the tasks they perform, is an equally important factor.

Autonomy at work is by no means given solely to this service class, being far more common in industrial settings than the bathos of proletarianization theory admits (see, for example, Fox 1974: 21–39; Friedman 1977: 78–9), but greater autonomy and authority are granted occupations of the service class. They are by definition "trusted workers" (see Whalley 1986). While they are subordinate to the ruling class which, as Goldthorpe notes (1982: 170), holds its position by virtue of its own economic, political, or military power and delegates its authority to them, they are superiors to those whose work they direct and whose affairs they supervise. Their interaction with their subordinates, their class standing, their institutional authority, and their certified expertise all figure in the invocation of deference and respect. By contrast, their relationship to their superiors, members of the ruling class, which is marked on the one hand by trust and respect elicited by both their reliable class standing and their expertise, is marked on the other hand, I suspect, by a degree of condescension, if not contempt, due to their lack of independent power. As Murphy (1988: 552) observes, there are "vastly different power and advantages accruing to [educational] credentials and to property."

7

Bodies of Knowledge

In chapter 1, I sketched the broad varieties of knowledge and skill found in complex societies and singled out as ideal-typical professional knowledge the kind of specialization considered to be both discretionary and based on abstract concepts and theories. In my characterization I relied on *official* definitions, not merely because I wanted to avoid the sea of multiple opinions and perspectives, but more importantly, because official conceptions have the greatest consequences for an occupation's position in a complex political economy. However, as we shall see in this chapter, it does not follow that popular conceptions of different bodies of knowledge and skill have no consequences at all. Indeed, an essential part of any comprehensive view of work and knowledge requires the investigation of their construction in the course of everyday life (Freidson 1994b: 13–24).

While many disciplines may claim to have that special type of professional knowledge and skill which is given official recognition, the particular substance or content of each and the institutional requirements for the performance of the tasks it claims as its own have critical bearing on its success in gaining the full political, economic, and social recognition and support necessary for establishing and consolidating professionalism. Some of those substantive differences stem from the intrinsic character of particular bodies of knowledge and skill; others from the economic, political, and social conditions required for the practice or application of the particular discipline; still others from the relationship of disciplines to the elite and popular culture of the time and place in which they exist. These are the topics of this chapter. I will show how variation in the substance or content of knowledge and skill that affects the conditions of practice is an important contingency of the process by which the ideal-typical position of professionalism can be gained and maintained.

Professional Knowledge

The notion that the knowledge of professionalism requires a foundation in abstract concepts or theories that must be learned in a school is a familiar one.[1] Goode (1969: 277), for example, specifies abstraction as an essential feature and goes on to discuss the importance of knowledge being organized into a codified body of principles in creating and sustaining the social status of an occupation. Larson (1977: 31) specifies knowledge that "must be formalized or codified enough to allow standardization ... and yet ... must not be so clearly codified that it does not allow a principle of exclusion [or discretion] to operate." There must be a sufficient degree of uncertainty or indeterminacy in the character of the knowledge and skill (Jamous and Peloille 1970; Boreham 1983) to require the use of discretionary judgment, but the uncertainty is justified less by ignorance than by the complexity of the task.

However, it is difficult if not impossible to establish truly objective criteria by which to characterize the knowledge and skill required to perform work, for all criteria seem to be contestable as either indefensibly evaluative or relative. As Abbott (1988: 9) noted in the case of abstraction, "what matters is abstraction effective enough to compete in a particular historical and social context, not abstraction relative to some supposed absolute standard." The criteria are not fixed and objective. Furthermore, they vary by social perspective: both consumers and managers are prone to perceive less indeterminacy and complexity in work than are those who actually perform it. The additional claim that esoteric, schooled *theory* is essential for performing the work adequately is also contestable, questioned not only by consumers and managers but even by practitioners themselves who chafe under the author-

---

1 For a recent review of sociological views of knowledge, including those of Abbott, Halliday, Larson, and Marxist and Foucauldian writers, see Macdonald 1995: 157–86. His usage is somewhat inconsistent, but on balance narrower than mine, emphasizing utilitarian knowledge. For a different, rather combative perspective, see Rossides 1998.

ity claimed by theorists who do not have to dirty their hands with reality. But even if these distinctions are not objective, they are socially and culturally real, serving as a major source of justification for the social status assigned to some kinds of work. As analytic distinctions, they are most viable in a comparative context which does not assume timeless, objective characteristics but instead examines the consequences of prevailing ideas about the characteristics of an occupation's body of knowledge and skill.

Epistemological Status

Some time ago Rueschemeyer (1964) protested the inclination of the literature on professions to hold modern medicine up as the prototype, for that leads to the conclusion that prototypical professional knowledge is scientific in character. He pointed out that while virtually every analyst considers law as well as medicine to be a fully established profession, the knowledge employed in law is significantly different from that of medicine. Law has no scientific foundation, and while everywhere it employs abstract concepts, it does not everywhere rely on a systematic body of abstract theory (see Merryman 1985). Since no one questions the status of law as a profession, it follows that a scientific foundation is not an essential characteristic of professional knowledge. This conclusion immediately raises the possibility of distinguishing different bodies of professional knowledge by their epistemological status.

A partial framework for exploiting these distinctions has been provided by Terence Halliday (1987: 28–55). He is concerned primarily with the legal profession, and more specifically the circumstances surrounding the exercise of political influence by the American Bar. He quite rightly criticizes the virtually exclusive emphasis of recent scholarly literature on the importance to the activities of professions of gaining and defending monopoly, arguing that once professions become economically and politically secure, their associations spend little energy on jurisdictional matters. Their attention turns outward and they devote much of their energy to influencing social policies relevant to their special expertise and disciplinary orientation. But professions differ considerably in the *areas* in which they can exercise influence and in the *kind* of influence they can exercise.

In attempting to conceptualize the source and nature of the influence that professions can exercise, Halliday advances the concept of knowledge mandate, which refers to the epistemological foundation of disciplines. Like Rueschemeyer before him, he points out that the most common analyses of professional influence take medicine as the prototype and assert that it is the scientific character of its knowledge which provides it with cognitive authority. But neither the legal nor clerical profession is based on positive science any more than are a great many others which have exercised considerable influence on policy and attained many of the institutions of professionalism. What is needed, he argues, is a more catholic mode of distinguishing bodies of knowledge and skill. He agrees that the optimal cognitive basis for a discipline is one whose claimed tasks are sufficiently distinctive to allow the drawing of clear jurisdictional boundaries, sufficiently codified that standards of competent performance can be established, though not so standardized that discretionary judgment appears to be unnecessary. But then he goes on to argue the need for a broader set of distinctions. He suggests that the epistemological foundation of disciplines can serve that need and proceeds to argue (with full awareness of the philosophical controversies surrounding it) that

> the professions divide into classes depending on whether the cognitive base is primarily of the descriptive or prescriptive. For *scientific* professions, which lie on one side of the logical divide, knowledge is empirically derived from observation and experimental inquiry in methods epitomized by the natural and biological sciences. For *normative* professions, which lie on the other side of the divide, the substance of their discourse and the manner in which it is derived are concerned primarily with matters of value – values in respect of how one should attain salvation, how [for example] salvation should mold individual and social ethics, and how individuals and groups should act in relation to each other and the state. (Halliday 1987: 32, italics added)

Recognizing that his distinction is too crude to match the variety of disciplines, he notes that the military is something in between the two because it incorporates science and technology on the one hand with normative military doctrine on the other. Furthermore, he points out that the academic profession contains both scientific and normative disciplines and disciplines that incorporate both. He suggests the term *syncretic* for such mixed forms.

These distinctions apply both to the substance of the knowledge of the various disciplines and to the "authoritative application of that [disciplinary] knowledge to public policy decisions, or even to everyday practice, where moral and ethical issues assume as much importance as ... technical information" (Halliday 1987: 37). He distinguishes between *technical authority*,[2] which is essentially the license granted a knowledgeable person or expert to employ or guide the employment of a discipline in performing a task (even if the task is only to provide understanding), and *moral authority*, which is the license to specify the norms that select and guide behavior. He suggests that "the more normative (or syncretic) the epistemological core of professional knowledge, the more readily that profession will be able to exercise moral authority in the name of expertise and thus the greater will be its potential breadth of influence" (Halliday 1987: 40). He singles out law as relatively unique among contemporary professions in that it has technical authority embedded in a normative system in which the determination of what is technical and what normative is opaque. This provides law with an unusual opportunity to employ moral authority in the guise of technical advice. In contrast, physical scientists on one side and moral philosophers or members of the clergy on the other are likely to be able employ only one form of authority.

While Halliday provides a useful basis for distinguishing among professions by the epistemological foundation of their knowledge, I believe his distinctions are too limited. The distinction between scientific and normative knowledge is too narrow because scientific knowledge is not the only kind that attempts to describe "the facts" while reserving consciously normative judgment. While the facts dealt with by science and its special methods may be more reliable than, say, those studied and narrated by historians, both are descriptive. Many non-scientific bodies of knowledge attempt to establish the facts about particular topics, so their practitioners are more appropriately treated as technical rather than moral authorities. Furthermore, while Halliday is perhaps correct in noting that the epistemological foundation of the martial discipline is syncretic, his delineation of a single academic profession is supported only by the fact that all professors make a living by teaching.[3] Otherwise, there are marked differences among them. What they teach, as well as what research and writing they do, sharply divides them into quite different specialties. The knowl-

2   Since many of the writers I cite use the term "authority" loosely, I will do so as well even though, strictly speaking, "influence" is the more appropriate term.
3   By that logic, all who make a living by consultation, whether physicians, lawyers, or advisors, are members of the same profession of consulting.

edge of some of those specialties is scientific in character, and most of the others are concerned with discovering and refining substantive knowledge rather than consciously analyzing and expounding values or norms.[4] At best a minority of the professorial disciplines has an essentially normative or syncretic focus. I prefer to call one group concerned with descriptive analysis scientific, and another scholarly or humanistic.

Just as we must distinguish scientific from scholarly disciplines among all those concerned with descriptive analysis of the facts, so must we distinguish among those that are normative in character. The most conspicuous normative disciplines – law and the clergy – are concerned with behavioral and social norms, or morality. But there are others concerned with norms which have little to do with morality but which are an important part of human life and culture. I refer to esthetic norms which are associated with the practice of the various arts.[5] Today the artistic occupations in many countries, certainly in the United States, are weakly organized, and the very notion of canonical art so deprecated that esthetic authority is weak. But this was not the case in some periods of the past (see Becker 1982; Freidson 1994a; Schneider 1997), when there were authoritative canons for the arts and when formal institutions like academies controlled and organized the work of officially recognized practitioners. Just as a comprehensive conception of epistemological authority must include descriptive knowledge associated with scholarship as well as science, so must it also include prescriptive knowledge associated with esthetic as well as moral norms.

The Scope of Epistemological Authority

There are, then, three forms of knowledge: descriptive forms, which include both science and scholarship claiming technical authority; prescriptive forms, secular and sacred, including law, religion, and ethics, which deal with social norms and claim moral

4 For an interesting discussion of contemporary epistemological disputes in literary theory, linking them with the practice of teaching undergraduates, see Schneider 1997.
5 It is patent that esthetic criteria direct technique in the arts. They are also central in distinguishing the profession of architecture (or design) from engineering, and they play a covert but important role in scientific disciplines where the term "elegance" is used to applaud the simplicity and quality of a technical or theoretical solution to a problem.

authority; and the arts, which deal with esthetic norms and claim normative esthetic authority.[6] As Halliday noted, these different forms of knowledge provide different kinds of authority – what he calls technical and moral authority, to which I add cultural and esthetic authority – that can be exercised both in everyday affairs and in the formation of social policy. Those who are experts on some substantive topic have authority that is more limited in scope than those whose stock in trade is normative. Scientists, for example, are more likely to exercise influence in the comparatively narrow and limited substantive areas of their science, and less in affairs lying outside, while those whose knowledge is essentially normative in character are able to exercise authority in a considerably broader range of affairs. These distinctions are not empirically exclusive, since it is possible to add moral authority directly to technical expertise, as Halliday asserts for law and, indirectly or implicitly, as I have argued in the case of medicine (Freidson 1988). Furthermore, it is possible for those whose knowledge is normative in character to develop empirical knowledge about which they can claim technical authority, as is the case for art historians, historians of religion, and perhaps theologians.

But the degree and scope of the authority of a discipline depend on the concrete historical circumstances surrounding its position – its relationship to other disciplines in the social division of labor and to the spirit of the times. Karpik (1988) has shown how the political influence of lawyers in France has changed over the past two centuries. And as Abbott's (1988) extended analysis of the contest for jurisdiction in divisions of labor shows, when jurisdictional boundaries change, so does the substance and scope of the authority of an occupation's practitioners. Indeed, authority can change even when the general content of a discipline remains constant. In the history of the United States, for example, Kimball (1992) argues that from colonial times to the recent past there has been a succession of professions which held and then lost positions of "architectonic" influence – the clergy in the eighteenth century displaced by lawyers in the nineteenth century, who then yielded to medicine and science, both of which appeared to be yielding to economics at the end of the twentieth century. In the light of

6 A more catholic typology would have to deal with the socially recognized knowledge provided by what is believed to be supernatural revelation – knowledge about the creation of the earth, for example. Such knowledge is certainly not empirical, as is that of science or secular history, but neither is it prescriptive. It has played an extremely important role in the past and is by no means insignificant in the present.

history it is clear that the epistemological status of disciplines does not tell us enough about them to allow us to understand their position in a political economy. To understand how and why bodies of knowledge can gain and lose influence requires closer examination of the variable historic and national circumstances in which they are practiced.

The Variety of Institutional Spheres

Classifying disciplines by their epistemological status has very general implications for the kind and scope of the authority they can exercise. But such a classification ignores the human institutions in which knowledge is exercised. Such institutions vary in important ways that can either restrict or facilitate the capacity of an occupation to exercise influence of any kind. Halliday rightly observes that professions, like any occupation, are practiced in particular institutional spheres, or core institutions, within which their members are considered to have legitimate interest and authority. Thus, medicine is practiced in the health system, engineering in the industrial system, and law in the legal system. But as he points out, this is not true for all members of a particular occupation, since some specialties within a relatively well-developed and complex profession are practiced in other than those core institutions: a minister, for example, may work at a youth center and not a church, a physician in an industrial plant and not in the consulting room of a community practice, and an engineer in a planning agency and not in an industrial firm. This leads Halliday to distinguish between primary institutional spheres, where the authority of a discipline's knowledge is central, and secondary spheres, where it is not. Thus, the capacity of individual professionals to exercise authority, whether technical or normative, will depend in part on whether or not they are working in their primary institutional spheres.

The distinction is well taken, but it points to a critical element of the power – both potential and actual – of disciplines. Disciplines must be *practiced* and the differences among the institutions in which they are practiced have momentous consequences for their privileges. While the minister who practices in a hierarchically (or episcopally) organized church may command knowledge of the same epistemological status as one practicing in a congregationally organized church, the effective influence of each differs considerably. The same may be said for the effective authority of a teacher working in a public school compared to one working as a tutor in a wealthy household.

Halliday is concerned with creating the conceptual tools to facilitate an orderly analysis of the areas in which professional associations may be able to influence state policy and the circumstances under which influence can be exercised. He is particularly concerned with the legal profession in the United States which, he argues, is in a more strategic position than many other professions to exercise influence over a broad range of policy issues, due in part to the normative character of its discipline and in part to its relationship to state institutions. The concepts that he advances create a strong skeleton to bear and give shape to the ordinarily diffuse and formless flesh of both Foucauldian analysis and conventional narrative histories of state policy formation. But although those concepts distinguish broad differences between disciplines, they are clearly not sufficient. While recognizing that the institutions in which a discipline is practiced condition the authority of its practitioners even when epistemological status is held constant, Halliday does not go on to analyze the implications. The institutional circumstances of practice have critical bearing on the capacity of disciplines to attract the support of others so as to secure privileges in the first place and, once secured, to exercise influence in public affairs. Those having the same epistemological status do not all gain the same degree of privilege and influence. And the same discipline, its epistemological status constant, may have differing degrees of influence on public affairs in different times and places. Patently, we need to examine additional criteria before we can understand how the character of disciplines bears on the gaining of economic or political privilege. We must go beyond epistemology to the substance or content of the tasks that disciplines perform and the conditions required for their performance.

The literature does not provide us with much help in distinguishing disciplines by their content or tasks. Abbott's (1988) analysis, which is perhaps the most sophisticated in recent years, purports to focus on work itself rather than the organization of work, but it is obvious that he has not developed a systematic rationale for distinguishing among different kinds of work. He refers to varied "task areas" which are distinguished at one point by "health, justice, emotions, and business" (Abbott 1988: 108), and at another by "education, medical area, legal/business area, social area, design, engineering science, print media, arts, entertainment" (1988: 172). Elsewhere, he speaks of "information professions," differentiated into qualitative and quantitative bodies of knowledge (1988: 216) and of a "personal problems jurisdiction" (1988: 280). Clearly, he has not developed a logical or systematic method of categorizing disciplines by their content – that is, by the particular work they perform. But so far as I know, neither has anyone else, crude official classification of industries or sectors of modern economies notwithstanding. Nothing more than common sense seems to be available, so I use pragmatic rather than abstract criteria, working inductively with those occupations which are generally recognized as professions. I will discuss the contingencies posed by the particular bodies of knowledge used by different professions and by the circumstances in which they must be practiced. Following the order of my analysis of professionalism in earlier chapters, I will discuss how the contingencies connected with the practice of different kinds of knowledge have differing consequences for the status of occupations in the official economy, their position in their division of labor and their labor market, and their control over their training institutions. Inevitably, this will require discussing the role of the state and of ideology.

The Contingencies of Knowledge

The official labor force. As I pointed out in chapter 1, any form of specialized knowledge and skill is embedded in a much larger universe of work. In some cases practitioners may be recognized and their skills employed in the informal or criminal economy without official sanction or awareness. That means, of course, that they have no official status and are wholly dependent upon their clients or customers. However, ideal-typical professionalism cannot develop without official recognition and support. In some cases, official recognition and support is a response to the existence of broad public concern with the problems or issues addressed by a particular discipline; in most cases, with or without broad public concern, it is a response to the concerns of politically or economically influential segments of the public, of the ruling class or party, or of a state agency.

There are a few disciplines whose tasks bear on issues of widespread interest and deep concern on the part of the general population. They might be called *core disciplines*, bodies of knowledge and skill which address perennial problems that are of great importance to most of humanity. Although they have quite different epistemological statuses, medicine, law, and religion exemplify such disciplines, dealing as they do with relief from pain, illness, and disability (see Parsons 1964), the just resolution of disputes and maintenance of social order, and a comforting relationship to the perennial misfortunes of life and the inevitable prospect of death. With official support, one version or another of those disciplines can become very securely established so long as it also has the support of the general population. But when general support from the population is fragmented by sectarianism or weakened by general skepticism or indifference, the official position of disciplines purporting to serve those concerns may become an empty shell and crumble over time, their position ultimately usurped by another more popular discipline or by schismatic movements which fragment if not dissolve the original.[7]

Apart from the core disciplines to which the state is virtually obliged to provide special recognition and status in the labor force, there are others – schoolteachers, social workers, and professors, for example – which are familiar to the general population because they provide services directly to many of its members. A special position for them in the labor force is not as dependent on widespread popular approval as are the core disciplines, but both activist and reactive states are likely to be concerned with establishing a special status for them. In many other instances, gaining professional status in the official labor force of complex political economies has little relationship to the interests and felt needs of the broad public. Many disciplines are granted such status because of their importance to special segments of society or to the state itself. Engineers are of patent functional importance to the design and production of goods no matter whether productive enterprises are controlled by the state or by private capital, and so are accountants to the management and evaluation of the financial affairs of both state and private organizations. From the nineteenth century on, both capital enterprise and the state came to recognize the importance of the physical sciences for economic development, as well as the importance of higher education for training the staff of modern governmental and private enterprises.

But not all disciplines likely to gain special status in the labor

---

7   The history of religion is of course rife with examples of the popular decline and displacement of orthodoxies, though largely successful religious conversion by force was not unimportant in the spread of Christianity and Islam. Revolutions represent the installation of new (though often temporary) legal institutions. In the case of medicine, some analysts claim that alternatives to physicians and "scientific medicine" are becoming so popular today that the public (if not official) status of medicine is weakening.

force are believed to be of immediate functional value to either the powers of the political economy or the public at large. Conspicuously without such value but privileged nonetheless are most of the academic disciplines. If clear functional value alone were invoked, a privileged professoriate would be composed solely of those disciplines directly related to the training of engineers, chemists, accountants, and physicians. Most of the academic disciplines having little relationship to the functional skills of practicing vocations are supported by the belief of political, social, and (in highly variable degree) economic elites that they have cultural importance. Those studying, writing, and teaching such disciplines as history, literature, esoteric languages, philosophy, and musicology, of varied epistemological status, must depend on the sufferance of elites to gain and maintain their official status in the labor force.

Divisions of labor.[8] Of course no occupation, no practiced body of knowledge and skill, exists in isolation. Most, if not all, disciplines are part of a particular division of labor organized, established, and enforced by some power external to it. The actual jurisdictional boundaries between concrete specializations, even when managerial authority rather than free occupational interaction organizes them, can be bitterly contested (in firms this is called "office politics") and may by no means be taken for granted. However, apart from the logical alternatives for organizing a division of labor that I discussed in chapter 2, different task areas, or economic sectors, vary considerably in the number and type of specializations needed for attaining their productive goals. The division of labor in today's hospital, for example, includes an extremely complex set of technical specialties both within medicine itself and in the occupations supporting its activities, and not all the occupations are subordinate to medicine, as was once the case. In the community outside the hospital, medical work takes place within a simpler division of labor, but an increasing number of other practitioners contend with medicine for jurisdiction over particular tasks. In contrast, the division of labor in religion is fairly simple by the very nature of the tasks its practitioners perform. Within

---

8 Taking the division of labor seriously requires undertaking the comprehensive analysis that Becker (1982) makes of the arts. Those devoted to studying professions usually limit their attention to occupations competing for the same tasks and privileges, which is a very small though admittedly important part of the division of labor in the arena in which they compete.

some religious denominations there are only ministers and unpaid, voluntary assistants. But even a hierarchical and bureaucratically organized religion like the Roman Catholic Church[9] displays a remarkably simple set of specializations in comparison with many disciplines in other sectors of the political economy. And of course, many of the academic scholarly professions involve little division of labor at all, either in the practice of teaching or of research and writing.

Thus, it is undeniable that because of the character of their knowledge, different disciplines participate in divisions of labor that vary in complexity and in the relationships that exist among participating occupations. The epistemological character of disciplines bears on the degree of the division of labor in that when they are empirical and technical rather than normative, a complex organization of many specialties and sub-specialties is likely. Complex divisions of labor can be organized hierarchically around a dominant occupation, as was the case for mid-twentieth-century medicine, while others are more simple and egalitarian, as in teaching. No doubt other features of the knowledge commanded by a discipline may be related to variation in the structure of the division of labor and the processes taking place within it, but the topic must be approached with caution because it cannot be separated from the character of the labor market upon which the very existence of a division of labor inevitably depends.

Labor markets. The physical, economic, and social resources required for practice differ from one discipline to another. Some of those differences vary by time and place, but others flow generically from the substantive character of the disciplines themselves. Practices differ by their relation to consumers, who are the indispensable source of economic support for workers. The practice of medicine, excepting some specialties like public health, requires access to individual patients. By contrast, others require access to groups: ministers need congregations, teachers classes, and military officers squads if not platoons, regiments, battalions, divisions, or armies. Needing a collective clientele for one's practice unavoidably creates an institutional dependency that need not exist for work with individuals. Still other disciplines have no direct relationship to those who ultimately consume their services or

---

9   For an analysis of the "dual labor market" of the Roman Catholic Church, see Wittberg and LaMagdeleine 1989.

products, but instead gain their living from those who use their labor to provide goods to consumers, as is the case for engineers.

The organization of the division of labor in which particular disciplines must work is reflected in their labor market. Thus, while the practice of architecture may begin with a drawing, a design created by an independent individual, the design ordinarily has no exchange value unless it is realized. Only personal time and expense may be expended to create a design, yet realizing it in a building requires a considerable amount of capital. Dependence on the wealthy and powerful to commission a design for a building is intrinsic to the labor market of most architects. So too for most engineers: with few exceptions, the various engineering specialties cannot be practiced independently, their position in their labor market depending on employment by a complex, heavily capitalized organization which supplies them with their income and the resources they need for their work.

These constraints on the requirements for practice in a labor market can of course be compounded by economic, technological, and other changes. For example, when it became possible to design buildings supported by reinforced steel rather than by walls or pillars of stone or brick, new kinds of workers were required. When refined surgical skills and new technologies allowed the routine performance of previously impossible procedures in medicine, larger capital investment in technology, as well as new and greater numbers of specialized assistants, became necessary. Simple scalpels, bone saws, clamps, and, before anesthesia, unskilled attendants to hold down the patient no longer sufficed. Changes in the mode of financing work create different contingencies: the physician still serves patients as individuals whether they are insured by a national health or private insurance program, as does the lawyer who serves individual citizens under state-financed legal assistance programs, but neither can negotiate fees individually and must instead make do with a living provided by a single mediating organization that is considerably more powerful than the unorganized aggregate of individual clients. Dissatisfied university professors can no longer march their students out of the city of Paris, or out of Oxford and across the River Cam to found Cambridge, nor can they collect fees from them individually as they could in Germany early in the twentieth century. With few exceptions today they depend on an employing institution to pay them and to recruit and organize students. However, it should not be assumed that dependence on an organization rather than bargaining with individual consumers necessarily means less freedom of action; some tutors, scholars, scientists, and artists who were once dependent on the goodwill of powerful and wealthy individuals gained considerably more freedom in the exercise of their disciplines when their sources of support became institutionalized.

Training institutions.   The substance of a discipline also has implications for attracting and training its recruits. Someone is said to have observed that the ideal arrangement for education is having an exemplary teacher like Mark Hopkins (the nineteenth-century American) at one end of a log and a student at the other. This is true enough for a tutorial arrangement, but it is possible only in the case of disciplines requiring no resource other than words. In so far as training can come to resemble the ideal-typical arrangement I discussed in chapter 4, in which research and scholarship are also supported, bulk teaching is required. This means classrooms and the capital investment they entail, as well as a regular source of economic support. Taking that as a given, different disciplines require markedly different material, economic, and social instructional resources. Since legal education, like education for many of the scholarly disciplines, is purely verbal, it requires little more than classrooms, a faculty, and a library, and thus demands a relatively small amount of capital.[10] Since the early twentieth century, on the other hand, medical education has come to require many far more expensive resources, including laboratories, increasingly complex and expensive technology, legally obtained cadavers, support personnel, and access to patients. The same contingencies distinguish different academic disciplines, the teaching and study of philosophy requiring only classrooms and a library, but modern physics requiring what has become extremely elaborate and expensive technology, laboratories, and support personnel. Such differences in the material requirements for educating recruits make some disciplines far more dependent on continuous large-scale support from state or private capital than others and their training programs far more vulnerable to fluctuations in support than those whose needs are more modest.

Ideologies.   Finally, I may note that by their very substance disciplines differ in the values they can claim, and that neither the

---

10   This is a major reason why legal education can be so expansive wherever there is no deliberate restriction imposed on the number of students that can enter law programs, such as the quota system of admission that is called *numerus clausus* in Europe.

general public nor elites nor the state are equally committed to all of them. The transcendent values of the core disciplines, Health, Justice, and Salvation, are of nearly universal attraction and can gain broad support for privilege, though the particular discipline which can claim custody of a value of course varies in time and place and is often in contention. Contention exists not only between disciplines struggling over jurisdiction, but also between disciplines and the public or an elite over the ideological claim that desirable goals can be realized only through the use of expertise.[11] Furthermore, the general public is less likely than elites to be concerned with such transcendent values as Beauty, Truth, or Knowledge.

Comparing the Consequences of Knowledge

Substantive differences in the content of disciplines are more important for their status than are their epistemological foundations, degree of abstraction, theorization, or indeterminacy. The most important handicaps to professionalism flow from the contingencies stemming from the particular tasks which the members of a discipline must perform in order to make a living. This may be illustrated concretely by comparing the consequences of differences in the knowledge of engineering, architecture, and physics, all of which have a scientific component.

In the case of engineering,[12] its major source of support was initially political because of its importance to both military and civil affairs – designing and supervising the construction of bridges, roads, and fortifications. During the Industrial Revolution, however, engineering not only grew but broke up into a number of different specialties, a process that continues to this day. The most conspicuous and populous engineering specialties today are those engaged in the technical planning and supervision of the production of the consumer goods and services that form the

---

11   In the case of law, popular justice has a short life. In the Soviet Union the pre-revolutionary Bar was eliminated in 1921 only to be reconstituted that same year, in part because Lenin believed that in order "to restore the confidence of the masses in the legal system as equitable and just, professional defense counsel were needed" (Huskey 1986: 81–2). Popular religion, on the other hand, is more persistent.

12   I have used a number of sources for this analysis, especially Arkell 1999, Armytage 1961, Crawford 1989, Lundgreen 1990, Meiksins and Smith 1996, Orzack 1989, Shinn 1980, Whalley 1986, and Zussman 1985.

foundation of the modern standard of living. From their beginning as an identifiable occupation, the very nature of their work barred most engineers from independent practice because of their dependence on large amounts of capital to realize their plans. It is true that some specialties, such as mechanical engineering in the United States (Calvert 1967), were first organized as individual entrepreneurial practices in small shops, but within a few decades most of their practitioners had become employees of industrial organizations, a few becoming managers or owners. Today, there are a few powerful and wealthy engineering corporations that are analogous to the autonomous professional organizations of large law and accounting firms, but by and large such independent practice in industrial nations is rare for all but civil engineers. The vast majority of engineers depend for their living on employment, some by state-owned but most by privately owned firms. This has obvious influence on their position in their labor markets.

While engineers are granted some special status in the official labor force of modern industrial nations, their institutions are only weak reflections of ideal-typical professionalism due to the contingencies connected to the kind of knowledge they command and the circumstances of their practice. All engineers may be said to design, plan, or coordinate some productive process, but the tasks that they perform vary by industry and specialty. Unlike physicians, lawyers, or accountants, who may dominate some of the organizations in which they work, engineers cannot. The work they do requires large sums of capital provided by others, and constitutes only one specialized and by no means dominant segment of the division of labor involved in production. While they are among the few specialists who can achieve executive positions in firms,[13] they can do so only by leaving the practice of their profession.

While the occupational title of engineer is familiar to most people and is sometimes used as an honorific title like "Doctor" in Latin nations, there is nonetheless no distinct set of tasks which the public associates with it. (For evidence of this in the United States, see Doble and Komarnicki 1986.) The public does have a notion, stereotyped and overdramatized as it may be, of what lawyers, physicians, and teachers do, but engineers have only the most general identity, certainly none that could arouse public interest and support. Given the variety of their specializations,

---

13 Other professions not trained as managers having a fair chance of becoming officers of firms are lawyers and accountants.

there is good reason for this vague image. Any effort engineers might make to gain special privilege, therefore, cannot count on mobilizing public sympathy; they must seek support solely from their employers or from the state.

They also hold a weak position in the economy because they serve as disparate specialists in many different industries. While the general roles of research, development, and production design may remain the same for all engineers no matter what the industry or specialty, just as managerial roles are the same everywhere in that very broad sense, each specialty contends with a differently constituted division of labor, one that is organized not by engineers but by managers and owners. Unlike the more homogeneous domains of health, law, and education, a standard model for organizing the division of labor for all engineers is impossible. Furthermore, the body of engineering knowledge is so exact that it is in constant danger of obsolescence through mechanization or advances in knowledge and technique, and its practitioners are susceptible to displacement by workers with lesser training. The division of labor between those called "technician" and those called "engineer" is likely to be relatively fluid, depending more on the personnel practices of particular organizations than on a legally required set of jurisdictional boundaries.[14]

It is the economic foundation of the labor markets in which engineers work that is decisive for the organization of their division of labor and for the possibility of establishing the independence of a stable labor market shelter. It is not to the advantage of employers to allow engineers to determine their own tasks and evaluate their own performance nor, most particularly, to allow them to establish labor market shelters. In fact, industrial employers in all Western nations have resisted the institution of shelters, wishing instead to have as much flexibility as possible in the assignment of tasks. Thus, while in some nations, such as France and Germany, engineers have succeeded in gaining legal protection for distinctive titles such as *ingénieur diplomé* or *Diplom-Ingenieur*, title protection by itself does not establish a secure monopoly over a defined set of tasks.[15] The general job title of "engineer" is one which employers can and do assign at will.

14 See for example the papers in Barley and Orr 1997a.
15 It is true that there is a hierarchy among engineers based on educational degrees, especially marked in Sweden, Germany, and France, where engineers with elite education are sharply distinguished from others. Nonetheless, they have no monopoly over high-level positions.

The absolute dependence of the practice of engineering on large capital investment is also reflected in engineering education. From the beginning of modern engineering, faculties have struggled for academic recognition – in Germany, for example, for university rather than vocational institute status. Consonant with the demands of professionalism, during the course of that struggle engineering faculties asserted their intellectual commitment to abstract theory and formed their training programs around such theory. But they had to contend with powerful opposition from governments concerned with modernizing and expanding their economies, and industrialists concerned with obtaining technical employees who were prepared to perform practical tasks at the lowest possible cost. This conflict between employers and engineering school faculties has been perennial for well over a century. It has been manifested in some countries, such as the United Kingdom until very recently, by a tendency for employers to avoid hiring engineering school graduates, preferring apprentices whose training they could control. In nineteenth-century France, employers used the lesser-trained *gadzart* to perform technical tasks; more recently such company-trained technical workers in France have had titles such as *ingénieur auto-didacte*, or *ingénieur-maison* (see Crawford 1989).

The state, of course, can be a powerful counterforce to capital, but apart from establishing and supporting engineering schools, particularly during the early stages of the Industrial Revolution, few if any nations have had any interest in supporting labor market shelters for engineers. State concern for developing and maintaining an adequate public infrastructure as well as a capable military has led most to develop their own corps of engineers. In France this evolved into an elite corps of high-level civil servants and managers, but that is not common elsewhere. In any case, states have provided little impetus or support for the development of the institutions of professionalism for engineering. State disinterest, together with public disinterest and the resistance of employers, has played a large part in the profession's weakness.

The engineering profession's own resources for organization and political action have also been weak due to its fragmentation into a variety of virtually unrelated specialties practicing in so many different industrial sectors that few common interests link its members. When they identify themselves as part of a broad class of middle management – as *cadres* in France[16] – the particular

16   See especially Boltanski 1987 and also Crawford 1989: 27–8, 172–95.

occupation they practice becomes unimportant. Furthermore, engineering associations are often dominated by engineers who have risen to managerial positions and exercise their influence in association activities to advance their company's interest rather than that of the rank and file.[17] It was possible in France to mobilize some[18] engineers as members of the large group of *cadres*, and in Germany engineers did create a strong union movement before the First World War, and they gained greater strength during the Nazi regime. In both countries they have finally gained legally protected titles, but the collective influence of engineering associations on state policies everywhere has been powerful only when narrowly technical (Freidson 1986: 184–208; Golden 1991) and unable to create strong versions of professionalism for itself.

Part of that impotence may stem not only from the intrinsic circumstances of engineering practice which prevent the development of occupational solidarity but also from the ideology of engineering itself. The only distinctive value to which the tasks of engineering can be attached is efficiency. While at first glance efficiency seems a powerfully attractive value, at second it is merely instrumental in character, with no real substance.[19] Efficiency is equally involved in designing and manufacturing microwave ovens and in designing a system for incinerating Jews, gypsies, and homosexuals. Furthermore, the criteria defining the terms of efficiency are arbitrary and established by the use of economic or political power external to the disciplines themselves.

It is instructive to compare engineering with architecture, which is a related and in some cases competing discipline of similar historical origins, but with a different epistemological authority. Architecture attempts to subordinate technology to design.[20] Like engineers, architects cannot realize their designs autonomously. Even before the development of modern construction techniques,

17 For a failed effort to change the orientation of an engineer association in the United States early in the twentieth century, see Layton 1971.
18 I use the word "some" advisedly, for everywhere the title of engineer is ambiguous enough to make the inclusiveness of various engineering associations and unions very difficult if not impossible to establish. Such a problem is itself testimony to the weakness of the profession. See Shinn 1980 for a brief, though now dated, history of the title in France.
19 Abbott (1988: 194–5) asserts that management claims to advance the goal of efficiency in order to legitimate a position which lacks any "obvious technical expertise."
20 Larson 1993 must be specially cited here because of her rich and sophisticated analysis of the interaction between the ideologies of architecture and changes in technology, political economy, and style.

building required the mobilization and coordination of a variety of occupations in the building trades who could realize the architect's plans. And like engineering projects, architecture requires a considerable amount of capital to pay for the building materials and the labor of the builders. This has almost always meant dependence upon a wealthy individual, the state, or a corporation. (For brief studies of architecture in various times and places, see Kostof 1977.) While broad comparative studies of architectural practice are not available,[21] the picture one gets is that architecture in general is in as weak a position, economically and legally, as engineering, and has succeeded in gaining little official privilege.

Yet in another sense it is considerably stronger than engineering. First, its epistemological mandate is, in Halliday's terms, syncretic rather than entirely scientific. At least since Vitruvius it has claimed a foundation in theory for its knowledge and skill and, like engineering, jurisdiction over the tasks of conception and supervision of execution. But unlike engineering, architecture's origins lie partly in the arts, and it claims authority over esthetic design. Furthermore, it can be practiced in the service of individuals (Gutman 1983: 216) rather than only the state or corporation, however restricted the opportunities and however poorly paid, so that its practitioners have the possibility of independent self-employment. Its tasks are focused around the design and construction of buildings rather than dispersed across a number of quite different industries, so that, stratified as the profession may be, all members share a common core of practice which fosters the development of solidarity and organization as a profession. Furthermore, the buildings architects design, sometimes monumental in character, are on public display, as are the names of their designers. And perhaps most important, the association of the profession with the arts[22] and with theory rather than with the merely practical, gains its practitioners much more public prestige than builders, developers, and construction engineers can attain

---

21   For French architects see Moulin and her associates (1973), for a brief German study see Clark 1990, and see the analyses of the American profession by Gutman (1983, 1988), Blau (1984), Blau et al. (1983), Larson (1983, 1993), Montgomery (1990), and Brain (1991).

22   The identification of architecture with art (at least in the context of the Romantic tradition) can lead to rejection of licensing or registration as an infringement of artistic freedom. At the turn of the nineteenth century, the Royal Institute of British Architects in fact opposed the statutory registration of architects on those grounds.

and permits the more successful of them to have social and cultural ties with the economic and political elite.

Consider the fact that while it is difficult if not impossible to think of engineers whose names are familiar to the public or even the industrial elite, the names of prominent architects and their firms are well known. They are known to the wealthy who commission them to design their homes, to government agencies and politicians charged with erecting public buildings as monuments, to large corporations seeking concrete emblems of their importance and good taste, and to educated middle-class consumers of high culture (Gutman 1988: 89–96). Of course, given the fundamentally weak economic position of the profession as a whole, none of these distinctions prevents rank-and-file architects from practicing under much the same circumstances as their engineering cousins, which frustrates their aspirations toward creativity. But unlike their cousins, they are not social and cultural ciphers; they not only aspire to creative tasks but can bask in some of the reflected glory of their creative elite.

A number of other disciplines with an epistemological mandate similar to that of engineering are in markedly different positions by virtue of having developed out of occupations which originally had no significant connection with commercial affairs. An example of such a discipline is physics, which had its origin in the observations and reasoning of philosophers concerned with explaining the nature of the material world. Apart from those whose work was financed by the largesse of powerful individuals or by personal wealth, since medieval times such people have gained their support from universities. They contributed to the liberal education of students by teaching them their discipline, pursued their own research, and in some cases trained their successors. The immediate justification for the living their university positions provided[23] lay in teaching others theories of the nature of the material world, the very act of which could include elaborating and refining those theories as well as creating new ones. By corresponding with colleagues, writing monographs, and presenting papers at public gatherings a collegial community was formed that extended outside the boundaries of the immediate university workplace. But unlike engineers, practitioners of the discipline could claim primary concern with "basic" or "pure" knowledge, an effort to understand the ultimate character of the universe

---

23 It is important to avoid exaggerating the level of economic support provided by university positions until very recently.

without direct interest in practical application and innovation. Thus, while engineers could claim the pursuit of efficiency, which is merely a facilitative value, scientists (and philosophers) could claim the pursuit of Knowledge or Truth, "pure research . . . done wholly for the love of truth" (Kevles 1979: 45). Their methodological criteria of parsimony and comprehensiveness are applied to understanding and explanation without any necessary connection to the practical world. This frees them from any obligation to serve the practical needs of their time.

Joseph Ben-David (1971: 31; see also Ben-David 1976) argues that, historically in Europe, the view of the elite "that scientific knowledge for its own sake was good for society" was essential to the institutionalization of science as an enterprise independent of religious or political affairs. Yet in so far as the physical and biological sciences aim at understanding the empirical world, they cannot fail to be summoned to practical uses when faith in the validity of their knowledge develops. And indeed, in the course of their development as disciplines in the nineteenth century and much more markedly in the twentieth, they have become associated, sometimes unwillingly, with industrial and state interests. In nineteenth-century France, when provincial university scientists could get little financial support from the state, they turned to local industrialists who were attracted to the possibility of practical benefits (Paul 1980), and in the United States there has been considerable pressure on university scientists to devote themselves to solving practical problems in industry and agriculture (see, for example, Bruce 1987; Kevles 1979; Daniels 1967; Mendelsohn 1964).

By the start of the twenty-first century the success of the positive sciences in applying their knowledge to practical affairs has created labor markets in which the various scientific professions are stratified like engineers, those with basic degrees assuming line positions in industry and, depending on the nation, those with higher degrees becoming entrepreneurs, managers, directors of research, and professors. Further, given the growth of knowledge, the laboratories, equipment, and research personnel required for research have become so expensive that it cannot be undertaken without considerable support from state or private capital. The consequences for research practice are complex and have not been fully documented, but it does seem that both physical and biological scientists now have much less freedom to carry out research for its own sake. Financial support is usually given for research that is useful for the military and economic development policies of the state or that offers potential for profit to private investment capital (Dickson 1984; Weingart 1982; Sassower 1996). In universities, independent choice of research problems remains possible, but only within the limits posed by the resources that are routinely available from the university itself.

Finally, I may mention academic disciplines which are more descriptive than prescriptive and more empirical than normative, yet are not scientific in the same sense as physics, chemistry, and other natural sciences. Unlike other professions, the public prestige of most of those disciplines depends less on the often obscure content of their practice than on their members' position as professors in universities to whom unusual erudition is ascribed and who may be seen as the custodians of privileged high culture.[24] With some exceptions, economics and psychology being perhaps the most prominent, these academic disciplines have little or no value in the market outside of education. Most of their practitioners have no alternative to making their living by teaching their disciplines in post-secondary institutions, their scholarly endeavors therefore being parasitic on their teaching duties.[25] This means that public or private authorities are the source of capitalization and administrative authority, representing a contingency of some importance. The faculties' employing institutions recruit students for them and provide the financing, physical plant, support personnel, and administrative framework for their teaching, sometimes leaving them free time to engage in research and writing. Unlike contemporary natural scientists, most need rather modest resources for their research, often only libraries, and while their research is usually of interest only to their disciplinary colleagues, it may nonetheless contribute to the reputation of their employing institutions. Like other disciplines, they have always been subject to political and economic constraints on their freedom to study and write about what they will.

The more esoteric of these scholarly disciplines in Western universities, which are least able to argue some practical value (Sanskrit, Egyptology, Latin, and classical Greek, for example), are most likely to depend upon elites for their continued existence. Virtually all scholarly disciplines, however, are dependent on a fragile general respect for high culture and more particularly on

24 Bourdieu 1989 provides a rich analysis of those disciplines in France.
25 I use the term analytically, not judgmentally, with ecology in mind. Some readers have deplored my use of this term, claiming that research is also expected of professors as part of their job. But the fact that only a very small proportion of professors ever publish anything implies that, except in elite universities, engaging in research is not in fact a prerequisite for holding their jobs.

their more robust value in providing cultural capital to the children of the middle and upper classes. But times change, and today some in the United States predict the death of many academic disciplines. A few may return to their amateur origins, but that is unlikely for most. Quite apart from the dead weight of tradition, predictions of doom not only overlook the importance of "impractical" disciplines to the cultural capital demanded by elites and those aspiring to them, but also overlook a long history of oscillation between the dominance of generalist and specialist ideologies of education. Furthermore, the pressure of multiculturalism that is emerging from globalization is, if anything, likely to expand rather than contract the number of impractical and unprofitable but ideologically privileged disciplines nurtured by universities.

Part III

The Fate of Specialized Knowledge

8

The Assault on Professionalism

The analytic strategy I have used in this book is based on my belief that a coherent standpoint for the study of professions and an intelligent and considered public policy toward them requires the use of a theoretical model. While my model makes little effort to fit the enormous variety of occupations resembling what are called professions in English, it is not pure invention, for it has been abstracted from concrete national and historical circumstances with which I am familiar. Because of its emphasis on logic over substance, however, it is partially freed from the parochial character of those circumstances.

In the broadest sense, this book is concerned with work, which is the practice of knowledge and skill, and the social, economic, and cultural circumstances surrounding its practice. Professionalism is conceived of as one of three logically distinct methods of organizing and controlling those circumstances. I have defined professionalism as the occupational control of work and have suggested an ideal-typical model of the institutional circumstances that embody the perfect or ideal-typical form of occupational control. Like Max Weber's model of rational-legal bureaucracy which represents managerialism and Adam Smith's model of the free market which represents consumerism, it specifies what can but may never fully be. Like those other models, it does not mirror the empirical world, yet is intended to provide a stable, logically articulated framework that can organize the way we look at the world and compare its wide variety of cases, including occupations that have nothing like the same control over their work as the professions.

Professionalism represents occupational rather than consumer or managerial control. The circumstances in which an occupation becomes able to organize and control its own work are generically different from the situation more common today in which an employer (or labor consumer) chooses who is to perform what tasks and how much will be paid, on what terms, for performing them. Labor consumers make these choices either as individual patrons in an ideally free market, or as managers of a formally constituted firm. I have elaborated on the differences among those three modes of control and their substantively different consequences, arguing that a model of occupational (or worker) control of work is quite as important theoretically as the better-known models of the perfectly free market and the rational-legal bureaucracy. It constitutes a distinct logical possibility, a third logic.

In elaborating the model of professionalism, I have distinguished between institutional constants, which I used to define professionalism ideal-typically, and a number of variables which are critical contingencies for establishing and supporting professionalism. The defining elements of the ideal type, the theoretical constants, are, first, a body of knowledge and skill which is officially recognized as one based on abstract concepts and theories and requiring the exercise of considerable discretion; second, an occupationally controlled division of labor; third, an occupationally controlled labor market requiring training credentials for entry and career mobility; fourth, an occupationally controlled training program which produces those credentials, schooling that is associated with "higher learning," segregated from the ordinary labor market, and provides opportunity for the development of new knowledge; and fifth, an ideology serving some transcendent value and asserting greater devotion to doing good work than to economic reward. The contingencies which are critical to realizing the institutions of the ideal type and which vary in time and place include the organization and policy positions of state agencies, the organization of occupations themselves, and the varying institutional circumstances required for the successful practice of different bodies of knowledge and skill.

Given the ideal type that establishes a stable framework for comparing empirical cases, and the historically variable institutions essential to it, the examination of their interaction allows making sense of the processes which establish and maintain the position of professions. It establishes, furthermore, a systematic method of analysis that can be applied to all forms of work, not only those organized as professions. And it provides a theoretical foundation for discussing social policy. Are the monopoly, credentialism, and elitism that are intrinsic to professionalism inimical to the public welfare? Should all vestiges of professionalism in present-day political economies be replaced by the free market or rational bureaucracy? Or should professionalism be reinforced?

It makes no sense to answer these questions without recognizing the inevitably partial manner in which any ideal type can be realized in the empirical world. It is common for ideologues to argue that empirical deficiencies in their policies are due to the incomplete realization of their model, and that removing all barriers to full realization would achieve utopia. I do not believe in utopias, on earth or elsewhere, now or in the future, so while I emphasize the rationale for the institutions of professionalism, I do not go on to argue for a policy that attempts to realize them in full at the expense of markets or firms. Reality is and should be a variable mix of all three logics, the policy issue being the precise composition of that mix. The issue should be whether the virtues of each are suppressed by emphasis on the others and their vices excessively stimulated. I believe that the emphasis on consumerism and managerialism has legitimized and advanced the individual pursuit of material self-interest and the standardization of professional work which are the very vices for which professions have been criticized, preserving form without spirit.

I will discuss the fate of professionalism in these concluding chapters. In order to give the issue substance I want to take as concrete example the fortunes of an occupation that is alternately praised and damned as the prototypical profession – American medicine. What makes medicine in the United States at the start of the twenty-first century an unusually good subject for examination (apart from the fact that I studied it intensively some time ago) is the dramatic way its position changed over the course of the twentieth century. At the beginning of the century it was in disarray. Before the First World War it was only beginning to gain significant professional status. In the fifty years that followed it gained such strength that it almost completely realized ideal-typical professionalism. But in the last quarter of the century its status was so weakened that some asserted its proletarianization. How and why did those changes occur and what are their implications?

The Golden Age of American Medicine[1]

Labor force status.   At its prime in the 1950s, medicine was the most highly respected occupation in the United States, excepting only that of Supreme Court Justice. The federal government was essentially passive in financing and organizing health care, restricting itself primarily to enforcing the recommendations of the organized profession. In the jargon of chapter 6, the American state was reactive-coordinative, with relatively modest and passive state agencies following a policy of enforcing rules created by private professional associations. The profession was granted special, protected status by the state, legally sustained by Supreme Court decisions which, by denying that medicine was a business or trade, granted it immunity from anti-trust action and sustained both its exclusive license to practice and its efforts to monopolize and control practice.

Division of labor.   Medicine dominated the division of labor in which it worked by controlling both the state institutions which licensed it and related occupations, and by successfully initiating the prosecution of other occupations for unlicensed practice. By the end of the Second World War, many potential competitors had been driven out of the official marketplace. Some, such as dentists and optometrists, were confined to narrowly limited practices; others, such as chiropractors, were restricted to marginal status; and still others, such as nurses, pharmacists, and laboratory technicians, were firmly subordinated, unable to perform their work without authorization by physicians.

Since only physicians could prescribe state-regulated drugs or order the use of diagnostic and treatment technology, both pharmaceutical and medical technology firms were dependent on their goodwill. Given that dependency, those firms, along with hospitals and the insurance industry, were political allies who supported the policy positions of the profession. In the absence of national legislation, the states were the major sources of legislation controlling health affairs, and there well-financed medical associations exercised considerable political influence. Legislative efforts to

1   My key sources are Alford 1975, Blair and Rubin 1980, Brennan and Berwick 1996, Derbyshire 1969, Freidson 1988, Garceau 1941, Gray 1991, Hyde and Wolff 1954, Imershein et al. 1992, Rodwin 1993, Rosenberg 1987, Rothstein 1987, Starr 1982, Stevens 1971 and 1989, and Wolinsky and Brune 1994.

establish national health insurance in the late 1940s were defeated by heavily financed resistance from the American Medical Association, aided by its pharmaceutical and other industrial allies.

The labor market. The labor market for the profession was organized primarily on a local and state rather than a national basis. Characteristically, a medical practice was established through the slow construction of an attractive reputation among patients within a local community as well as mutually supportive referral relations among colleagues dependent on each other's goodwill in local referral networks. The arduous character of that process tended to lock physicians into their communities, since the social and economic cost of leaving and starting a new practice was prohibitive. Outside of large cities, and with the exception of positions in government health programs, medical schools, and a few nationally known practice institutions like the Mayo Clinic, physicians had no other career option but a local practice. This gave local community practitioners considerable power to establish and enforce economic as well as medical norms of practice. Competition for patients was constrained by both professional etiquette and mutual dependence. And in the absence of national licensing boards, county and state medical associations had considerable power to control both the number of physicians admitted to practice and the economic organization of their practice. "Liberal," fee-for-service self-employment was the enforced norm. Collective or group forms of practice were condemned, as was any economic arrangement involving services prepaid by insurance.

The labor market was organized by two institutions. One was individual, fee-for-service general practice with a direct and often long-term relationship with individuals and families. Located in neighborhoods and communities, it was linked by referral relations to specialized practices that were financed and organized the same way, and to private, usually non-profit hospitals. The practice characteristic of the time was completely financed by the patient paying fees out of pocket to the doctor, who decided what fees to charge. Medical or surgical treatment which could not be performed or followed up in private consulting rooms needed the services and facilities of the hospital, which was the second institution organizing the labor market.

The hospital had greatly increased in importance since the 1920s. By the middle of the century it had become the doctor's workshop, administered for the convenience of the physicians of the community and largely controlled by them. Unlike hospitals in many

European countries, which excluded primary care physicians practicing in the community and relied on their own medical staff, in the United States community physicians, both generalists and specialists, provided the services for those they hospitalized. Hospitals were dependent on them as virtually the only source of paying patients. While physicians conducted the bulk of their practice in their private offices, as "attending physicians" they were responsible for diagnosis of their patients in hospital, ordering tests and the like, and performing whatever surgical or medical procedures they deemed necessary. Nurses and other hospital-based personnel (including physicians in training in teaching hospitals) were charged with carrying out their orders for treatment and care.

During this Golden Age, physicians had virtually complete control over the terms, conditions, and content of their work. They were free to charge all that the pockets of their patients could yield and to decide how much charity or free care to provide to whom. In the years following the Second World War, they received the highest average income of any occupation, though within the profession there were marked income differences between generalists and specialists, physicians and surgeons, and practitioners in rural and urban areas. They were free to follow their own clinical judgment, for neither state licensing boards, state medical societies, nor local community colleagues examined their work. Only the most grossly incompetent or negligent behavior led to official disciplinary action. The major source of redress for patient grievances lay in the courts, but the effectiveness of malpractice suits was limited because few physicians could be induced to testify against colleagues, and medical matters themselves were treated by the courts as beyond the comprehension and judgment of lay juries. Furthermore, the courts used as the basis for judging physician performance local medical community standards rather than those advocated in medical schools, textbooks, or by national medical authorities. This meant that forms of treatment that would be frowned upon in one community might be entirely acceptable in another and thus defensible in court.

Professional schooling. The medical degree and the literal and figurative state license attendant on it served as the essential credential required for performing medical work in the labor market. Free-standing, proprietary schools having been successfully shut down in the first quarter of the century, medical education had become firmly attached to universities and (unlike most

European nations, where an academically oriented secondary education alone was required for admission) generally required a four-year college education preceding professional training. The medical faculty was composed largely of physicians, in earlier years often serving part-time while continuing outside practices, but later serving full-time with private practice (and fee-collecting) privileges. Some of the faculty was engaged primarily in clinical teaching, but the most prominent were heavily engaged in research, supported by both public and private funds. Medical schools usually had their own hospitals where their faculty and students could have access to patients who were the major source of fees and also provided the "training material" on which advanced and postgraduate students could hone their skills and "subjects" for clinical research and experimental procedures.

After the Golden Age

The labor force.   During the last third of the twentieth century the virtually ideal-typical professionalism of American medicine was eroded, though it is still probably closer to the ideal type than are all other occupations. Medicine has not lost its pre-eminent position in the official labor force. True, there has been some reduction of its high prestige in the eyes of the general public, but compared to other professions medicine still occupies the highest rank. All American institutions, professional, commercial, and political, have suffered a decline in public respect and confidence since the 1960s. Some loss of public confidence and trust in medicine may stem from the growth of public ambivalence toward scientific medicine itself, something that extends beyond medicine to science in general. It is manifested in greater willingness, even eagerness, to employ purportedly natural, non-medical remedies for everyday ills, an enthusiasm that supports an increasingly large market for food supplements, herbal remedies, and the like whose consumption is neither regulated by the state nor recommended by physicians. It would not be well to make too much of this, however, for while a large segment of the American public now seeks out both "alternative" practitioners and "natural" remedies, the general public continues to flock to physicians in search of well-publicized, newly discovered, or invented remedies and procedures which only physicians have the license to provide. The public has not reduced its consumption of medical resources so much as increased its consumption of non-medical resources and supported the growth and official recognition of some, though hardly all, of that very diverse group of practitioners of alternative medicine.

Division of labor. The growth of support for non-medical practitioners and products to which access is not controlled by physicians has complicated both the health-related division of labor and the capacity of medicine to control it as closely as it did during the Golden Age. While medicine still exercises exclusive command over the central tasks of treatment, a number of new jurisdictions have risen outside it and at least some of the older jurisdictions, the most obvious being chiropractic and acupuncture, have gained wider official recognition (see Saks 1995). Furthermore, remarkable innovations in medical technology and surgical procedures have spawned a greater number of medical specialties and sub-specialties and specialized technicians, both in the hospital and in free-standing treatment centers and laboratories. This increasing complexity has made it considerably more difficult for medicine to dominate and control many of the occupations in the health division of labor.

Part of that complexity and jurisdictional ambiguity has been nourished by pressures created by the massive expansion of health insurance. Previously, consumers paid out of pocket for all their ambulatory care, including what they sought from non-medical practitioners: they made a personal decision to choose and pay for a service. But once health insurance rather than the individual patient paid physicians, consumers who patronized non-medical practitioners, as well as those practitioners' own associations, pressed for extending insurance to their services as well. Obviously, this potential additional cost raises counter-pressures from employers and others who would have to pay for it, but the very existence of third-party payment creates political pressures from consumers, as yet unrecognized practitioners, and their political representatives to expand coverage.

The labor market. The initiation of national health insurance for the elderly in 1968 and the expansion of employer-financed health insurance to a large segment of the working population (the poor and marginal, as usual, being excluded) meant that payment for both physician and hospital services became more reliable than when it was made by individuals. Assured of payment, investment in the provision of services therefore became highly attractive to private parties seeking profit. Once the state had licensed the selling of services by investor-owned enterprises, many for-profit hospitals, clinics, and specialized facilities such as those for kidney dialysis were established. The bureaucratic management of government agencies, private insurance companies, and investor-owned health service facilities came to mediate the relationship between doctor and patient. Although they did not necessarily employ doctors, they gained the power to determine how much the doctor would be paid and for which services. Many physicians have become employees, and virtually all are bound by some sort of contractual agreement with those who pay for their patients' services.

Initially, physician and patient reimbursement claims were honored without serious question, but the extraordinary increase in costs that occurred during the 1970s led to increasingly stringent efforts to restrict coverage and, more importantly, to develop ostensibly objective medical criteria by which to appraise the propriety of paying claims. On their face, such efforts did not limit the freedom of consumers to seek whatever services they wished or of physicians to provide whatever their judgment dictated, but in so far as some services, drugs, and procedures were banished to a "not covered" limbo requiring out-of-pocket payment, they were effectively discouraged unless organized political pressure resulted in their legitimation. Furthermore, contrary to the permissiveness of the past, administrative review of laboratory test results, diagnoses, and procedures was initiated and some form of peer review required. This created significant constraints on the freedom of physicians to do their work however they wished, and replaced the hegemony of local community practitioner standards of practice with national academic standards. With the development of managed care later in the century, administrative control of both patients' and doctors' choices increased, though never without professional legitimation by authoritative research findings and medical opinion.

A number of contingencies were responsible for changes in the medical labor market. First, the political influence of the American Medical Association was seriously weakened. Once federal health insurance had been established for the elderly, the state was forced to become more activist and hierarchical. Both the legislative and executive branches began to take active steps to control the increasing cost to taxpayers and to take some responsibility for the quality of the care paid for by federal programs. Federal agencies staffed largely by physicians and economists were created to do so. Furthermore, the medical profession's legal position changed:

whereas in earlier times the Supreme Court judged medicine and other professions to be something other than trades and therefore not subject to anti-trust legislation, a series of decisions so whittled away its special status that many time-honored, professionally initiated restrictions on advertising, fee-bills, and other economically protective measures were abolished. In the political struggles surrounding this process, the organized medical profession lost much of its previous support. Having very large sums of money at stake, large insurance companies and corporate employers who pay for the health insurance of their employees were not inclined to protect physicians' freedom to order whatever services they thought best and to bill for whatever they had established as the going rate. Members of the public, while wishing to choose their own physicians and obtain whatever services they desired, were less concerned with the position of the profession than with their own freedom to choose, their out-of-pocket expense, and the cost of health insurance premiums.

In addition, corporate and to a lesser degree government interests have been much more free to take political action than has the American Medical Association, which has been riven by conflicting interests among specialties and sub-specialties, primary care and specialized practices, and rural and urban practices. Moreover, the pharmaceutical, medical technology, and hospital industries, once the profession's allies, have found good economic and political reasons to adopt independent, even opposing, positions. In the past, because they were the legal gatekeepers who controlled the consumption of medical products and use of facilities, those industries sought primarily to persuade physicians to prescribe their products, use their technologies, and patronize their facilities. However, once they had gained state regulatory agency permission to do so they began to advertise directly and aggressively to consumers, aiming at minimizing their dependence on physicians as gatekeepers by persuading patients to demand what they want from their physicians. Presumably they believe consumers to be the more easily influenced and physicians likely to give in to their patients' demands.

These important changes in the medical labor market have been greatly stimulated by changes in the ideological winds. Over the past decades the ideology of consumerism has come to dominate policy discourse, supplemented by the ideology of managerialism. Part of the ideology of consumerism asserts that participants in the market are motivated much more by material self-interest than by dedication to service or good work. The unusually large income of physicians during their Golden Age, and well-documented revelations of the economically self-interested activities of professional associations seemed to confirm the truth of the ideology and negate the professional ideology of disinterested service. Aside from that, the strength of economism has been due to the convergence of two separate movements. First, there is the steady growth of neo-conservatism, which denigrates the capacity of the state to deal effectively with social problems of health, welfare, education, and living conditions, emphasizing instead the beneficent outcome of the efforts of individuals and localities to manage their own affairs when free from state interference. This political ideology is closely connected to that of neo-liberal economics, which asserts that individual competition in a free market, freed of state regulation, will lead to a better (or at least more affluent) society. Neo-liberal economics has led to the development of a highly influential school of legal thought called "law and economics" (see Barreto et al. 1984), which created the intellectual foundation for judicial rulings that modified and in some cases reversed earlier court decisions assigning professions a special position in the political economy.[2] Those rulings reduced protection for the profession and increased the freedom of for-profit firms and entrepreneurs to finance, organize, and administer health care. It also lay behind court and state agency policies that reduced constraints on commercial advertising and extended anti-trust restrictions to the actions of professional associations.

Contributing to the strength of the neo-liberal ideology in public policy decisions has been the consumer movement, which opposes professional and other monopolies that limit consumer choice and are thought to keep prices inappropriately high. The two are not entirely compatible, however, for neo-liberal ideologues seek greater freedom from state regulation of the marketplace while consumer advocates, preoccupied with the inadequate and inaccurate information about products and services that is provided in the market, advocate strong state action requiring the provision of full information to consumers, together with the establishment and enforcement of rigorous state standards to prevent fraud and the sale of faulty or dangerous products. In opposition, corporations spend large sums lobbying to protect themselves from legislative and administrative actions that would, they claim, raise prices and restrict the consumer's right of free choice. Their public advocacy

2 My guess is that it was only because Supreme Court justices are themselves lawyers that they do not eliminate all protection of professions from market forces.

of free consumer choice is less an endorsement of the consumer movement than a reflection of their assurance that, if they are freed from regulation, their enormous advertising resources can determine what consumers will choose.

The enthusiasm for these ideologies during the past few decades has seriously weakened the appeal of the professional ideology. The ideology of professionalism challenges the consumer's movement by claiming that ordinary people cannot make their own choices without danger to themselves and that therefore there is no sensible alternative to trusting the professional's judgment; it challenges consumerism by asserting its need for a monopoly in the market; it challenges managerialism by claiming self-direction and the necessity to employ discretionary judgment. But the economically self-interested actions of the profession and its failure to undertake responsibility for assuring the quality of its members' work weakened its claims and appeared to confirm the truth of the assumptions of consumerism and managerialism.

The consequence of the change in financing medical care in conjunction with the massive growth of specialized knowledge and complex technology is that the labor market for medicine changed greatly over the last three decades of the twentieth century. Medical service has of course always been a commodity sold in the marketplace, but in the past its practice was organized into small shops by practitioners who ran their own neighborhood businesses. As late as the 1960s such practice required only a modest capital investment; it was stocked with affordable instruments, a modest support staff, and supplemented by what could be ordered from a pharmacist. Perhaps those simple conditions of traditional liberal practice were what led Marxist analysts until recently to consider professions part of the *petite bourgeoisie*. They were seen only as small shopkeepers, the special character of their work and training that sets them markedly apart from those selling more ordinary goods or services being ignored.

In any case, the development over the past half-century of the discipline's knowledge and technique has created a technology and corpus of skills whose capital and personnel requirements have become far too complex and expensive to be financed and organized by individual practitioners. Independently of the shift from individual to third-party payment, the small shop can no longer accommodate the provision of any but the most modest routine services. Instead, the labor market has come to include a variety of institutions, some bureaucratic in form, some linking together individual practitioners by formal contract, and some collective. However, as the credential from medical school and the legal license to practice continue to be the mandatory prerequisites for entering that labor market, the *profession* may still be said to control it even though individual practice is no longer independent and fixed in a single locality but is increasingly organized by firms.

Professional schooling and research. Medical schools have also felt the impact of changes in the American political economy. First, some of their insulation from the universities with which they are affiliated has been stripped away by scientific advances in the biological sciences and technological developments in engineering and computer science. Whereas during the Golden Age the faculty of medical schools was dominated by physicians, with a few PhDs teaching the science courses of the first years of training, now a growing proportion of faculty members, particularly those engaged in research, do not have medical degrees. The monopoly provided by the MD degree remains an essential prerequisite for those whose research requires access to patients (which sometimes makes physicians mere front men for PhDs), but neither epidemiological research nor that requiring only human blood or tissue is monopolized by physicians. There is thus a weakening of the dominance of physicians within their own schools.

Changes in the credentials of the research faculty in American medical schools are less important for medical control than changes in the financing and direction of research. In earlier decades, medical schools obtained generous financing for their training programs from both state and federal governments. Significant subsidy for research came from cost shifting in the teaching hospitals attached to medical schools, by which some proportion of the fees charged for patient care was allocated to support research and on-site postgraduate medical education. In addition, private foundations supported research on their favorite diseases and disabilities, as did legislatively mandated federal research support programs. More recently, however, proportionately less public support for research has been available, while the cost of doing research has increased. This is making the research programs of medical schools dependent to an unprecedented degree on support by pharmaceutical and privately capitalized, for-profit corporations. Some medical schools have entered into contracts with corporations which agree to finance particular programs of research in exchange for first rights to exploit the economic potential of their findings. In other cases, members of the faculty have left their positions in medical schools to start up their own for-profit research firms as entrepreneurs or to work in laboratories financed by pharmaceutical and other corporations of the health industry.

Of course the financing (and therefore direction) of health-related research has always been selective, its choice of particular disabilities, diseases, and conditions heavily influenced by well-organized political movements and by the personal fears of the wealthy, of influential politicians, and of the affluent middle class. Those forces continue to influence the direction of research, but over the past twenty years the potential for profit has become a much more powerful source of direction, the emphasis being on pharmaceutical, electronic, biogenetic, and other advanced technologies that can be patented. This emphasis on discovering what can be highly profitable is a distinct departure from the past in medicine, when considerations of broad human need and public benefit were more prominent. Furthermore, emphasis on research with immediate practical value to those who can afford to pay for it reduces support for "basic" or "pure" research that can make no short-term promises. Recent evidence suggests that concern for the potential for profit has reduced, or at least slowed, the communication of both theoretical thinking and research findings to the medical/scientific community at large. Increasingly, quite apart from their findings, research designs themselves become commercial trade secrets. Knowledge becomes the private property of capital rather than lodged in the public domain where it is shared by the entire disciplinary community and used for the benefit of all.

Despite this reduction in the strength of professionalism in medicine, we must never forget that in the background there is deep and broad support from both the general public and the state for medicine as a discipline, even if not as an organized profession. The knowledge and skills of medicine are of profound interest to virtually every member of the public, dealing as they do with the truly fundamental human problems of health, disability, and illness. Health rivals and may even surpass sports, sex, and entertainment for attention by the popular media. Health is also of deep concern to states irrespective of their particular policies, for illness and disability are critical handicaps to the maintenance of an effective military and a productive labor force. As De Swaan 1989 and Stone 1984, for example, have shown, and as Parsons (1951: 428–47) has argued on a theoretical basis, the certified diagnosis of illness and disability provides both individuals and the state with a defensible foundation for obtaining and assigning special benefits to segments of the population. Medicalization is as often a process initiated by those desiring the benefits of being classified and treated as ill or disabled as it is the outcome of medical imperialism. (See Broom and Woodward 1996 and Lowenberg and Davis 1994 for recent appraisals of medicalization.) Quite apart from its objective effectiveness in dealing with human ills, the powerful human appeal and the administrative value of medicine for state policy are too important and pervasive to allow one to believe that the status of medicine can decline precipitously. It has hardly lost all control over its work, and its institutions can still be said to resemble those of the ideal type, if less closely at the start of the twenty-first than at the middle of the twentieth century.

The Present Status of Professions

The general changes I have described for medicine are also taking place for the other major professions in the United States. All have suffered some loss of public confidence and trust, and many have come under financial pressure to reduce the cost of their services to consumers and the state, as well as to create and increase financial return to investors in some cases. The academically based sciences, like medical research, have come under tremendous pressure to work on applied problems that can attract extra-academic financing and yield lucrative patents to their university employers. Many academic researchers have been moving outside the university to work in well-equipped and financed corporate research programs whose primary interest is to investigate potentially profitable areas. Others have started their own firms as entrepreneurs.

By contrast, the academically based humanities and social science disciplines are criticized for preoccupation with theoretical rather than practical problems, and for making little effort to communicate with the general public. Some disciplines, such as classical studies, are losing support and shrinking, perhaps even disappearing from some colleges and universities. The professoriate is under attack for what are said to be its politically leftist tendencies, and for neglecting its teaching duties in favor of esoteric scholarship and research that is of interest only to colleagues. The propriety of protection by tenure in universities is being seriously questioned, and in any case is being limited to a shrinking proportion of full-time faculty, while an increasing proportion of teaching is being performed by part-time employees who have little or no security.

Of the major professions, perhaps law has seen the least change, though in some nations its division of labor has been reorganized. Those practicing law dealing with corporate affairs are working in firms and corporate legal departments of increasing size and administrative complexity, which has changed markedly the division of labor and the labor market in which they participate. Furthermore, significant inroads into their jurisdiction are being made by the accounting profession. By contrast, however, personal legal services in the United States (the "hemisphere" of the profession serving individuals and small businesses which Heinz and Laumann [1982] view as virtually a separate profession) retains its traditional form of solo or small partnership practice. Lawyers in those practices now often adopt previously proscribed methods of obtaining clients such as advertising on television and in commercial telephone directories (Seron 1996), and, as they always have, make their living by dealing with fairly routine issues. Still, they have greater freedom in their work than do any of the other major professions today excepting, perhaps, dentists and accountants working outside large firms, both of whom remain independent practitioners, seldom paid by third parties.

The extension of private capital into the domains of the major professions has also been taking place in the other Western industrial nations, though as yet to nowhere near the same degree as in the United States. The unique history and culture of each nation are reflected in the varied character of its professions and their institutions, but I think that the governments of all European nations are losing their capacity and willingness to protect the professions from market forces and to underwrite their services. Since medicine is the greatest source of public expense, it has everywhere been subjected to the greatest pressure to rationalize its services and reduce costs. (For a number of European nations, see e.g. Freddi and Bjørkman 1989.)

An additional source of change for all European professions stems from the efforts of the emerging European Union to remove barriers to the free movement of labor across national boundaries (see Evetts 1999). This has led to the "harmonization" of national credential requirements for the professions and has changed some of the traditional characteristics of professions within their own nations. Jurisdictional boundaries in their division of labor have been altered in some cases, as have the curricula of their training institutions. Excepting engineering, for which there have long been large firms operating internationally, and some large law and accounting firms which have already developed a transnational presence, few professions have moved across national boundaries to practice outside their own nations. Both globalization of investment and production, as well as the development of such entities as the European Union, are certain to stimulate new forms of practice and professional association, though it is much too early for us to be able to do more than note the fertile ground, some of the seeds, and the few seedlings. At this date it is by no means certain that they will germinate, grow vigorously, and displace old growth. Nor, if they do survive, are we in a position today to forecast the character of their mature form.

In order to alter traditional arrangements decisively, the emerging forces I have been discussing must continue to develop at the same pace, in the same direction, and with the same strength for decades in the face of volatile technological, political, and economic circumstances that can shift to discourage any further change in the direction it has taken thus far. Since such development is by no means certain now, at the beginning of the twenty-first century it is possible to raise only highly speculative questions about the future position of professions in national and international labor forces, divisions of labor, labor markets, and intellectual life. What can be asserted with little fear of contradiction is that change cannot affect all professions alike, if only because of the varied contingencies of the work they do. Some cannot escape dependence on large amounts of capital for their work, yet it may make a great difference to their fate whether capital is supplied by the state, or by private investors, or by national or transnational organizations. Some may not have a popular constituency that can be mobilized to provide them with political support separate from capital and the state, while others may. And some may be able to survive independently of state programs and large firms by providing personal services to individual consumers willing to pay out of pocket, even if survival is only at the fringes of their economy and yields only a modest income. In light of these different possibilities, I do not believe that Elliott Krause (1996) is correct in his sweeping conclusion that the guild-like characteristics of the traditional professions will disappear.[3] The very work

3 It is with sympathy rather than derision that I quote from Parsons' superb essay (1968: 546) in which he predicts decline in the powers of both state and capital and the rise of the power of professional expertise: "The professional complex has already not only come into prominence but has even begun to dominate the contemporary scene in such a way as to render obsolescent the primacy of the old issues of political authoritarianism and capitalistic exploitation." Let all prophets beware!

that some professions do provides them with resources to resist total control by capital and the state. Furthermore, I believe that a relatively neglected but decisive factor in the changes I have described is ideological and political rather than economic. I touched on that factor briefly in discussing the changes going on in medicine, but in my final chapter I will concentrate on the ideologies that justify the pressure for change today and suggest the course by which professionalism may be able to strengthen its position.

9

The Soul of Professionalism

How can we make sense of the changes that have been occurring in the position of professions throughout the advanced industrial world? What is their source and what are their consequences for professionalism as a logically distinct way of organizing and controlling work? What, furthermore, can be done by the proponents of professionalism to strengthen their position in the future? These are the questions I shall confront in this final chapter of my book.

Doubtless much of the change taking place in the organization and direction of professional work today is economically inspired and reflects the material interests of both private capital and the state. But it is politics that advances and protects such change, and in politics ideology is a critical factor. Indeed, I believe that the assault on the credibility of the professional ideology has been a major factor in weakening the voice of professions as they seek to influence that change.

I want to begin by examining the substance of the ideological attacks on professionalism that have become very prominent over the past few decades and show that by concentrating on only one aspect of professional institutions they sweep away any serious consideration of other issues which cannot be avoided in a world that is profoundly dependent upon organized bodies of specialized knowledge and technique. I will suggest that the major consequence of their assault is to create an atmosphere of distrust that has weakened the credibility of professional claims to an independent moral voice in evaluating social policies. This strengthens the power of capital and the state to control the use to which professionalized disciplines are put. Contrary to many prophets, I will suggest that the assault on professionalism will not in fact seriously weaken the organization and operation of professional institutions but rather the control over their ends. Finally, I will suggest ways by which the proponents of professionalism may regain some of their credibility and raise an effective third voice for choosing social policies that provide benefit to all.

In order to defend itself, professionalism must have a persuasive rationale that confronts and explains what are ordinarily considered unpleasant truths. One of those truths is that the crux of its institutions, the heart of what must be defended, is its economic privilege. The claim of privilege was at the center of the ideological struggles of the past and remains at the heart of the struggle today. The privilege consists in holding a monopoly over the exclusive right to perform a particular kind of work in the marketplace, thereby creating a labor market shelter. The social instrument which sustains that shelter is a credential testifying to the successful completion of professionally controlled training. *Monopoly and credentialism are the key elements of professionalism's economic privilege.*

Ideological Shibboleths Surrounding Monopoly

The monopoly of professionalism is not over real property, wealth, political power, or even knowledge, but rather over the *practice* of a defined body of intellectualized knowledge and skill, a discipline. It has become difficult to evaluate because the term is frequently used as a shibboleth – that is, a word used as a slogan that lacks real meaning. Thus, in attacking professionalism, critics use the word monopoly stereotypically, the implication being that it serves only one purpose dominated by only one overriding motive. They ignore the fact that the institutions of professionalism are grounded not only in an economy but also in a social enterprise of learning, advancing, and practicing a body of specialized knowledge and skill. The institutions of professionalism organize and advance disciplines by controlling training, certification, and practice on the one hand, and by supporting and organizing the creation and refinement of knowledge and skill on the other. While those institutions do privilege the economic position of professions, critics nearly always overlook the fact that they also privilege the disciplinary coherence of professions in an organized division of labor.

If we assume that the practice of disciplines is worthwhile even when their economic value in the ordinary market is small, as is the case for many of the academic professions, then the problem is how they can be institutionalized so that practitioners can make a living doing their work and developing the formal bodies of knowledge connected with that work. Monopoly provides a solution to this problem. Whether monopoly is enforced by law, administrative regulation, or established custom, it necessarily limits the freedom of consumers by preventing them from hiring anyone they want to do a particular kind of work, restricting their choice to qualified members of the occupation. It also restricts the freedom of workers to offer their services to consumers, for only those who are qualified may do so. Here is where Max Weber's notion of social closure becomes relevant. Invoked most conspicuously by Frank Parkin (1979) in the context of class theory, and later by Raymond Murphy (1988), it refers to the formation of groups which exclude all those who fail to possess some characteristic important to its members. A social closure has broader scope than monopoly, which generally refers to a privileged economic position. It can be based on a variety of criteria – the possession of property, common ancestry, gender, race, in theory almost anything. Its rewards to its members need not be economic but can be cultural, social, or psychological. Collins (1979: 59, 171) refers to groups created by social closure as associational or consciousness communities. The particular social closure of professionalism is based upon competence attested to by the special educational credentials without which one is excluded from membership.

"Monopoly" and "social closure" are almost always used invidiously rather than neutrally or descriptively. Economists consider monopoly to be by definition a conspiracy against consumers, assuming that the primary intent of those who establish it is to keep prices and their own incomes higher than they would be under free competition. Sociologists link social closure, on the other hand, to inequality by the fact that it involves exclusion. Parkin asserts that "all forms of exclusion are exploitative, by *whatever* criteria they are justified" (Parkin 1979: 71, his emphasis), though he does not explain how exclusion is exploitative or whether all criteria for exclusion are exploitative in the same way or to the same degree. Murphy states that "an exclusionary code is by its nature a means of *domination*" (1988: 48, my emphasis), though he does not discuss how a code can be used to dominate the excluded, or whether different codes result in different kinds and degrees of domination. In a Foucauldian mode, Bauman (1987: 19–20) equates dominance with the position of specialized experts upon whose advice or assistance people depend. In all cases, the presumed intent is domination or exploitation.

In evaluating these charges, it is important to remember that they do not apply only to doctors, lawyers, and certified public accountants. They apply also to academic scholars and scientists, who can all be accused of conspiring to maintain a monopoly by restricting practice and teaching to those with the proper academic degrees. By excluding uncredentialled people from university jobs the closure restricts their freedom to teach, let us say, classical Greek, if for some bizarre reason they want to do so. Thus, academicians too can be said to conspire, dominate, and exploit, their aim being to monopolize jobs and their economic rewards.

The assumption that economic self-interest dominates human motivation has a powerful appeal. Even Max Weber (1978: 1000) advanced it when he charged contemptuously that the growing demand for educational credentials by the German bourgeoisie was motivated more by the lucrative careers they provide than by a "thirst for education."[1] He would no doubt have dismissed such students as *Brotstudenten*, an epithet current in his time among the university elite who were preoccupied with *Bildung* as the proper aim of education. Such charges are countered by the professional ideology that the goal of monopoly and exclusive membership is to maintain standards of work performance high enough to assure consumers that those they consult or employ are competent to do the work of the discipline adequately, if not necessarily brilliantly. True, no one can deny that all professions, like all workers, have an economic interest in making what they regard as a good living (though what is considered a good living varies considerably from one profession to another). But the professional ideology also asserts another primary interest – commitment to the quality of work. We can see this commitment clearly in the case of the academic professions in the United States which, more than elsewhere, are subject to strong economic pressures. Their members *do* worry about maintaining the student enrollment which indirectly supports them, but as their administrative supervisors often complain, they worry even more about the theories, concepts, and data that are their primary interest, and about publishing articles in journals which yield no income and are read only by each other. Furthermore, in the interest of improving the quality of their work, they sometimes try to raise standards so as to reduce rather than

---

1 I wonder whether he would have been consistent enough to make the same assumption about the motives of the faculty of German universities.

expand the number of their student consumers, often to the detriment of their economic self-interest.[2] Paradoxically, they are criticized for *not* making any effort to realize any income from their work in the ordinary marketplace.

Interestingly enough, at least a seed of doubt about the motives of professionals was acknowledged by Milton Friedman, neo-liberal ideologue par excellence. He explicitly recognized the possibility that concern for the integrity and quality of practice might figure in professional efforts at monopoly, though he dismissed it as an inappropriate preference for what he called technical rather than economic efficiency. In the end his loyalty to his ideology won out and he concluded that expression of concern for the quality of work is in fact mere rationalization masking self-interest (Friedman 1962: 153). But I would argue that both aims must be acknowledged in evaluating the ideological struggle over professionalism. Concern with preserving and improving the quality of work by establishing and maintaining social closures based on training cannot be waved away.

Monopoly, Social Closure, and Disciplinary Community

One of Adam Smith's most famous and oft-quoted assertions is simply false – that "people of the same trade seldom meet together, even for merriment and diversion, but the conversation ends in a conspiracy against the public, or in some contrivance to raise prices" (Smith 1976a: 144). On the contrary, when people of any trade meet together they are far more likely to talk shop than conspire to improve their economic situation. They are more likely to tell war stories, gossip about colleagues, compare working conditions, and trade new information, theories, and tricks of the trade. Doing the same work creates common intellectual and social as well as economic interests. This seems to be especially true of those who go through a longer than average period of vocational training or schooling, who do relatively complex discretionary work in which they take great interest, and who see their work as a long-term career. If only because of their sunk costs in that extensive training, they become committed to their body of know-

---

2 Of course, by the very nature of the theory a committed ideologue can argue that material self-interest operates there also, though indirectly. Ultimately, there is no way of contradicting such assumptions.

ledge and skill, and wish to advance it and protect its integrity. They do so by forming social closures without which their knowledge and skill cannot become formalized. Their work is institutionalized by the drawing of jurisdictional boundaries so that it can be maintained and cultivated as a coherent, or at least recognizable, discipline. *Without closure there can be no disciplines.*

The development of a specialized body of formal knowledge and skill requires a group of like-minded people who learn and practice it, identify with it, distinguish it from other disciplines, recognize each other as colleagues by virtue of their common training and experience with some common set of tasks, techniques, concepts, and working problems, and are inclined to seek out each other's company, if only to argue with each other. In so far as such a group is what Collins called a "consciousness community" (1979: 58), "formed on the basis of common and distinctive experiences, interests, and resources" (1979: 134), it cannot help but be exclusive. If it did not exclude from membership those who lacked any consciousness of common experience, interest, and commitment, it would be an entirely different kind of group, perhaps not a group at all.

While such a group is exclusive, what may be more important is that it is *inclusive*. The formation of boundaries or exclusive jurisdictions allows members to focus on a common body of formal knowledge and skill, or discipline. Without boundaries, nothing that could be appropriately called even an occupation, let alone a formal discipline, could exist. Those boundaries create a mutually reinforcing *social* shelter within which a formal body of knowledge and skill can develop, be nourished, practiced, refined, and expanded. They create a social environment within which there can well be a great deal of disagreement and debate, but which nonetheless establishes a pale outside of which stand both different disciplinary communities and the public at large. This, after all, is what a division of labor is all about.

Furthermore, without social closures the work of professions may not even survive as distinct disciplines. Consider that in a free market economic survival requires that price competition be central and that work always be calibrated to the demands and desires of consumers. Prices must be kept as low as possible and, in so far as cost is associated with the quality of work, quality must be as low as it can be and still sell. This is what Friedman advocates as economic rather than technical efficiency. However, apart from circumstances in which providers create new consumer needs, economically successful goods and services are those that satisfy what consumers understand, desire, and are interested in. If disciplines could survive at all without shelter, therefore, they would be popularized and lose some if not most of their disciplinary character and value. It is economic monopoly that reduces this necessity for modifying or at least diluting disciplinary knowledge and skill so as to gain a greater resemblance to everyday knowledge.[3]

An economic monopoly also encourages the development and maintenance of a discipline by tempering competition among colleagues. When supply is well calibrated to demand (which is actually empirically rare), a monopoly may assure that all qualified members of the discipline gain at least a modest living. If the qualified compete with each other for work with some economic security assured, competition is less likely to be predatory. This can strengthen a different focus: competition for collegial respect, even acclaim, awarded for the quality of work and for contributions made to the practice and improvement of the discipline. Such competition was what Talcott Parsons (1949) had in mind when he asserted that professionals are just as self-interested and competitive as people in business, but they differ from them by competing for symbolic rewards. That is possible, of course, only if an adequate income can be taken for granted, for while it is true that one does not live by bread alone, it is also true that without bread one cannot live at all. Obviously, if the valuation of collegial honors is high, considerable effort will be expended in employing, refining, and developing the chosen body of knowledge and skill in a way that, as they say, "advances the discipline."

Those using monopoly and social closure as shibboleths with which to attack professions have not looked closely enough at professional institutions (or looked at themselves in their own professions) to see that these practices are more than modes of exploitation or domination: they are also social devices for supporting the growth and refinement of disciplines and the quality of their practice. Historically, most professions achieved social closure during the nineteenth and twentieth centuries. Before then, few organized disciplines could be said to exist, and the discovery and development of new knowledge and techniques rested largely in the hands of admirable but unorganized amateurs. Efforts were scattered and movement slow. Since then, the social closures

---

3 I do not mean to be an apologist for the frequently scandalous consequences of complete protection from public desires and understandings. I mean only to follow the logic of the argument.

embodied in exclusive chairs, schools, departments, societies, and associations have become essential institutions for the systematic application, development, refinement, and expansion of the formal bodies of knowledge and skill that now exist.

Credentialism

As Bridges (1996: 173) noted in his recent review of the literature on credentialism, "much, but not all, of the empirical investigation of educational credentials has been colored by a polemical tone." Credentialism, the device that sustains monopoly and social closure in the professional labor market, has also spawned a shibboleth enabling attacks on professionalism. But a social closure is intended to include only those who have effective command over a defined body of knowledge and skill, so that some method must be used to determine qualifications for admission and the right to practice. The characteristic method of selection for professionalism is the training credential. Its possession earns both inclusion in the ranks of the elect and exclusive right to practices or jobs requiring a defined set of skills.

Without contesting the very general findings of Ivar Berg's *Education and Jobs* (1970) or Randall Collins' (1979) sustained criticism of the indiscriminate role of credentialism in employment, and without considering contemporary controversies over the value of educational testing, one must ask what alternatives to credentialism exist for selecting workers to consult or employ. Trial and error consultation or employment of anyone who offers to perform a particular set of tasks is at the very least expensive in time and money, and in some cases, such as surgery or bridge construction, very risky. Nor is credentialism as vulnerable to the charge of injustice, exploitation, or inefficiency as is the use of such common criteria for employment as kinship, ethnicity, gender, race, sexual orientation, political persuasion, personal recommendations, highly doctored and undocumented résumés or, what is the same thing, attractive advertising. For all its failings, credentialism is far less likely than its alternatives to be an unfair basis for exclusion from particular jobs.

Nonetheless, economists espousing the neo-liberal market ideology are almost automatically opposed to the constraint on freedom of employment that credentialism imposes on the market. A few, such as Kenneth Arrow (1963; see also Akerlof 1970), believe that exception to the rule should be made for services dealing with life-threatening conditions such as those provided by surgeons, if not also physicians in general. Implicitly or explicitly, they accept the professional argument that some kinds of work are too complex or esoteric for the untrained to understand, so that in circumstances where the wrong choice can be fatal, the range of choices must be limited to safe ones. Milton Friedman, however, characteristically wedded to the free market, argues to the contrary that credentialism should not be mandatory because consumers are capable of making choices in their own interest when "the relevant information" is made available to them (Friedman 1962: 149). Full information is of course one of the conditions considered essential for the operation of a truly free market. Only fully informed consumers are effectively equipped to choose among available goods and services in their own best interest. It is admitted that without full information they may be at the mercy of others.

Unfortunately, full information is conspicuously absent for many goods and services in the empirical marketplace. Much of what is available is only the attractively distorted and selected information of commercial advertising. Furthermore, economists have paid little attention to the extremely high transaction costs of time and effort that consumers must pay if they are to shop really carefully in complex and opaque markets. And sometimes choices must be made too quickly for full investigation, as in a medical or legal emergency. Most important is the fact that even if full information were available about much of the work that professionals do now, not even the educated middle class could understand it and make fully informed choices. This is especially the case for the 21 percent of American adults who are functionally illiterate and the additional 25 percent who are marginally illiterate.[4] While it is true, as Giddens noted, that "technical expertise is continuously reappropriated by lay agents as part of their routine dealings with abstract systems, [nonetheless] no one can become an expert . . . in more than a few small sectors. . . . The lay person – and all of us are lay persons in respect of the vast majority of expert systems – must ride the juggernaut" (Giddens 1990: 144–5).

Certainly no one can deny that consumers should be provided with much more complete and reliable information than is avail-

---

4   About 21 per cent of adults, or 40–44 million people, are functionally illiterate, reading at or below a fifth-grade level, according to the US Department of Education's 1993 National Adult Literacy Survey. An additional 25 percent of adults, another 50 million people, are only marginally literate, meaning they cannot understand, interpret, and apply written material to accomplish daily tasks.

able to them at present, and that many will sometimes make good use of some of it. By the same token, it cannot be denied that most of the formal (even if not the tacit) knowledge of present-day disciplines is freely available in textbooks and monographs for anyone inclined to make the considerable effort needed to command it. But it is blind denial of the quantity, complexity, and opacity of present-day specialized knowledge, as well as widespread functional and marginal illiteracy, to assume that consumers need only more information to become competent to make their own unconstrained choices in the marketplace. In light of the large gap between specialized knowledge and the capacity of non-specialists to deal with it intelligently, let alone the massive and sophisticated commercial efforts to manipulate choice, it is sometimes reasonable to restrict consumer choice to credentialled workers. As Dingwall and Fenn (1987: 53) put it, "professional licensure is a theoretical solution to certain organizational problems which are intrinsic to any complex society." It is not the *principle* of professional monopoly based on training credentials that is unjustified and exploitative, but only particular instances where it is either unnecessary or abused. The only reasonable position lies not in damning the principle but in determining where it is both appropriate and reliable, and where it is not.

Elitism

In sum, I believe that the assumptions underlying the invidious uses of the terms monopoly, social closure, or their major instrument, credentialism, cannot survive critical scrutiny. Furthermore, a close look at the circumstances in which complex, fairly abstract bodies of knowledge and skill develop into organized disciplines, and at the social, political, and economic conditions that sustain or discourage their growth, is likely to reveal virtues in social, economic, and political shelters. However, since the professional ideology questions the capacity of consumers to make choices to their own benefit it is often labeled "elitist." This shibboleth reflects a position that Williams (1983: 114–15) describes as "a general opposition to all kinds of social distinction, whether formally constituted or practiced or not." Thus, it is believed that to argue privilege for specialized knowledge deprecates the reliability and validity of everyday or lay knowledge and demeans the capacities of ordinary people.

A number of critics support this argument, which expresses

what, in chapter 5, I called populist generalism. For writers like Ivan Illich (1977), and in more sophisticated though qualified form, Bauman (1987: 19–20) and Frankford (1997), it is anathema that people need defer to the practitioners of complex, specialized knowledge, for this makes them dependent and disables their capacity to manage their own affairs. Thus, by definition experts dominate and exploit others. Conversely, while neoclassical economists would probably avoid the word elitism like the plague, in reality they take a position similar to that of the populists and revolutionary egalitarians who use it freely. Economists do differ from them in that they reason about individual choice based on economic self-interest while populists and egalitarians reason about collective choice on the basis of a common good, yet both base their arguments on similar assumptions about people as consumers and as citizens. Economists assume that consumers have the intrinsic capacity to gather and analyze all market information without special training so that they can in fact make rational choices in their own best interest independently of experts. Populists and radical egalitarians assume that people have an intrinsic human capacity to learn all that is necessary for managing their collective affairs without deference to specialized expertise.

Ideologies invoked to attack the fundamental institutions of professionalism deprecate claims of exclusive cognitive authority on the part of those creating and practicing a discipline. Implicitly they deny that specialized bodies of knowledge and skill are any more reliable or valid than everyday knowledge. The epithet "elitist" expresses that denial and colors it with the charges of inequality, exploitation, domination, and injustice. However, not only today but in any time or place, surely a large proportion of specialized knowledge is more reliable and valid than everyday or popular knowledge. True inequality of knowledge and judgment in specialized affairs exists by virtue of the very existence of a division of labor. Those who have had intensive training and then work full-time at a specialty can hardly fail to know more about that work than others.

But such inequality is not unjust, as would be inequality based on race, gender, or other criteria. Nor does such inequality necessarily provide justification for political or economic inequality. According to Benn, "Aristotle's celebrated account of justice in Book III of the *Ethics* amounts to this: no distinction ought to be made between men who are equal *in all respects relevant to the kind of treatment in question*, even though in other (irrelevant) respects they may be unequal" (Benn 1967: 39, his italics). The ideology of professionalism argues that expertise properly warrants special influence in certain affairs because it is based on sustained systematic thought, investigation, or experiment, and in the case of individuals, accumulated experience performing specialized work for which they had long and appropriate training. Serious appraisal of that claim is avoided by invoking the shibboleth of elitism. It turns us away from considering the real problems surrounding the role of specialized knowledge in human affairs. Such knowledge exists and is indispensable in present-day societies, so that institutional arrangements which will protect and nourish it as well as prevent its abuse are essential. Of course, some disciplines may indeed deserve no deference or privilege, and some of the content of every discipline may indeed be false, unreliable, or unduly inflated in importance. To recognize that, however, does not justify sweeping away all specialized knowledge and rejecting all cognitive authority.

I believe that some version of monopoly cannot be avoided, nor can credentialism or expert authority. They are essential for the nurturance of specialized knowledge. The real issue is not whether those institutions should exist, but what are their proper limits and the uses to which they should be put. They are certainly subject to abuse and have in fact been abused to some degree by the professions. But they are not, as the assault by shibboleths charges, merely masks for self-interest and illegitimate power. They play a legitimate role in protecting valuable specialized knowledge and providing the means by which it can be developed and practiced well. But while the shibboleths assaulting professionalism are mostly empty rhetoric, they have succeeded nonetheless in increasing public suspicion of professionalism and weakening the credibility of its claim to have more than a material interest in its work. This has strengthened the power and increased the legitimacy of the ideologies of consumerism and managerialism that underlie the activities of both capital and the state. It has also liberated many individual professionals from the ideology of service, freeing them to devote themselves to single-minded efforts to maximize their own incomes.

But if that rhetoric has weakened the credibility of the professional ideology, it has barely weakened the institutions it has attacked. The institutions of professionalism remain largely intact because complex, esoteric knowledge and skill is difficult to organize in any other way than by some kind of protective monopoly and expert authority. Agents of both capital and the state recognize the value of monopoly for preserving the coherence of disciplines, of credentialism for providing a convenient and reasonably accurate way of identifying competence, and above all of the practical value of professional knowledge. Consequently, they have no inclination to make serious changes in the institutions of professionalism. The net effect of the assault on professionalism by the shibboleths of monopoly, credentialism, and elitism, therefore, has only been to weaken its credibility with the public, and its capacity to fend off the pressures of capital and the state.

Professional Privilege in the Future

What is the likely outcome of this situation? I assume that the aim of both state and capital, each in its own way, is to reduce the cost and the independence of professional services. If we make the shaky assumption that the policies of the state and organized private capital will continue to move in the same direction and at the same pace as in the recent past, and that the ideologies of consumerism and managerialism will continue to be the dominant sources for legitimizing change, then we can make some reasonable guesses about the way the institutions of professionalism and the practice of disciplines will change in the future. In doing so, however, we must remember that change will certainly not be uniform because the balance between state activism and the power of private investment capital varies in different nations and times, as do the needs and tactics of each. And it will not be exactly the same for every profession because of differences in the contingencies of their knowledge. But though changes will differ from place to place, they are likely to differ only in degree, not in substance.

First, we can assume that recent jurisdictional boundaries will be altered by reassigning many now professional tasks to less qualified workers, a process that was common long before recent events. This does not mean that professionals will be stripped of all their tasks, however, for some traditional ones are likely to remain part of their jurisdiction and newly invented ones based on new knowledge will probably be added. There is no reason to assume that all teaching, health care, legal counseling and advocacy, accounting, and other professional activities will be reduced to semi-skilled work. The worst and not unlikely possibility is that professionals will be slowly transformed into especially privileged technical workers. This is what is implied by Brint's (1994) careful analysis of the changes that have been taking place in the political positions of American professions. He believes that professionals, once considered trustees of socially important knowledge designed to contribute to the public good and servants of values transcending the immediate and practical, are on a course of changing into neutral technical experts. This is also implied by Abbott's (1991b) analysis both of the commodification of some expert knowledge and, more important, of the way the professions are being drawn into organizations where they become well-paid workers of high status who exercise a relatively large degree of independence, but only within boundaries, channels, and goals carefully established by their employers.

Greater control by capital and the state over both performance and cost is likely to be gained in part by intensifying the trend toward a two-tier professional system composed of a permanent, relatively small elite corps of professionals who do research and set standards of performance in practice organizations and an often floating population of qualified practitioners who may be employed on a temporary and sometimes part-time basis. This pattern is similar to what Doeringer and Piore (1971) observed in industrial firms, where there was a primary or core sector of relatively permanent employees with stable careers and benefits and a transient, poorly paid secondary sector. The division of labor associated with this is likely to be one in which the transient professionals will be generalists, performing comparatively routine but nonetheless fully professional, discretionary tasks demanding conceptualization and theory. More specialized and complex tasks will be performed by the permanent cadre of professionals.

Employing organizations are likely to intensify efforts to standardize the work of rank-and-file professionals in order to reduce their cost and better control and supervise them. Standardization of work in universities, for example, can occur by mandating standard syllabi and examinations for courses taught by part-time instructors, or in health-care organizations by establishing standard protocols for primary care examination, treatment, and referral. Such standardization is certain to require legitimation by using authoritative professional knowledge, some of it formulated by the professional cadre of the organization which is familiar with its special needs, others by national cognitive elites empowered to create binding rules to govern the work of practitioners. Purely administrative procedures designed to control costs and standardize management can, of course, be formulated and enforced by lay managers of the employing firms or state agencies.

If jurisdictions and jobs are reorganized in the way I suggest, professional monopoly over particular tasks is certain to be preserved. Credentialism is also likely to remain the primary mechanism for entering and moving through the labor market. In the case of previously professional tasks which have been reassigned to workers of more modest status, there may be less reliance on credentials and more on training by firms themselves, though most firms are likely to prefer that training costs be borne by the state or by individual workers. It is likely that the increasing technical needs of both state agencies and private firms will lead to the burgeoning of educational policies resembling the German model, in which training programs are shaped by close collaboration between industry and school. This will of course reduce though not eliminate the power of school faculties and professional associations to formulate training and research programs according their own criteria and disciplinary interests.

Disciplinary control of professional training is likely to narrow, therefore, though as in the case of the other institutions of professionalism, it will hardly disappear. I have no doubt that the faculty will remain composed primarily of credentialled professionals, but the curricula they create and administer will have to respond more than previously to the demand for practical training, equipping students to perform the particular tasks required by employers after matriculation. The period of time required for the completion of some curricula may be reduced, becoming less expensive and broad, more specialized and narrow. Some of the humanistic disciplines which have no clear vocational value may not survive at all, and those that do will be pressed by students to be entertaining. Neither "pure" or "disinterested" research and scholarship which follows out the logic of abstract questions raised by theory nor idle curiosity will be forbidden in principle, but in the scientific disciplines their prominence is likely to be discouraged by shrinking support and respect. The scholarly disciplines would be less handicapped than the scientific disciplines by the absence of generous financial support, yet given the increasing influence of commercialized popular culture and, especially in the United States, the decline of economic and political elites who value traditional high culture, it is possible that even basic institutional support may be lost and some of their practitioners may become, once again, amateurs. The educational climate created by strong emphasis on practical service to profitable private investment or the state or on relevance to mass popular culture will probably make universities and professional schools less hospitable to faculty members who devote themselves to clarifying and extending the traditional intellectual problems of their disciplines, and to debating moral and intellectual goals.

I believe that should current trends continue without pause, subject to no strong countervailing forces,[5] professionals will indeed become merely technical experts in the service of the political and cultural economy. Still, they are likely to continue to be called professionals and their occupations called professions in English-speaking nations; their official status in the labor force is likely to remain high; they will continue to dominate some but not all other occupations in their particular division of labor; their labor market shelters are also likely to remain, and while their average incomes may be somewhat lower than they are today, they will still be high compared to those of others in the labor force.[6] Support for disciplines will be limited to those specialties or fields of expertise which are thought to have economic or political value or those which contribute to commercialized popular culture. Within each individual profession, the gap in income between rank-and-file practitioners and the elite in supervisory, cognitive, and consulting specialist positions is almost certain to become greater, as will tension and possibly conflict between them, but all will remain recognizable "professionals."

Such changes will have three major consequences. First, the quality of service to individual clients will change due to the minimization (though certainly not the elimination) of discretion in everyday disciplinary work. This will reduce the satisfaction of "line" practitioners with their work, particularly those who are part-time and transient. Consumers will sense perfunctory, bureaucratic service because their individual problems or needs will be forced into standardized administrative and epidemiological molds to be dealt with by predetermined methods; this may lead to the increased use of alternative practitioners.[7] Second, emphasis

5   The current rebirth of nationalism, ethnic identity, and religious fundamentalism is a contingency that could have profound effects on changes in education and especially research and teaching in the humanistic disciplines.
6   What is often overlooked in discussing the income of the professions is the importance of the *range* of income. Professions are likely to have a wider range of income than most other occupations, excepting those that have ambiguous titles like "manager." The range for law in the United States is especially wide, and the range for medicine much wider than the popular stereotype of rich doctors would lead us to suppose.
7   The paradox here is that the more "alternative," "lay," or "paraprofessional" workers are used, the more likely is it that they will become regulated. This is especially the case if they desire officially recognized and approved status, and

on service to the practical needs of the state, the discovery and development of profitable goods and services by private capital, and satisfaction of what the public believes to be its needs may restrict and narrow the direction of the development of knowledge by limiting it to what is presently known and believed and what can be anticipated by the passive projection of trends. No one can predict what may be lost when idle curiosity and purely theoretical interest are discouraged, but it could be substantial. Finally, and most importantly for the professionalized disciplines, if the activities of members become wholly organized around immediately practical service, they will have lost the spirit of ideal-typical professionalism. Their protective economic institutions will have survived, if in somewhat attenuated form, but they will have lost what has provided them with something more than technical authority. Serving only immediate political, economic, and popular interests cripples both the intellectual development of disciplines and their distinctive moral position that considers the use of their knowledge in light of values that transcend time and place. Should that occur, the character of their responsibility and their relationship to their societies will have gone through a momentous change.

In all, because those in power understand that productivity and profit depend on protecting disciplines from the everyday market and administrative forces to which most workers are subject, the occupations labeled professions in some Western industrial nations are likely to remain privileged. They will continue to exercise greater control over their work than most occupations because, with some exceptions, both capital and the state have found no other way to organize their work. What is likely to be most at risk for the professions is their freedom to set their own agenda for the development of their discipline and to assume responsibility for its use. Thus, the most important problem for the future of professionalism is neither economic nor structural but cultural and ideological. The most important problem is its soul.

Trust and Ethics

I have emphasized again and again that professionalism is based on specialized bodies of knowledge and skill that have no coercive power of their own but only what may be delegated to them by

---

compensation from third-party funds. I might also predict that the better established they become, the less accommodating they will be to their clientele.

the state or capital. They gain their protected status by a project of successful persuasion, not by buying it or capturing it at the point of a gun. They must persuade others that the discipline is of special value either to the public at large or to an important interest of the state or an influential elite. But because of the special nature of the knowledge and skill imputed to professionals as well as the fact that their practice is protected, friendly commentators have long invoked the need to trust their intentions. Adam Smith himself defended the privileged position of professions on the ground that the nature of their work requires trust. (See Dingwall and Fenn 1987 for a discussion of Smith's position. On trust more generally, see examples in Barber 1983, Shapiro 1987, Dasgupta 1988, Veatch 1991, and Seligman 1997.) There is a long tradition of observers who claim that professionals place the good of the client, the public, or the development of a discipline over their own economic self-interest (see the reviews and discussions of altruism by such varied writers as Merton and Gieryn 1982, Haskell 1984, Elster 1990, and Frankford 1997).

Apart from the assumption of good intentions, the increasing complexity of specialized knowledge and skill as well as the problems entailed in their practice has led to an enormous growth in the attention given to the way intentions are translated into action in the various professions – attention, that is, to ethics. Editorials in professional journals and public addresses by officers of various professional associations call for greater concern with ethics, and professional ethics has become a special topic for philosophers (for example, Kultgen 1988; Sullivan 1995). Critics deplore instances of unethical behavior by professionals, whether the exploitation of patients (see Wolinsky and Brune 1994 and Rodwin 1993 for American medicine), of research subjects, law clients, students, or junior faculty. In medicine, previously unimaginable possibilities made available by advanced technologies and techniques have produced complex problems in decision-making that have spawned the specialty of medical ethics in academic philosophy (see Pellegrino et al. 1991) and full-time careers for some in medical institutions. Formal codes of ethics have been written for some disciplines for the first time, while for others they have been greatly revised and expanded. They aim not at creating manuals of administrative procedure, or regulations embodied in law, but at providing guidance for practitioners by clarifying the ethical issues arising in their work.

Part of the purpose of such codes is without doubt to persuade the public that the formulation of ethical standards justifies trust.

In addition to that, however, they provide practitioners with considered opinions, sometimes very detailed and systematic, about the ethics of actions taken in the course of their work. The general principles underlying such codes are not much different from those of everyday life, for they proscribe lying, cheating, stealing, exploiting others, killing, and other sins familiar to us all. But while in everyday life the Ten Commandments and civil and criminal codes may be sufficient guide, for professions there is a genuine problem of determining how they apply to the special circumstances surrounding their specialized practices. To take a comparatively simple issue, while one might believe that lying is wrong, is it wrong for a physician to honor the request of a patient with a fatal but not immediately disabling condition that her family be lied to about her condition until final arrangements must be made? And while one might agree that it is wrong to fail to give people credit for their work, what kind of authorship credit, if any, is appropriate for those who work in different capacities on a research project? Sensitive answers to those questions cannot be given by lay people unfamiliar with the variety of circumstances and issues involved in the practice of a discipline. Only when that concrete, specialized context is taken into account can the ordinary moral norms of daily life be translated into the ethics of practice.

The largest part of professional codes of ethics performs that translation function, dealing with the use of specialized skills in circumstances not familiar to lay people but involving familiar sins. Perhaps the most important of them for the legitimation of professional institutions are those which deal with circumstances of work in which the possibility of conflict of interest exists. This is a critical test of professionalism in that in order to justify a monopoly over practice it must be assumed that it will not be used for selfish advantage. In order to create and sustain trust, therefore, it is essential that codes of ethics specify in detail and condemn all those actions and circumstances in which the privileged position of practitioners is employed to generate profit beyond the value of the work that is performed. The nature of the work of some disciplines – law and accounting, for example – provides a great many opportunities for conflict of interest – but all disciplines provide some.

However, I want to emphasize that if professionals mean to lay successful claim to independence of judgment and action and justify trust in that independence, the formulation of codes of ethics is not adequate by itself to allay public suspicion. Codes may guide those practitioners who wish to have guidance, but they are mere rhetoric if they are not vigorously (though sensitively) enforced. While some ethical issues involve the violation of law, many others involve violations of trust that are not, perhaps cannot, be taken to law, so no code of ethics can mean much if it is not supported by professional institutions that undertake both the vigorous investigation of violations and whatever corrective action is finally deemed appropriate. The conspicuous absence of activities conscientiously enforcing professional codes of ethics in all the advanced industrial nations has contributed to the credibility of the intellectually impoverished shibboleths that are used to attack professional privilege and to the general decline in trust. If professionalism is to be reasserted and regain some of its influence, it must not only elaborate and refine its codes of ethics but also strengthen its methods of adjudicating and correcting their violation.

Institutional Ethics

Without intending to demean that component of professional codes which guides and judges the conduct of professional practitioners at work and which in another paper (Freidson 1999b) I called "practice ethics," I suggest that it may not be the most essential part of professional ethics. Practice ethics deal with the problems of work that are faced by individual practitioners, addressing ethical issues familiar to everyone but which have assumed exotic guises that need sorting out and recognizing. Institutional ethics are rather different. They deal with the economic, political, social, and ideological circumstances which *create* many of the moral problems of work. The issues with which they are concerned include the way practice itself is financed, administered, and controlled in the concrete places where professionals work, and the social policies which establish and enforce the broader legal and economic environment within which practice takes place. Institutional ethics are concerned with the moral legitimacy of the policies and institutions that constrain the possibility to practice in a way that benefits others and serves the transcendent value of a discipline. They are animated by moral concern for the ultimate purpose of disciplines. It is the institutional ethics of professionalism, not the practice ethics, that have been most seriously undermined by the assault on professionalism, and it is particularly institutional ethics that must be re-examined and forcefully asserted if the professions are to be more than well-paid technical experts. The freedom to judge and choose the ends of work is what animates the institutions of the third logic. It expresses the very soul of professionalism.

The ideology of professionalism asserts above all else devotion to the use of disciplined knowledge and skill for the public good. Individual disciplines are concerned with different aspects of that good, in some cases the immediate good of individual patients, students, or clients, in others of firms and groups, and in others the general good. But such service must always be judged and balanced against a still larger public good, sometimes one anticipated in the future. Practitioners and their associations have the duty to appraise what they do in light of that larger good, a duty which licenses them to be more than passive servants of the state, of capital, of the firm, of the client, or even of the immediate general public.

The proponents of professionalism must necessarily exercise a strong, principled voice both in broad policy-making forums and in the communities where practice takes place. This voice cannot be left to individuals, however, for the most influential source of evaluation and protest comes from a collegial body which provides authoritative support to individuals and expresses forcefully the collective opinion of the discipline. Because some practice arrangements may prevent professionals from providing their services to all who may benefit from them, it is appropriate to declare social policies which deny equal access to such services as health care, education, legal defence, and education to be professionally unethical. It should also be declared unethical for practice institutions to provide working conditions that prevent the performance of good work – conditions such as over-heavy caseloads and inadequate space, equipment, and support personnel. Such conditions clearly provide ethical justification for collective public action against practice organizations, though whether or not issues of compensation do is moot.

The administrative policies of practice organizations bring up the matter of the relation of professionalism to the hierarchical control and standardization of procedure and production that is generic to ideal-typical bureaucracy and is advanced by the power of the state and of large private firms. Fully realized, ideal-typical bureaucracy is intrinsically at odds with professionalism, since its aim is to reduce discretion as much as possible so as to maximize the predictability and reliability of its services or products. True, like the fluid and free competition of the ideal-typical market, bureaucracy does have its own positive virtues as a corrective to inappropriate or irresponsible discretion. However, when its logic is fully developed in dealing with professional tasks that require discretion based on schooled knowledge as well as experience, it transforms those tasks and in the course of doing so transforms their outcome. Where service is being provided to individual humans in need, standardization runs the risk of degrading the service to some and failing to serve appropriately those who fall outside the norm. Where research and development are involved, rational-legal administration may gain its immediate ends but, due to its constraints, point nowhere further than management can imagine. Unanticipated knowledge will be lost. The institutional ethics of professionalism should suggest ways in which disciplinary practice can be organized so as to maximize the use of responsible and accountable discretion, assuring the virtues of rational-legal bureaucracy while restraining its vices.

On a broader level, the ideological assertion of economism that the primary purpose of work is to maximize personal gain should be viewed as a frontal assault on professionalism. It should be declared unethical for professionals, whether self-employed or employed, to aim at maximizing gain at the expense of the quality of their work and the broadest possible distribution of its benefits. It should also be considered unethical to invest capital in professional services with the aim of maximizing returns on profit. When maximizing gain is the dominant goal, attention and effort are directed toward the most profitable activities and away from the less profitable, whatever their benefit to others. When work is organized by the free market, the maximization of gain follows from its logic, but because professional work is sheltered from ordinary market processes, maximizing gain is clearly a violation of the terms legitimizing that shelter. There can be no ethical justification for professionals who place personal gain above the obligation to do good work for all who need it, even at the expense of some potential income. The strengthening of the legitimacy of professionalism requires clear recognition of the ethical implications of professional privilege and strong resistance to institutional arrangements for practice which emphasize economic incentives over others. Of course, it is not profit itself which is unethical, for all workers must gain a living: it is the *maximization* of profit that is antithetical to the institutional ethics of professionalism, as is a political economy which protects and stimulates it.

The free market emphasis on maximizing profit is especially destructive of professionalism when portions of the specialized knowledge and skill of disciplines become proprietary, when they become private property withheld from others until a fee or "rent" is paid to the owner. It is even more destructive when knowledge or technique is withheld as a legally defined and protected trade secret rather than becoming part of the common body of knowledge held by all practitioners. Secrecy is anathema to the growth of knowledge and technique, preventing independent testing and validation by others, creating a destructive and divisive form of collegial competition and, most important of all, preventing those not privy to the trade secret from providing its benefits to their clients. In professionalism, the knowledge and skill of disciplines have not been private property, nor closely held. They may be opaque and masked in jargon, but they have been publicly available to all who wish to learn and understand. More particularly, they have been available to all practitioners, not withheld one from another for competitive advantage as has sometimes occurred in the past. While there may be some occasions when secrecy is legitimate, the very principle endangers professionalism and its values, and can easily become grossly unethical.

More complex and difficult to appraise, but perhaps even more important because of its enormous growth toward the end of the twentieth century, is the conversion of knowledge and skill into intellectual property, patented or copyrighted and exploited for maximum profit so that practitioners cannot use it to benefit those they serve without someone paying for the privilege. Making private property of knowledge and skill attacks the fundamental assumptions and aims of professionalism. It should be vigorously and unremittingly opposed, for it means impoverishing the public domain of knowledge and skill that is freely available for all. Taking professionalism seriously requires critical examination of the very concept of private property and the promulgation of an institutional ethic that resists, even attempts to reverse, its extension into the fruits of disciplinary endeavors. Property rights are not "natural": they are established by social and political decisions and cannot be sustained without support by the state. Just as in times past political and legal decisions freed blacks, women, and children from the chains of ownership, so can they free knowledge.

It is true that the matter of intellectual property should not be oversimplified, for those whose disciplinary work has created valuable knowledge and technique and those who financed them are entitled to economic reward as well as honor. In considering the appropriate level of reward, however, it must be kept in mind that effective property rights depend upon protection by the state.

Were this not the case for copyrights and patents, competitors in a free market would quickly infringe them. As in professionalism, therefore, there can be no justification for taking advantage of that protection by maximizing profit. The exclusive right to sell, like the exclusive right to practice, is a privilege easily subject to abuse. The ethical principle governing it should be that profits from such property shall be properly controlled and limited. Beyond that broad principle, there are knotty but by no means insoluble issues of detail. It may be that some things, such as genes, should never be allowed to become private property at all and that others can be, but under limited circumstances. The amount and kind of reward appropriate for the discovery and development of new knowledge is debatable, as is the length of time a patent or copyright protecting its economic exploitation should hold before it is required to become part of the public domain freely available for all. These are not merely economic and legal issues, but also fundamental ethical issues for professionalism.

The Soul of Professionalism

In this concluding chapter I have analyzed and then discarded the criticism of professions that has become increasingly common over the past few decades. I do not deny the more than occasional truth of that criticism nor that there is a need to make professional institutions more honest, but it fails to deal with the central problem: how to nurture and control occupations with complex, esoteric knowledge and skill, some of which provide us with critical personal services, others with functional knowledge without which much of our standard of living could not exist, and others with enlightenment without which we would be culturally impoverished. The criticism has succeeded in weakening the credibility of the professional ideology, which has made the institutions that support the professions more vulnerable to market and bureaucratic forces and less able to resist their pressure toward the maximization of profit and the minimization of discretion. Still, those institutions remain and professionals retain their special position, though somewhat modified. What *has* been seriously undermined is what I believe to be much more important – the ideology that claims the right, even the obligation, of professionals to be independent of those who empower them legally and provide them with their living.

The functional value of a body of specialized knowledge and

skill is less central to the professional ideology than its attachment to a transcendent value that gives it meaning and justifies its independence. By virtue of that independence members of the profession claim the right to judge the demands of employers or patrons and the laws of the state, and to criticize or refuse to obey them. That refusal is based not on personal grounds of individual conscience or desire but on the *professional* grounds that the basic value or purpose of a discipline is being perverted. For example, the codes of ethics of national and international medical associations declare it unethical for a physician to act as an executioner of convicted criminals condemned to death by the state. Those codes do not declare that capital punishment is unethical or that physicians as individuals are all opposed to it, but rather that the deliberate use of the specialized knowledge and skill of medicine for killing subverts its ethical purpose to heal, give relief, or, in the traditional injunction attributed to Hippocrates, above all to do no harm. Ethical physicians would refuse to participate in what is an entirely legal state-mandated execution because it is a perverse use of their skill. Their personal opinion about such punishment is entirely irrelevant to their professional obligation. As we saw in chapter 6, it was primarily the inability or unwillingness of professionals in Nazi Germany and the Soviet Union to exercise that independence which justified considering them deprofessionalized. It was not any decisive interference with their immediate control over their work or any significant change in the institutions that sustained their position. Professional ethics must claim an independence from patron, state, and public that is analogous to what is claimed by a religious congregation.

This conclusion may seem extravagant when attached to the average weary professional who puts in many more hours a week than most other workers, who has become accustomed to a standard of living and a level of respect that are becoming increasingly difficult to sustain, and whose workload constantly presses toward routinization, the cutting of corners, and the loss of any pleasure from work. Give or take here or there, that is the condition of all of us who work. But those with the status of professions in advanced industrial nations are still in a position of symbolic as well as economic privilege. It is no accident that for well over a century in the iconography of popular media it is professionals who are the "crusaders" seeking Justice, Health, Truth, and Salvation. While it is common to see physicians and lawyers, scientists and professors, and sometimes journalists and politicians, in that principled role one does not see bankers, stockbrokers, or business executives.[8] There is, then, still some popular foundation for the professional's claim of license to balance the public good against the needs and demands of the immediate clients or employers. Transcendent values add moral substance to the technical content of disciplines. Professionals claim the moral as well as the technical right to control the uses of their discipline, so they must resist economic and political restrictions that arbitrarily limit its benefits to others. While they should have no right to be the proprietors of the knowledge and technique of their disciplines, they are obliged to be their moral custodians.

<hr />

8   It is true that in popular iconography one finds doctors, lawyers, scientists, and professors in very unflattering roles as well, but it is extremely rare to find stockbrokers, business executives, bankers, and others connected with commerce in any flattering roles at all.

References

Abbott, A. 1988: *The System of Professions: An Essay on the Division of Expert Labor*. Chicago: University of Chicago Press.

Abbott, A. 1991a: The order of professionalization: an empirical analysis. *Work and Occupations*, 18, 355–84.

Abbott, A. 1991b: The future of occupations: occupations and expertise in the age of organization. *Research in the Sociology of Organizations*, 8, 17–42.

Abel, R. L. 1989: Comparative sociology of legal professions. In Abel, R. L. and Lewis, P. S. C. (eds), *Lawyers in Society*. Volume 3, *Comparative Theories*. Berkeley: University of California Press, 80–153.

Abel, R. L. and Lewis, P. S. C. (eds). 1989: *Lawyers in Society*. Volume 3, *Comparative Theories*. Berkeley: University of California Press.

Akerlof, G. A. 1970: The market for "lemons": quality uncertainty and the market mechanism. *Quarterly Journal of Economics*, 84, 488–500.

Alford, R. 1975: *Health Care Politics*. Chicago: University of Chicago Press.

Alston, P. L. 1969: *Education and the State in Tsarist Russia*. Stanford: Stanford University Press.

Althauser, R. P. 1989: Internal labor markets. *Annual Review of Sociology*, 15, 143–61.

Althauser, R. and Appel, T. 1996: Education and credentialing systems, labor market structure and the work of allied health occupations. In Kerkhoff, A. C. (ed.), *Generating Social Stratification: Toward a New Research Agenda*. Boulder, CO: Westview Press, 223–55.

Althauser, R. P. and Kalleberg, A. L. 1981: Firms, occupations and the structure of labor markets: a conceptual analysis. In Berg, I. (ed.),

Sociological Perspectives on Labor Markets. New York: Academic Press, 119–49.

Anderson, M. J. 1988: *The American Census: A Social History.* New Haven: Yale University Press.

Anthony, P. D. 1977: *The Ideology of Work.* London: Tavistock Publications.

Applebaum, H. 1992: *The Concept of Work, Ancient, Medieval and Modern.* Albany, NY: SUNY Press.

Archer, M. S. 1979: *Social Origins of Educational Systems.* Beverly Hills: Sage Publications.

Arendt, H. 1959: *The Human Condition: A Study of the Central Dilemmas Facing Modern Man.* Garden City, NY: Doubleday Anchor.

Arkell, J. 1999: International engineering practices: adapting to multiple jurisdictions. *International Review of Sociology,* 9, 101–15.

Armytage, W. H. G. 1961: *A Social History of Engineering.* London: Faber & Faber.

Aronson, R. L. 1991: *Self-Employment: A Labor Market Perspective.* Ithaca, NY: Cornell University Press.

Arrow, K. 1963: Uncertainty and the welfare economics of medical care. *American Economic Review,* 53, 941–73.

Attewell, P. 1990: What is skill? *Work and Occupations,* 17, 422–48.

Auerbach, J. S. 1971: Enmity and amity: law teachers and practitioners, 1900–1922. *Perspectives in American History,* 5, 551–601.

Auerbach, J. S. 1976: *Unequal Justice: Lawyers and Social Change in Modern America.* New York: Oxford University Press.

Balzer, H. D. (ed.). 1996: *Russia's Missing Middle Class: The Professions in Russian History.* Armonk, NY: M. E. Sharpe.

Barber, B. 1983: *The Logic and Limits of Trust.* New Brunswick, NJ: Rutgers University Press.

Barley, S. R. and Orr, J. E. (eds). 1997a: *Between Craft and Science: Technical Work in U.S. Settings.* Ithaca, NY: Cornell University Press.

Barley, S. R. and Orr, J. E. 1997b: Introduction: the neglected workforce. In Barley, S. R. and Orr, J. E. (eds), *Between Craft and Science: Technical Work in U.S. Settings.* Ithaca, NY: Cornell University Press, 1–19.

Barreto, H., Husted, T. A., and Witte, A. D. 1984: Review essay: The new law and economics: present and future. *American Bar Foundation Research Journal,* 253–66.

Bauman, Z. 1987: *Legislators and Interpreters: On Modernity, Post-Modernity and Intellectuals.* Cambridge: Polity Press.

Becker, H. S. 1970: *Sociological Work: Method and Substance.* Chicago: Aldine Publishing Company.

Becker, H. S. 1982: *Art Worlds.* Berkeley: University of California Press.

Becker, H. S. 1998: *Tricks of the Trade: How to Think About Your Research While You're Doing it*. Chicago: University of Chicago Press.

Becker, H. S. et al. 1960: *Boys in White: Student Culture in Medical School*. Chicago: University of Chicago Press.

Belitsky, A. H. 1969: *Private Vocational Schools and their Students*. Cambridge, MA: Schenkman.

Bell, D. 1976: *The Coming of Post-Industrial Society*. New York: Basic Books.

Benavot, A. et al. 1991: Knowledge for the masses: world models and national curricula, 1920–1986. *American Sociological Review*, 56, 85–100.

Ben-David, J. 1971: *The Scientist's Role in Society: A Comparative Study*. Englewood Cliffs, NJ: Prentice-Hall.

Ben-David, J. 1976: Science as a profession and scientific professionalism. In Loubser, J. J. (ed.), *Explorations in General Theory in Social Science: Essays in Honor of Talcott Parsons*. New York: The Free Press, 874–88.

Benn, S. I. 1967: Equality, moral and social. In Edwards, P. (ed.), *The Encyclopedia of Philosophy*, vol. 3. New York: Macmillan and The Free Press, 38–42.

Berezin, M. 1991: The organization of political ideology: culture, state, and theater in fascist Italy. *American Sociological Review*, 56, 639–51.

Berg, I. 1970: *Education and Jobs*. New York: Praeger.

Berlant, J. L. 1975: *Profession and Monopoly: A Study of Medicine in the United States and Great Britain*. Berkeley: University of California Press.

Berry, J. W. and Irvine, S. H. 1986: Bricolage: savages do it daily. In Sternberg, R. J. and Wagner, R. K. (eds), *Practical Intelligence: Origins of Competence in the Everyday World*. New York: Cambridge University Press, 271–306.

Bielby, W. T. and Bielby, D. D. 1999: Organizational mediation of project-based labor markets: talent agencies and the careers of screenwriters. *American Sociological Review*, 64, 64–85.

Black, A. 1984: *Guilds and Civil Society in European Social Thought from the Twelfth Century to the Present*. Ithaca, NY: Cornell University Press.

Blair, R. D. and Rubin, S. (eds). 1980: *Regulating the Professions: A Public Policy Symposium*. Lexington, MA: Lexington Books.

Blau, J. R. 1984: *Architects and Firms: A Sociological Perspective on Architectural Practice*. Cambridge, MA: MIT Press.

Blau, J., La Gory, M. E., and Pipkin, J. S. (eds). 1983: *Professionals and Urban Form*. Albany, NY: SUNY Press.

Bledstein, B. J. 1976: *The Culture of Professionalism*. New York: Norton.

Bledstein, B. 1985: Discussing terms: professions, professionals, professionalism. *Prospects: An Annual of American Cultural Studies*, 10, 1–15.

Block, F. 1990: *Postindustrial Possibilities: A Critique of Economic Discourse*. Berkeley: University of California Press.

Bögenhold, D. 1995: Continuities and discontinuities in the sociology of the division of labor. In Littek, W. and Charles, T. (eds), *The New Division of Labour: Emerging forms of Work Organization in International Perspectives*. Berlin: Walter de Gruyter.

Boltanski, L. 1987: *The Making of a Class: Cadres in French Society*. New York: Cambridge University Press.

Boreham, P. 1983: Indetermination: professional knowledge, organization and control. *Sociological Review*, 31, 693–718.

Boris, E. 1986: *Art and Labor: Ruskin, Morris, and the Craftsman Ideal in America*. Philadelphia: Temple University Press.

Bourdieu, P. 1989: *Homo Academicus*. Stanford: Stanford University Press.

Brain, D. 1991: Practical knowledge and social control: the professionalization of architecture in the United States. *Sociological Forum*, 6, 239–68.

Brennan, T. and Berwick, D. 1996: *Regulation, Markets and the Quality of American Health Care*. San Francisco: Jossey Bass.

Bridges, W. P. 1996: Educational credentials and the labor market: an inter-industry comparison. In Kerckhoff, A. C. (ed.), *Generating Social Stratification: Toward a New Research Agenda*. Boulder, CO: Westview Press, 173–99.

Brint, S. 1994: *In an Age of Experts: The Changing Role of Professionals in Politics and Public Life*. Princeton, NJ: Princeton University Press.

Brint, S. and Karabel, J. 1989: *The Diverted Dream: Community Colleges and the Promise of Educational Opportunity in America, 1900–1985*. New York: Oxford University Press.

Broom, D. H. and Woodward, R. V. 1996: Medicalisation reconsidered: toward a collaborative approach to care. *Sociology of Health and Illness*, 18, 357–78.

Bruce, R. V. 1987: *The Launching of Modern American Science, 1846–1876*. New York: Knopf.

Bücher, C. 1907: *Industrial Evolution*. New York: Henry Holt.

Bucher, R. and Strauss, A. 1961: Professions in process. *American Journal of Sociology*, 66, 325–34.

Burchell, B. et al. 1994: Management and employee perceptions of skill. In Penn, R., Rose, M., and Rubery, J. (eds), *Skill and Occupational Change*. Oxford: Oxford University Press, 159–88.

Burrage, M. 1984: Practitioners, professors and the state in France, the USA and England. In Goodlad, S. (ed.), *Education for the Professions: Quis custodiet . . .?*, Guildford: SRHE & NEER-Nelson, 26–37.

Burrage, M. 1993: From practice to school-based professional education: patterns of conflict and accommodation in England, France, and the United States. In Rothblatt, S. and Wittrock, B. (eds), *The European and American University since 1800: Historical and Sociological Essays*. Cambridge: Cambridge University Press, 142–87.

Calvert, M. 1967: *The Mechanical Engineer in America: 1830–1910, Professional Cultures in Conflict*. Baltimore, MD: Johns Hopkins University Press.

Campbell, J. L. and Lindberg, L. N. 1990: Property rights and the organization of economic activity by the state. *American Sociological Review*, 55, 634–47.

Caplan, J. 1990: Profession as vocation: the German civil service. In Cocks, G. and Jarausch, K. H. (eds), *German Professions, 1800–1950*. New York: Oxford University Press, 163–82.

Caplow, T. 1954: *The Sociology of Work*. Minneapolis: University of Minnesota Press.

Carle, S. D. 1999: Lawyers' duty to do justice: a new look at the history of the 1908 canons. *Law and Social Inquiry*, 24, 1–44.

Carr-Saunders, A. M. and Wilson, P. A. 1933: *The Professions*. Oxford: Clarendon Press.

Casey, C. 1995: *Work, Self and Society after Industrialism*. London: Routledge.

Childe, V. G. 1965: *What Happened in History*. Baltimore, MD: Penguin Books.

Clark, B. R. (ed.). 1985: *The School and the University: An International Perspective*. Berkeley: University of California Press.

Clark, V. 1990: A struggle for existence: the professionalization of German architects. In Cocks, G. and Jarausch, K. H. (eds), *German Professions, 1800–1950*. New York: Oxford University Press, 143–60.

Clemente, F. 1972: The measurement problem in the analysis of an ecological concept: the division of labor. *Pacific Sociological Review*, 15, 30–40.

Collins, R. 1979: *The Credential Society: An Historical Sociology of Education and Stratification*. New York: Academic Press.

Conk, M. A. 1980: *The United States Census and Labor Force Change: A History of Occupation Statistics*. Ann Arbor, MI: UMI Research Press.

Crawford, S. 1989: *Technical Workers in an Advanced Society: The Work, Careers and Politics of French Engineers*. New York: Cambridge University Press.

Crouch, C. and Dore, R. 1990: Whatever happened to corporatism? In Crouch, C. and Dore, R. (eds), *Corporatism and Accountability: Organized Interests in British Public Life*. Oxford: Clarendon Press, 1–43.

Crozier, Michel. 1971: *The World of the Office Worker*. Chicago: University of Chicago Press.

Dahl, R. 1956: *A Preface to Democratic Theory*. Chicago: University of Chicago Press.

Damaška, M. R. 1986: *The Faces of Justice and State Authority: A Comparative Approach to the Legal Process*. New Haven: Yale University Press.

D'Amico, R. 1984: Industrial feudalism reconsidered: the effects of unionization on labor mobility. *Work and Occupations*, 11, 407–37.

Daniels, G. H. 1967: The process of professionalization in American science: the emergent period, 1820–1860. *Isis*, 58, 151–66.

Danielson, R. 1979: *Cuban Medicine*. New Brunswick, NJ: Transaction Books.

Darrah, C. 1994: Skill requirements at work: rhetoric versus reality. *Work and Occupations*, 21, 64–84.

Dasgupta, P. 1988: Trust as a commodity. In Gambetta, D. (ed.), *Trust: Making and Breaking Cooperative Relations*. New York: Blackwell, 49–72.

De Swaan, A. 1989. The reluctant imperialism of the medical profession. *Social Science and Medicine*, 28, 1165–70.

Derber, C., Schwartz, W. A., and Magrass, Y. 1990: *Power in the Highest Degree: Professionals and the Rise of a New Mandarin Order*. New York: Oxford University Press.

Derbyshire, R. C. 1969: *Medical Licensure and Discipline in the United States*. Baltimore, MD: Johns Hopkins University Press.

Desrosières, A. and Thévenot, L. 1988: *Les Catégories socio-professionnelles*. Paris: Éditions La Découverte.

Dickson, D. 1984: *The New Politics of Science*. New York: Pantheon Books.

Dingwall, R. 1983: "In the beginning was the work . . .": reflections on the genesis of occupations. *The Sociological Review*, 31, 605–24.

Dingwall, R. and Fenn, P. 1987: "A respectable profession?" Sociological and economic perspectives on the regulation of professional services. *International Review of Law and Economics*, 7, 51–64.

DiPrete, T. A. 1989: *The Bureaucratic Labor Market: The Case of the Federal Civil Service*. New York: Plenum Press.

Doble, J. and Komarnicki, M. 1986: *Engineering and Technology: The Public's Perspective*. Washington, DC: National Academy of Engineering.

Doeringer, P. B. and Piore, M. J. 1971: *Internal Labor Markets and Manpower Analysis*. Lexington, MA: D. C. Heath & Co.

Durkheim, E. 1957: *Professional Ethics and Civic Morals*. London: Routledge & Kegan Paul.

Durkheim. E. 1964: *The Division of Labor in Society*. Glencoe, IL: The Free Press.

Eckstein, M. A. and Noah, H. J. 1993: *Secondary School Examinations: International Perspectives on Policies and Practice.* New Haven: Yale University Press.

Edwards, R. 1979: *Contested Terrain.* New York: Basic Books.

Ehrenreich, B. and Ehrenreich, J. 1997a: The professional-managerial class. Part 1. *Radical America*, 2 (March–April), 7–31.

Enrenreich, B. and Ehrenreich, J. 1977b: The professional-managerial class. Part 2. *Radical America*, 2 (May–June), 7–22.

Elbaum, B. 1984: The Making and shaping of job and pay structures in the iron and steel industry. In Osterman, P. (ed.), *Internal Labor Markets.* Cambridge, MA: MIT Press, 71–104.

Elliott, P. 1972: *The Sociology of Professions.* London: Macmillan.

Ellul, J. 1964: *The Technological Society.* New York: Vintage Books.

Elster, J. 1990: Selfishness and altruism. In Mansbridge, J. A. (ed.), *Beyond Self-Interest.* Chicago: University of Chicago Press, 44–52.

Engel, A. 1983: The English universities and professional education. In Jarausch, K. H. (ed.), *The Transformation of Higher Learning 1860–1930.* Chicago: University of Chicago Press, 293–305.

Epstein, S. R. 1998: Craft guilds, apprenticeship, and technological change in preindustrial Europe. *Journal of Economic History*, 58, 684–713.

Etzioni, A. (ed.). 1969: *The Semi-Professions and their Organization: Teachers, Nurses, Social Workers.* New York: The Free Press.

Eurich, N. P. 1985: *Corporate Classrooms.* Princeton, NJ: Carnegie Foundation for the Advancement of Teaching.

Evans, M. D. and Laumann, E. O. 1983: Professional commitment: myth or reality? *Research in Social Stratification and Mobility*, 2, 3–40.

Evetts, J. 1999: Professions: changes and continuities. *International Review of Sociology*, 9, 75–85.

Field, M. 1957: *Doctor and Patient in Soviet Russia.* Cambridge, MA: Harvard University Press.

Fischer, F. 1990: *Technocracy and the Politics of Expertise.* Newbury Park, CA: Sage Publications.

Fisher, L. 1953: *The Harvest Labor Market in California.* Cambridge, MA: Harvard University Press.

Fisher, T. 1986: The "upright official" as a model in the humanities. In Hamrin, C. L. and Cheek, T. (eds), *China's Establishment Intellectuals.* Armonk, NY: M. E. Sharpe, 155–84.

Fligstein, N. and Byrkjeflot, H. 1996: The logic of employment systems. In Baron, J. N., Grusky, D. B., and Treiman, D. J. (eds), *Social Differentiation and Social Inequality: Essays in Honor of John Pock.* Boulder, CO: Westview Press, 11–35.

Form, W. M. 1968: Occupations and careers. In *International Encyclo-*

pedia of the Social Sciences, vol. 11. New York: The Free Press and Macmillan, 245–53.

Form, W. M. 1981: Resolving issues in the division of labor. In Blalock, H. M. Jr. (ed.), *Theory and Research in Sociology*. New York: The Free Press, 140–55.

Form, W. M. and Huber, J. A. 1976: Occupational power. In Dubin, R. (ed.), *Handbook of Work, Organization and Society*, Chicago: Rand-McNally, 751–806.

Foucault, M. 1979: *Discipline and Punish: The Birth of the Prison*. New York: Vintage Books.

Fox, A. 1974: *Beyond Contract: Work, Power and Trust Relationships*. London: Faber & Faber.

Frankford, D. M. 1997: The normative constitution of professional power. *Journal of Health Politics, Policy and Law*, 22, 185–221.

Freddi, G. and Bjørkman, J. W. (eds). 1989: *Controlling Medical Professionals: The Comparative Politics of Health Governance*. Newbury Park, CA: Sage Publications.

Freedman, M. 1976: *Labor Markets: Segments and Shelters*. Montclair, NJ: Allanheld, Osmun.

Freidson, E. 1970: *Professional Dominance: The Social Structure of Medical Care*. New York: Atherton Press.

Freidson, E. 1986: *Professional Powers: A Study of the Institutionalization of Formal Knowledge*. Chicago: University of Chicago Press.

Freidson, E. 1988 (1970): *Profession of Medicine: A Study in the Sociology of Applied Knowledge*. Chicago: University of Chicago Press.

Freidson, E. 1990: Labors of love in theory and practice: a prospectus. In Erikson, K. and Vallas, S. P. (eds), *The Nature of Work: Sociological Perspectives*. New Haven: Yale University Press, 149–61.

Freidson, E. 1994a: Pourquoi l'art ne peut pas être une profession. In Menger, P.-M. and Passeron, J.-C. (eds), *L'Art de la recherche: Essais en l'honneur de Raymonde Moulin*. Paris: La Documentation Française, 117–35.

Freidson, E. 1994b: *Professional Reborn: Theory, Prophecy, and Policy*. Chicago: University of Chicago Press.

Freidson, E. 1999a: Theory of professionalism: method and substance. *International Review of Sociology*, 9, 117.

Freidson, E. 1999b: Professionalism and institutional ethics. In Baker, R. et al. (eds), *The American Medical Ethics Revolution: How the AMA's Code of Ethics has Transformed Physicians' Relationships to Patients, Professionals, and Society*. Baltimore, MD: Johns Hopkins University Press, 124–43.

Frenk, J. and Durán-Arenas, L. 1993: The medical profession and the state. In Hafferty, F. W. and McKinlay, J. B. (eds), *The Changing*

Medical Profession: An International Perspective. New York: Oxford University Press, 25–42.

Friedman, A. L. 1977: *Industry and Labor.* London: Macmillan.

Friedman, M. 1962: *Capitalism and Freedom.* Chicago: University of Chicago Press.

Friedmann, G. 1964: *The Anatomy of Work.* New York: The Free Press.

Garceau, O. 1941: *The Political Life of the American Medical Association.* Cambridge, MA: Harvard University Press.

Garfinkel, H. 1967: *Studies in Ethnomethodology.* Englewood Cliffs, NJ: Prentice-Hall.

Geer, B. (ed.). 1972: *Learning to Work.* Special Issue of *American Behavioral Scientist,* 16/1, 1–138.

Geertz, C. 1983a: Common sense as a cultural system. In *Local Knowledge: Further Essays in Interpretive Anthropology.* New York: Harper Torchbooks, 73–93.

Geertz, C. 1983b: The way we think now: toward an ethnography of modern thought. In *Local Knowledge: Further Essays in Interpretive Anthropology.* New York: Harper Torchbooks, 146–63.

Gibbs, J. C. and Martin, W. T. 1962: Urbanization, technology, and the division of labor: international patterns. *American Sociological Review,* 27, 667–77.

Giddens, A. 1975: *The Class Structure of the Advanced Societies.* New York: Harper Torchbooks.

Giddens, A. 1990: *The Consequences of Modernity.* Stanford: Stanford University Press.

Gispen, K. 1989: *New Profession, Old Order: Engineers and German Society, 1815–1914.* Cambridge: Cambridge University Press.

Golden, W. T. (ed.). 1991: *Worldwide Science and Technology: Advice to the Highest Levels of Government.* New York: Pergamon.

Goldman, H. 1988: *Max Weber and Thomas Mann: Calling and the Shaping of the Self.* Berkeley: University of California Press.

Goldthorpe, J. 1982: On the service class, its formation and its future. In Giddens, A. and Mackenzie, G. (eds), *Social Class and the Division of Labour.* Cambridge: Cambridge University Press, 162–85.

Gonzales, Juan L. 1985: *Mexican and Mexican American Farm Workers: The California Agriculture Industry.* New York: Praeger.

Goode, W. J. 1957: Community with a community. *American Sociological Review,* 25, 902–14.

Goode, W. J. 1969: The theoretical limits of professionalization. In Etzioni, A. (ed.), *Professions and Semi-Professions.* New York: The Free Press.

Gordon, R. W. 1988: The independence of lawyers. *Boston University Law Review,* 68, 1–83.

Gouldner, A. 1979: *The Future of Intellectuals and the Rise of the New Class*. London: Macmillan.

Graham, L. R. 1967: *The Soviet Academy of Sciences and the Communist Party*. Princeton, NJ: Princeton University Press.

Granfield, R. 1992: *Making Elite Lawyers: Visions of Law at Harvard and Beyond*. New York: Routledge.

Granovetter, Mark S. 1974: *Getting a Job: A Study of Contacts and Careers*. Cambridge, MA: Harvard University Press.

Gray, B. H. 1991: *The Profit Motive and Patient Care: The Changing Accountability of Doctors and Hospitals*. Cambridge, MA: Harvard University Press.

Green, A. 1992: *Education and State Formation: The Rise of Education Systems in England, France and the USA*. London: Macmillan.

Green, P. 1983: Considerations on the democratic division of labor. *Politics and Society*, 12, 445–85.

Gritzer, G. and Arluke, A. 1985: *The Making of Rehabilitation: A Political Economy of Medical Specialization*. Berkeley: University of California Press.

Grusky, D. B. and Sørensen, J. B. 1998: Can class analysis be salvaged? *American Journal of Sociology*, 103, 1187–234.

Guroff, G. 1983: The red-expert debate: continuities in the state–entrepreneur tension. In Guroff, G. and Carstensen, F. V. (eds), *Entrepreneurship in Imperial Russia and the Soviet Union*. Princeton, NJ: Princeton University Press, 201–22.

Gutman, R. 1983: Architects in the home-building industry. In Blau, J., La Gory, M. E., and Pipkin, J. S. (eds), *Professionals and Urban Form*. Albany, NY: SUNY Press, 208–23.

Gutman, R. 1988: *Architectural Practice: A Critical View*. Princeton, NJ: Princeton Architectural Press.

Hafferty, F. W. 1971: *Into the Valley: Death and the Socialization of Medical Students*. New Haven: Yale University Press.

Haller, Max et al. 1985: Patterns of career mobility and structural positions in advanced capitalist societies: a comparison of men in Austria, France, and the United States. *American Sociological Review*, 50, 579–603.

Halliday, T. C. 1987: *Beyond Monopoly: Lawyers, State Crises, and Professional Empowerment*. Chicago: University of Chicago Press.

Halliday, T. C. 1989: Legal professions and politics: neocorporatist variations on the pluralist theme of liberal democracies. In Abel, R. L. and Lewis, P. S. C. (eds), *Lawyers in Society*. Volume 3, *Comparative Theories*. Berkeley: University of California Press, 375–426.

Halpern, S. A. 1987: Professional schools in the American university. In Clark, B. R. (ed.), *The Academic Profession: National, Disciplinary, and Institutional Settings*. Berkeley: University of California Press, 304–30.

Harper, D. 1987: *Working Knowledge: Skill and Community in a Small Shop*. Chicago: University of Chicago Press.

Haskell, T. L. 1984: Professionalism versus capitalism: R. H. Tawney, Emile Durkheim, and C. S. Peirce on the disinterestedness of professional communities. In Haskell, T. L. (ed.), *The Authority of Experts: Studies in History and Theory*. Bloomington, IN: Indiana University Press, 180–225.

Haworth, L. 1977: *Decadence and Objectivity*. Toronto: University of Toronto Press.

Heidenheimer, A. J. 1989: Professional knowledge and state policy in comparative historical perspective: law and medicine in Britain, Germany and the United States. *International Social Science Journal*, 122, 529–53.

Heinz, J. P. and Laumann, E. O. 1982: *Chicago Lawyers: The Social Structure of the Bar*. Chicago: Russell Sage Foundation and the American Bar Foundation.

Hinz, B. 1979: *Art in the Third Reich*. New York: Pantheon.

Hobsbawm, E. 1984: *Workers: Worlds of Labor*. New York: Pantheon Books.

Holzner, B. 1968: *Reality Construction in Society*. Cambridge, MA: Schenkman.

Hughes, E. C. 1971: *The Sociological Eye: Selected Papers*. Chicago: Aldine-Atherton.

Huskey, E. 1986: *Russian Lawyers and the Soviet State: The Origins and Development of the Soviet Bar, 1917–1939*. Princeton, NJ: Princeton University Press.

Hutchinson, J. F. 1996: Politics and medical professionalization after 1905. In Balzer, H. D. (ed.), *Russia's Missing Middle Class: The Professions in Russian History*. Armonk, NY: M. E. Sharpe, 89–116.

Hyde, D. R. and Wolff, P. 1954: The American Medical Association: power, purpose, and politics in organized medicine. *Yale Law Journal*, 63, 938–1022.

Illich, I. et al. 1977: *Disabling Professions*. London: Marion Boyars.

Imershein, A. W., Rond, P. C. III, and Mathis, M. P. 1992: Restructuring patterns of elite dominance and the formation of state policy in health care. *American Journal of Sociology*, 97, 970–93.

Irvine, J., Miles, I., and Evans, J. 1975: *Demystifying Social Statistics*. London: Pluto Press.

Jacoby, Sanford M. 1984: The development of internal labor markets in American manufacturing firms. In Osterman, P. (ed.), *Internal Labor Markets*. Cambridge, MA: MIT Press, 23–69.

Jamous, H. and Peloille, B. 1970: Changes in the French university-hospital system. In Jackson, A. J. (ed.), *Professions and Professionalization*. Cambridge: Cambridge University Press, 111–52.

Jarausch, K. H. 1990: *The Unfree Professions: German Lawyers, Teachers, and Engineers, 1900–1950*. New York: Oxford University Press.

Johnson, T. 1972: *Professions and Power*. London: Macmillan.

Johnson, T. 1993: Expertise and the state. In Johnson, T. and Gain, M. (eds), *Foucault's New Domains*. London: Routledge.

Johnson, T. 1995: Governmentality and the institutionalisation of expertise. In Johnson, T., Larkin, G., and Saks, M., *Health Professions and the State in Europe*. London: Routledge, 7–24.

Johnson, W. R. 1978: *Schooled Lawyers: A Study in the Clash of Professional Culture*. New York: New York University Press.

Josephson, P. R. 1988: Physics, Stalinist politics of science and cultural revolution. *Soviet Studies*, 40, 245–65.

Josephson, P. R. 1992: Soviets scientists and the state: politics, ideology, and fundamental research from Stalin to Gorbachev. *Social Research*, 59, 589–614.

Kalleberg, A. L. 1996: Changing contexts of careers: trends in labor market structures and some implications for labor force outcomes. In Kerckhoff, A. C. (ed.), *Generating Social Stratification: Toward a New Research Agenda*. Boulder, CO: Westview Press, 343–58.

Kalleberg, A. L. and Sørensen, A. B. 1979: The sociology of labor markets. *Annual Review of Sociology*, 5, 351–79.

Karpik, L. 1988: Lawyers and politics in France, 1814–1950: the state, the market, and the public. *Law and Social Inquiry*, 13, 707–36.

Keefe, J. and Potosky, D. 1997: Technical dissonance: conflicting portraits of technicians. In Barley, S. R. and Orr, J. E. (eds), *Between Craft and Science: Technical Work in U.S. Settings*. Ithaca, NY: Cornell University Press, 53–81.

Kemper, T. D. 1972: The division of labor: a post-Durkheimian analytic view. *American Sociological Review*, 37, 739–53.

Kendall, P. L. 1965: The relationships between medical educators and medical practitioners. *Journal of Medical Education*, 40/2, 137–245.

Kerckhoff, A. C. 1996. Building conceptual and empirical bridges between studies of educational and labor force careers. In Kerckhoff, A. C. (ed.), *Generating Social Stratification: Toward a New Research Agenda*. Boulder, CO: Westview Press, 37–55.

Kerr, C. 1950: Labor markets: their character and consequences. *American Economic Review*, 40, 278–91.

Kerr, C. 1954: The Balkanization of labor markets. In Bakke, E. W. (ed.), *Labor Markets and Economic Opportunity*, New York: Wiley, 92–110.

Kevles, D. J. 1979: *The Physicists: The History of a Scientific Community in Modern America.* New York: Vintage Books.

Kimball, B. A. 1986: *Orators and Philosophers: A History of the Idea of Liberal Education.* New York: Teachers College, Columbia University.

Kimball, B. A. 1992: *The "True Professional Ideal" in America: A History.* Cambridge, MA: Blackwell.

Knoke, D. and Kalleberg, A. L. 1994: Job training in U.S. organizations. *American Sociological Review,* 59, 537–46.

Konttinen, E. 1991: Professionalization as status adaptation: the nobility, the bureaucracy, and the modernization of the legal profession in Finland. *Law and Social Inquiry,* 16, 497–526.

Kostof, S. (ed.). 1977: *The Architect: Chapters in the History of the Profession.* Oxford: Oxford University Press.

Kraft, P. 1977: *Programmers and Managers.* New York: Springer-Verlag.

Kranzberg, M. and Gies, J. 1975: *By the Sweat of Thy Brow.* New York: G. P. Putnam's Sons.

Krause, E. A. 1996: *Death of the Guilds: Professions, States, and the Advance of Capitalism, 1930 to the Present.* New Haven: Yale University Press.

Kultgen, J. 1988: *Ethics and Professionalism.* Philadelphia: University of Pennsylvania Press.

Kusterer, K. 1978: *Know-how on the Job: The Important Working Knowledge of "Unskilled" Workers.* Boulder, CO: Westview Press.

La Vopa, A. J. 1988: *Grace, Talent, and Merit: Poor Students, Clerical Careers, and Professional Ideology in Eighteenth Century Germany.* Cambridge: Cambridge University Press.

Labovitz, S. and Gibbs, J. P. 1964: Urbanization, technology and the division of labor: further evidence. *Pacific Sociological Review,* 7, 3–9.

Larrain, J. 1979: *The Concept of Ideology.* Athens, GA: University of Georgia Press.

Larson, M. S. 1977: *The Rise of Professionalism: A Sociological Analysis.* Berkeley: University of California Press.

Larson, M. S. 1983: Emblem and exception: the historic definition of the architect's professional role. In Blau, J. L., La Gory, M. E., and Pipkin, J. S. (eds), *Professionals and Urban Form.* Albany, NY: SUNY Press, 49–86.

Larson, M. S. 1993: *Behind the Postmodern Facade: Architectural Change in Late Twentieth Century America.* Berkeley: University of California Press.

Laski, H. 1931: *The Limitations of the Expert.* Fabian Tract No. 235, 1–14. London: The Fabian Society.

Lavoie, D. 1991: The discovery and interpretation of profit opportunities: culture and the Kirznerian entrepreneur. In Berger, B. (ed.), *The Culture of Entrepreneurship*. San Francisco: ICS Press, 33–51.

Layton, E. T. 1971: *The Revolt of the Engineers: Social Responsibility and the American Engineering Profession*. Cleveland, OH: The Press of Case Western Reserve University.

Lee, D. J. 1981: Skill, craft and class: a theoretical critique and a critical case. *Sociology*, 15, 56–78.

Lévi-Strauss, C. 1966: *The Savage Mind*. London: Weidenfeld & Nicolson.

Lichtheim, G. 1967: The concept of ideology. In Lichtheim, G. (ed.), *The Concept of Ideology and Other Essays*. New York: Vintage Books, 3–46.

Liedman, S.-E. 1993: In search of Isis: general education in Germany and Sweden. In Rothblatt, S. and Wittrock, B. (eds), *The European and American University Since 1800*. Cambridge: Cambridge University Press, 74–105.

Light, D. W. 1983: The development of professional schools in America. In Jarausch, K. H. (ed.), *The Transformation of Higher Learning 1860–1930*. Chicago: University of Chicago Press, 345–65.

Lindblom, C. E. 1977: *Politics and Markets: The World's Political Economic Systems*. New York: Basic Books.

Lioger, R. 1993: *Sourciers et radiesthésistes ruraux*. Lyons: Presses Universitaires de Lyon.

Lioger, R. 1996: Du don comme origine du savoir faire. *Cahiers du travail social*, 32, 55–61.

Litt, E. 1969: *The Public Vocational University: Captive Knowledge and Public Power*. New York: Holt, Rinehart & Winston.

Littek, W. and Charles, T. (eds). 1995: *The New Division of Labor: Emerging Forms of Work Organization in International Perspective*. Berlin: Walter de Gruyter.

Littek, W. and Heisig, U. 1991: Competence, control, and work redesign: die Angestellten in the Federal Republic of Germany. *Work and Occupations*, 18, 4–28.

Littler, C. R. 1982: *The Development of the Labour Process in Capitalist Societies: A Comparative Study of the Transformation of Work Organization in Britain, Japan, and the USA*. London: Heinemann Educational Books.

Lowenberg, J. S. and Davis, F. 1994: Beyond medicalisation-demedicalisation: the case of holistic health. *Sociology of Health and Illness*, 16, 579–99.

Lukes, S. 1974: *Power: A Radical View*. London: Macmillan.

Lukes, S. 1977: *Emile Durkheim: His Life and Work. A Historical and Critical Study*. New York: Penguin Books.

Lundgreen, P. 1990 Engineering education in Europe and the USA, 1750–1930: the rise to dominance of school culture and the engineering professions. *Annals of Science*, 47, 33–75.

Macdonald, K. M. 1984: Professional formation: the case of Scottish accountants. *British Journal of Sociology*, 35, 174–89.

Macdonald, K. M. 1995: *The Sociology of the Professions*. London: Sage Publications.

Machlup, F. 1962: *The Production and Distribution of Knowledge in the United States*. Princeton, NJ: Princeton University Press.

MacKenzie, D. and Spinardi, G. 1995: Tacit knowledge, weapons design, and the uninvention of nuclear weapons. *American Journal of Sociology*, 101, 44–99.

Mackenzie, G. 1973: *The Aristocracy of Labor: The Position of Skilled Craftsmen in the American Class Structure*. Cambridge: Cambridge University Press.

Macrakis, K. 1993: *Surviving the Swastika: Scientific Research in Nazi Germany*. New York: Oxford University Press.

Marsden, D. 1986: *The End of Economic Man? Custom and Competition in Labor Markets*. New York: St Martin's Press.

Marx, K. 1963: *The Poverty of Philosophy*. New York: International Publishers.

Marx, K. 1967: *Capital: A Critique of Political Economy*. Volume 1, *The Process of Capitalist Production*. New York: International Publishers.

Massie, J. L. 1965: Management theory. In March, J. G. (ed.), *Handbook of Organizations*. Chicago: Rand-McNally, 387–422.

Maurice, M., Sellier, F., and Silvestre, J.-J. 1986: *The Social Foundation of Industrial Power*. Cambridge, MA: MIT Press.

McClelland, C. E. 1983: Professionalization and higher education in Germany. In Jarausch, K. H. (ed.), *The Transformation of Higher Learning 1860–1930*. Chicago: University of Chicago Press, 306–20.

McCormick, K. 1988: Engineering education in Britain and Japan: some reflections on the use of the best practice model in international comparison. *Sociology*, 22, 583–605.

McLellan, D. 1986: *Ideology*. Minneapolis: University of Minnesota Press.

Meakin, D. 1976: *Man and Work: Literature and Culture in Industrial Society*. London: Methuen.

Meek, R. L. and Skinner, A. S. 1973: The development of Adam Smith's ideas on the division of labor. *Economic Journal*, 83, 1094–116.

Meiksins, P. and Smith, C. (eds). 1996: *Engineering Labour*. London: Verso.

Mendelsohn, E. 1964: The emergence of science as a profession in nineteenth-century Europe. In Hill, K. (ed.), *The Management of Scientists*. Boston, MA: Beacon Press, 3–47.

Merryman, J. H. 1985: *The Civil Law Tradition: An Introduction to the Legal Systems of Western Europe and Latin America.* Stanford: Stanford University Press.

Merton, R. K. 1957: *Social Theory and Social Structure.* New York: The Free Press.

Merton, R. K. and Gieryn, T. F. 1982: Institutionalized altruism: the case of the professions. In Rosenblatt, A. and Gieryn, T. F. (eds), *Social Research and the Practicing Professions.* Cambridge, MA: Abt Books, 109–34.

Millerson, G. 1964: *The Qualifying Associations: A Study in Professionalisation.* London: Routledge & Kegan Paul.

Mills, C. W. 1951: *White Collar: The American Middle Class.* New York: Oxford University Press.

Miner, A. S. 1991: Organizational evolution and the social ecology of jobs. *American Sociological Review,* 56, 772–85.

Montgomery, A. C. 1990: Space, time and architects: careers in the architectural profession. *Current Research on Occupations and Professions,* 5, 91–109.

Moore, B. J. 1966: *Social Origins of Dictatorship and Democracy: Lord and Peasant in the Making of the Modern World.* Boston, MA: Beacon Press.

Moulin, R. 1992: *L'Artiste, l'institution et le marché.* Paris: Flammarion.

Moulin, R. et al. 1973: *Les Architectes: Metamorphose d'une profession libérale.* Paris: Calmann-Levy.

Mueller, H. E. 1984: *Bureaucracy, Education, and Monopoly: Civil Service Reforms in Prussia and England.* Berkeley: University of California Press.

Murphy, R. 1988. *Social Closure: The Theory of Monopolization and Exclusion.* Oxford: Clarendon Press.

Oberschall, A. and Leifer, E. M. 1986: Efficiency and social institutions: uses and misuses of economic reasoning in sociology. *Annual Review of Sociology,* 12, 233–53.

OED (*Oxford English Dictionary*). 1971: Oxford: Oxford University Press (compact edition).

Offe, Claus. 1985: *Disorganized capitalism.* Cambridge: Polity Press.

Ollman, B. 1976–7: Marx's vision of communism: a reconstruction. *Critique,* 8, 4–38.

Orzack, K. H. 1989: Engineers in Europe: 1992 and beyond. *Technology Studies,* 6–8.

Osterman, P. 1984: White-collar internal labor markets. In Osterman, P. (ed.), *Internal Labor Markets.* Cambridge, MA: MIT Press, 163–89.

Ouchi, W. G. 1980: Markets, bureaucracies, and clans. *Administrative Science Quarterly,* 25, 129–41.

Parkin, F. 1979: *Marxism and Class Theory: A Bourgeois Critique.* New York: Columbia University Press.

Parnes, H. S. 1968: Labor force: markets and mobility. In *International Encyclopedia of the Social Sciences*, vol. 8. New York: The Free Press and Macmillan, 481–7.

Parry, N. C. A. and Parry, J. 1976: *The Rise of the Medical Profession: A Study of Collective Social Mobility*. London: Croom Helm.

Parsons, T. 1949. The motivation of ecnomic activities. In *Essays in Sociological Theory, Pure and Applied*. New York: The Free Press, 200–17.

Parsons, T. 1951: *The Social System*. New York: The Free Press.

Parsons, T. 1964: Definitions of health and illness in the light of American values and social structure. In *Social Structure and Personality*. New York: The Free Press, 258–91.

Parsons, T. 1968: Professions. *International Encyclopedia of the Social Sciences*, vol. 12. New York: The Free Press and Macmillan, 536–47.

Paul, H. W. 1980: *Apollo Courts the Vulcans: The Applied Science Institutes in Nineteenth Century French Science Faculties*. Cambridge: Cambridge University Press.

Paul, H. W. 1985: *From Knowledge to Power: The Rise of the Science Empire in France, 1860–1939*. Cambridge: Cambridge University Press.

Peck, J. 1996: *Work Place: The Social Regulation of Labor Markets*. New York: The Guilford Press.

Pellegrino, E. D. 1991: Trust and distrust in professional ethics. In Pellegrino, E. D., Veatch, R. M., and Langan, J. P. (eds), *Ethics, Trust, and the Professions: Philosophical and Cultural Aspects*. Washington: Georgetown University Press, 69–89.

Peneff, J. 1997: Le travail du chirurgien: les opérations à cœur ouvert. *Sociologie du Travail*, 3, 265–96.

Penn, R., Rose, M., and Rubery, J. (eds). 1994: *Skill and Occupational Change*. New York: Oxford University Press.

Perkin, H. 1983: The pattern of social transformation in England. In Jarausch, K. H. (ed.), *The Transformation of Higher Learning 1860–1930: Expansion, Diversification, Social Opening, and Professionalization in England, Germany, Russia, and the United States*. Chicago: University of Chicago Press, 207–18.

Perrow, C. 1986: *Complex Organizations: A Critical Essay*. New York: Random House.

Persons, Stow. 1973: *The Decline of American Gentility*. New York: Columbia University Press.

Pinch, T., Collins, H. M., and Carbone, L. 1997: Cutting up skills: estimating difficulty as an element of surgical and other abilities. In Barley, S. R. and Orr, J. E. (eds), *Between Craft and Science: Technical Work in U.S. Settings*. Ithaca, NY: Cornell University Press, 101–12.

Podolny, J. M. and Page, K. L. 1998: Network forms of organization. *Annual Review of Sociology*, 24, 57–76.

Polanyi, K. 1944: *The Great Transformation*. New York: Rinehart & Co.

Polanyi, M. 1964: *Personal Knowledge: Towards a Post-Critical Philosophy*. New York: Harper Torchbooks.

Polanyi, M. 1967: *The Tacit Dimension*. Garden City, NY: Doubleday Anchor.

Porter, S. 1996: Contra-Foucault: soldiers, nurses, and power. *Sociology*, 30, 59–78.

Powell, M. J. 1988: *From Patrician to Professional Elite: The Transformation of the New York City Bar Association*. New York: Russell Sage Foundation.

Powell, W. W. 1990: Neither market nor hierarchy: network forms of organization. *Research in Organizational Behavior*, 12: 295–336.

Price, D. 1961: *Science since Babylon*. New Haven: Yale University Press.

Pring, R. A. 1992: *Academic Respectability and Professional Relevance*. Oxford: Clarendon Press.

Ramsey, M. 1988: *Professional and Popular Medicine in France, 1770–1830*. Cambridge: Cambridge University Press.

Rapaport, Elizabeth. 1976: Anarchism and authority in Marx's socialist politics. *Archives Européennes de Sociologie*, 17, 333–43.

Rattansi, A. 1982: *Marx and the Division of Labor*. London: Macmillan.

Reader, W. J. 1966: *Professional Men: The Rise of the Professional Classes in Nineteenth-Century England*. New York: Basic Books.

Rees, Albert. 1966: Labor economics: effects of more knowledge. Information networks in labor markets. *American Economic Review*, 56, 559–66.

Reinhardt, U. E. 1992: Reflections on the meaning of efficiency: can efficiency be separated from equity? *Yale Law Policy Review*, 10, 302–15.

Ringer, F. K. 1979: *Education and Society in Modern Europe*. Bloomington, IN: Indiana University Press.

Ringer, F. K. 1992: *Fields of Knowledge: French Academic Culture in Comparative Perspective*. Cambridge: Cambridge University Press.

Robert, P. 1978: *Dictionnaire alphabétique et analogique de la langue française*. Paris: Société du Nouveau Littré.

Rodgers, D. T. 1978: *The Work Ethic in Industrial America, 1850–1920*. Chicago: University of Chicago Press.

Rodwin, M. 1993. *Medicine, Money, and Morals: Physicians' Conflicts of Interest*. New York: Oxford University Press.

Rosenbaum, J. E. 1984: *Career Mobility in a Corporate Hierarchy*. Orlando, FL: Academic Press.

Rosenberg, C. E. 1987. *The Care of Strangers: The Rise of America's Hospital System*. New York: Basic Books.

Rossides, D. W. 1998: *Professions and Disciplines: Functional and Conflict Perspectives*. Upper Saddle River, NJ: Prentice-Hall.

Rothblatt, S. 1968: *The Revolution of the Dons: Cambridge and Society in Victorian England*. Cambridge: Cambridge University Press.

Rothblatt, S. 1976: *Tradition and Change in English Liberal Education: An Essay in History and Culture*. London: Faber & Faber.

Rothblatt, S. 1993: The limbs of Osiris: liberal education in the English-speaking world. In Rothblatt, S. and Wittrock, B. (eds), *The European and American University since 1800: Historical and Sociological Essays*. Cambridge: Cambridge University Press, 19–73.

Rothstein, W. G. 1987. *American Medical Schools and the Practice of Medicine: A History*. New York: Oxford University Press.

Rueschemeyer, D. 1964: Doctors and lawyers: a comment on the theory of professions. *Canadian Journal of Sociology and Anthropology*, 1, 17–30.

Rueschemeyer, D. 1986: *Power and the Division of Labor*. Stanford: Stanford University Press.

Rushing, W. A. 1968: The hardness of material as related to division of labor in manufacturing industries. *Administrative Science Quarterly*, 13, 229–45.

Ryan, P. 1984: Job training, employment practices, and the large enterprise: the case of costly transferable skills. In Osterman, P. (ed.), *Internal Labor Markets*. Cambridge, MA: MIT Press, 191–229.

Sabel, C. 1995: Meta-corporations and open labor markets: some consequences of the reintegration of conception and execution in a volatile economy. In Littek, W. and Charles, T. (eds), *The New Division of Labour: Emerging Forms of Work Organization in International Perspective*. Berlin: Walter de Gruyter, 57–94.

Saks, M. 1995. *Professions and the Public Interest: Medical Power, Altruism, and Alternative Medicine*. London: Routledge.

Salz, A. 1933: Specialization. *Encyclopedia of the Social Sciences*, vol. 14. New York: Macmillan, 279–85.

Sassower, R. 1996: *Knowledge without Expertise. On the Status of Scientists*. Albany, NY: SUNY Press.

Sayer, A. and Walker, R. 1992: *The New Social Economy: Reworking the Division of Labor*. Cambridge: Blackwell.

Schmitter, P. C. 1979: Still the century of corporatism? In Schmitter, P. C. and Lehmbruch, G. (eds), *Trends Toward Corporatist Intermediation*. London: Sage Publications, 7–52.

Schneider, M. A. 1997: Social dimensions of epistemological disputes: the case of literary theory. *Sociological Perspectives*, 40, 243–63.

Schnore, L. F. 1958: Social morphology and human ecology. *American Journal of Sociology*, 63, 620–34.

Schön, D. A. 1982: *The Reflective Practitioner: How Professionals Think in Action*. New York: Basic Books.

Schurmann, F. 1968: *Ideology and Organization in Communist China*. Berkeley: University of California Press.

Schutz, A. 1970: *On Phenomenology and Social Relations: Selected Writings*. Chicago: University of Chicago Press.

Sciulli, D. 1990: Challenges to Weberians' treatment of collegiality: comment on Waters. *American Journal of Sociology* 96, 186–92.

Scribner, S. 1986: Thinking in action: some characteristics of practical thought. In Sternberg, R. J. and Wagner, R. K. (eds), *Practical Intelligence: Nature and Origins of Competence in the Everyday World*. New York: Cambridge University Press, 13–30.

Seligman, A. B. 1997: *The Problem of Trust*. Princeton, NJ: Princeton University Press.

Seron, C. 1996: *The Business of Practicing Law: The Work Lives of Solo and Small-Firm Attorneys*, Philadelphia: Temple University Press.

Shapiro, Susan P. 1987: The social control of impersonal trust. *American Journal of Sociology*, 93, 623–58.

Shinn, T. 1978: La profession d'ingénieur, 1750–1920. *Revue française de sociologie*, 19, 39–71.

Shinn, T. 1980: *From Corps to Profession: The Emergence and Definition of Industrial Engineering in Modern France*. Cambridge: Cambridge University Press.

Siegrist, H. 1990: Professionalization as a process: patterns, progression and discontinuity. In Burrage, M. and Torstendahl, R. (eds), *Professions in Theory and History: Rethinking the Study of the Professions*. London: Sage Publications, 177–202.

Smith, A. 1976a: *An Inquiry into the Nature and Causes of the Wealth of Nations*, vol. 1. Chicago: University of Chicago Press.

Smith, A. 1976b: *An Inquiry into the Nature and Causes of the Wealth of Nations*, vol. 2. Chicago: University of Chicago Press.

Smith, D. L. and Snow, R. E. 1976: The division of labor: conceptual and methodological issues. *Social Forces*, 55, 520–8.

Smith, V. 1997: New forms of work organization. *Annual Review of Sociology*, 23, 315–39.

Spence, A. M. 1974: *Market Signaling: Informational Transfer in Hiring and Related Screening Processes*. Cambridge, MA: Harvard University Press.

Spenner, K. I. 1990: Skill: meanings, methods and measures. *Work and Occupations*, 17, 399–421.

Spilerman, S. 1977: Careers, labor structure, and socioeconomic achievement. *American Journal of Sociology*, 83, 551–93.

Spilerman, S. 1986: Organizational rules and the features of work careers. *Research in Social Stratification and Mobility*, 5, 41–102.

Stansky, P. 1985: *Redesigning the World: William Morris, the 1880s, and the Arts and Crafts*. Princeton, NJ: Princeton University Press.

Stark, D. 1986: Rethinking internal labor markets: new insights from a comparative perspective. *American Sociological Review*, 51, 492–504.

Stark, D. 1989: Bending the bars of the iron cage: bureaucratization and informalization in capitalism and socialism. *Sociological Forum*, 4, 637–64.

Starr, P. 1982: *The Social Transformation of American Medicine: The Rise of a Sovereign Profession and the Making of a Vast Industry*. New York: Basic Books.

Starr, P. 1987: The sociology of official statistics. In Alonso, W. and Starr, P. (eds), *The Politics of Numbers*. New York: Russell Sage Foundation, 7–57.

Steiner, P. O. 1968: Markets and industries. In *International Encyclopedia of the Social Sciences*, vol. 9. New York: The Free Press and Macmillan, 575–81.

Sternberg, R. J. and Wagner, R. K. 1986: *Practical Intelligence: Origins of Competence in the Everyday World*. New York: Cambridge University Press.

Stevens, R. 1971. *American Medicine and the Public Interest*, New Haven: Yale University Press.

Stevens, R. 1989. *In Sickness and in Wealth: American Hospitals in the Twentieth Century*. New York: Basic Books.

Stinchcombe, A. L. 1959: Bureaucratic and craft administration of production: a comparative study. *Administrative Science Quarterly*, 4, 168–87.

Stinchcombe, A. L. 1990: Reason and rationality. In Cook, K. S. and Levy, M. (eds), *The Limits of Rationality*. Chicago: University of Chicago Press, 285–317.

Stone, D. A. 1984: *The Disabled State*. Philadelphia: Temple University Press.

Strang, D. and Baron, J. N. 1990: Categorical imperatives: the structure of job titles in California state agencies. *American Sociological Review*, 55, 479–95.

Strauss, A. 1985: Work and the division of labor. *The Sociological Quarterly*, 26, 1–19.

Streeck, W. and Schmitter P. 1985: Community, market, state – and associations? The prospective contribution of interest governance to social order. In Streeck, W. and Schmitter, P. (eds), *Private Interest Government: Beyond Market and State*. London: Sage, 1–29.

Stymeist, D. 1979: Controlling the job: levels of organization in casual labour. In Wallman, S. (ed.), *Ethnicity at Work*. London: Macmillan, 193–212.

Suleiman, E. N. 1977: The myth of technical expertise: selection, organization, and leadership. *Comparative Politics*, 10, 137–58.

Sullivan, W. M. 1995: *Work and Integrity: The Crisis and Promise of Professionalism in America*. New York: Harper Collins.

Swidler, A. and Arditi, J. 1994: The new sociology of knowledge. *Annual Review of Sociology*, 20, 305–29.

Tilgher, A. 1958: *Homo Faber: Work Through the Ages*. Chicago: Henry Regnery.

Timberlake, C. E. 1983: Higher learning, the state, and the professions in Russia. In Jarausch, K. H. (ed.), *The Transformation of Higher Learning 1860–1930*. Chicago: University of Chicago Press, 321–44.

Tomaney, J. 1994: A new paradigm of work organization and technology? In Amin, A. (ed.), *Post-Fordism: A Reader*. Oxford: Blackwell, 157–94.

Torstendahl, R. 1993: The transformation of professional education in the nineteenth century. In Rothblatt, S. and Wittrock, B. (eds), *The European and American University since 1800: Historical and Sociological Essays*. Cambridge: Cambridge University Press, 109–41.

Trépos, J.-Y. 1996. *La Sociologie de l'expertise*. Paris: Presses Universitaires de France.

Turner, J. 1985: *Herbert Spencer: A Renewed Appreciation*. Beverly Hills, CA: Sage Publications.

Veatch, R. M. 1991: Is trust of professionals a coherent concept? In Pellegrino, E. D., Veatch, R. M., and Langan, J. P. (eds), *Ethics, Trust, and the Professions: Philosophical and Cultural Aspects*. Washington: Georgetown University Press, 159–73.

Veblen, T. 1983: *The Engineers and the Price System*. New Brunswick, NJ: Transaction Books.

Vucinich, A. 1984: *Empire of Knowledge: The Academy of Sciences of the USSR (1917–1970)*. Berkeley: University of California Press.

Wagner, R. K. and Sternberg, R. J. 1986: Tacit knowledge and intelligence in the everyday world. In Sternberg, R. J. and Wagner, R. K. (eds), *Practical Intelligence: Nature and Origins of Competence in the Everyday World*. New York: Cambridge University Press, 51–79.

Wallace, A. F. C. 1961: Schools in revolutionary and conservative societies. In Gruber, F. (ed.), *Anthropology and Education*. Philadelphia: University of Pennsylvania Press, 29–54.

Waters, M. 1989: Collegiality, bureaucratization, and professionalization: a Weberian analysis. *American Journal of Sociology*, 94, 945–72.

Weber, M. 1946a: The Chinese literati. In Gerth, H. H. and Mills,

C. W. (eds), *From Max Weber: Essays in Sociology*. New York: Oxford University Press, 416–44.

Weber, M. 1946b: Science as a vocation. In Gerth, H. H. and Mills, C. W. (eds), *From Max Weber: Essays in Sociology*. New York: Oxford University Press, 129–56.

Weber, M. 1978. *Economy and Society*. Berkeley: University of California Press.

Weick, K. E. and Berlinger, L. R. 1989: Career improvisation in self-designing organizations. In Arthur, M. B., Hall, D. T., and Lawrence, B. S. (eds), *Handbook of Career Theory*. New York: Cambridge University Press, 313–28.

Weingart, P. 1982: The scientific power elite a chimera: the de-institutionalization and politicization of science. In Elias, N., Martins, H., and Whitley, R. (eds), *Scientific Establishments and Hierarchies*. Dordrecht, Netherlands: D. Reidel, 71–87.

Weiss, D. D. 1976: Marx versus Smith on the division of labor. *Monthly Review*, 28, 104–18.

Whalley, P. 1986: *The Social Production of Technical Work: The Case of British Engineers*. Albany, NY: SUNY Press.

Whalley, P. and Barley, S. R. 1997: Technical work in the division of labor: stalking the wily anomaly. In Barley, S. R. and Orr, J. E. (eds), *Between Craft and Science: Technical Work in U.S. Settings*. Ithaca, NY: Cornell University Press.

Whitehead, A. N. 1963: *Science in the Modern World*. New York: Mentor Books.

Wilensky, H. 1961: Orderly careers and social participation: the impact of work history on social integration in the middle mass. *American Sociological Review*, 26, 521–39.

Wilensky, H. L. 1964: The professionalization of everyone? *American Journal of Sociology*, 70, 137–58.

Wilkinson, R. 1964: *Gentlemanly Power: British Leadership and the Public School Tradition. A Comparative Study in the Making of Rulers*. London: Oxford University Press.

Williams, R. 1983: *Keywords: A Vocabulary of Culture and Society*. New York: Oxford University Press.

Williamson, O. E. 1975: *Markets and Hierarchies: Analysis and Anti-Trust Implications*. New York: The Free Press.

Williamson, P. J. 1989: *Corporatism in Perspective: An Introductory Guide to Corporatist Theory*. London: Sage Publications.

Wilsford, D. 1991: *Doctors and the State: The Politics of Health Care in France and the United States*. Durham, NC: Duke University Press.

Wittberg, P. and LaMagdeleine, D. R. 1989: The dual labor market in the Catholic Church: expanding a speculative inquiry. *Review of Religious Research*, 30, 287–90.

Wolinsky, H. and Brune, T. 1994. *The Serpent on the Staff: The Unhealthy Politics of the American Medical Association*. New York: G. P. Putnam's Sons.

Wright, E. O. 1979: Intellectuals and the class structure of capitalist society. In Walker, P. (ed.), *Between Labor and Capital*. Hassocks: Harvester Press, 191–211.

Wright, R. and Jacobs, J. A. 1994: Male flight from computer work: a new look at occupational resegregation and ghettoization. *American Sociological Review*, 59, 511–36.

Wrong, D. H. 1988: *Power: Its Forms, Bases, and Uses*. Chicago: University of Chicago Press.

Zabusky, S. E. 1997: Computers, clients, and expertise: negotiating technical identities in a nontechnical world. In Barley, S. R. and Orr, J. E. (eds), *Between Craft and Science: Technical Work in U.S. Settings*. Ithaca, NY: Cornell University Press, 129–53.

Zabusky, S. E. and Barley, S. R. 1996: Redefining success: ethnographic observations in the careers of technicians. In Osterman, P. (ed.), *Broken Ladders: Managerial Careers in the New Economy*. New York: Oxford University Press, 185–213.

Zborovskiy, D. d. E. and Karpova, G. A. 1984: The pedagogical training of engineering instructors: o podgotovke inzhenerno-pedagogicheskikh kadrov. *Sotsiologicheskie Issledovaniya*, 11, 139–42, abstracted in *Sociological Abstracts*.

Zussman, R. 1985: *Mechanics of the Middle Class: Work and Politics Among American Engineers*. Berkeley: University of California Press.

Index